Contract Law

WEEK 1

D1471295

OPTIMIZE LAW REVISION

The Optimize series' academic advisors are:

- Michael Bromby, Higher Education Academy Discipline Lead for Law 2011–2013, Reader in Law, GCU.

'The use of visualisation in Optimize will help students to focus on the key issues when revising.'

- Emily Allbon, Law Librarian and creator of Lawbore, City University.

'Partnering well-explained, comprehensive content with visual tools like maps and flowcharts is what makes the Optimize series so unique. These books help students take their learning up a notch; offering support in grappling with the subject, as well as insight into what will help make their work stand out.'

- Sanmeet Kaur Dua, Lecturer in Law, co-creator of Lawbore, City University.

'This series sets out the essential concepts and principles that students need to grasp in a logical way by combining memorable visual diagrams and text. Students will find that they will not easily forget what they read in this series as the unique aim higher and interaction points will leave a blueprint in their minds.'

- Zoe Swan, Senior Lecturer in Law, University of Brighton.

'The wide range of visual material includes diagrams, charts, tables and maps enable students to check their knowledge and understanding on each topic area, every step of the way... When combined with carefully explained legal principles and solid, understandable examples, students will find this series provides them with a win- win solution to the study of law and developing revision techniques.'

Optimize Contract Law

Tracey Hough and Kathrin Kühnel-Fitchen

Routledge
Taylor & Francis Group
LONDON AND NEW YORK

First published 2014
by Routledge
2 Park Square, Milton Park, Abingdon, Oxon OX14 4RN

and by Routledge
711 Third Avenue, New York, NY 10017

Routledge is an imprint of the Taylor & Francis Group, an informa business
© 2014 Tracey Hough & Kathrin Kühnel-Fitchen

British Library Cataloguing in Publication Data
A catalogue record for this book is available from the British Library

Library of Congress Cataloging in Publication Data
A catalog record for this book has been requested

ISBN: 978-0-415-70969-9 (pbk)
ISBN: 978-1-315-84897-6 (ebk)

Typeset in TheSans
by RefineCatch Limited, Bungay, Suffolk

MIX
Paper from
responsible sources
FSC
www.fsc.org   FSC® C013604

Printed and bound by CPI Group (UK) Ltd, Croydon, CR0 4YY

Contents

Optimize – Your Blueprint for Exam Success

Why Optimize?

In developing the Optimize format, Routledge has spent a lot of time talking to law students like you, and to your lecturers and examiners about assessment, teaching and learning, and about exam preparation. The aim of our series is to help you make the most of your knowledge to gain good marks – to optimize your revision.

Students

Students told us that there was a huge amount to learn, and that visual features such as diagrams, tables and flowcharts made the law easier to follow. Learning and remembering cases was an area of difficulty, as was applying them in problem questions. Revision guides could make this easier by presenting the law succinctly, showing concepts in a visual format and highlighting how important cases can be applied in assessment.

Lecturers

Lecturers agreed that visual features were effective to aid learning, but were concerned that students learned by rote when using revision guides. To succeed in assessment, they wanted to encourage them to get their teeth into arguments, to support their answers with authority, and show they had truly understood the principles underlying their questions. In short, they wanted them to show they understood how they were assessed on the law, rather than repeating the basic principles.

Assessment Criteria

If you want to do well in exams, it's important to understand how you will be assessed. In order to get the best out of your exam or essay question, your first port of call should be to make yourself familiar with the marking criteria available from your law school; this will help you to identify and recognise the skills and knowledge you will need to succeed. Like course outlines, assessment criteria can differ from school to school, so if you can get hold of a copy of your own criteria, this will be invaluable. To give you a clear idea of what these criteria look like, we've collated the most common terms from 64 marking schemes for core curriculum courses in the UK.

research

reading

Evidence

Understanding

Structure Critical Argument

Engagement

Organisation

Application Use

sources

Analysis

Accuracy

Originality

Knowledge

Presentation

Common Assessment Criteria, Routledge Subject Assessment Survey

Optimising the law

The format of this *Optimize Law* volume has been developed with these assessment criteria and the learning needs of students firmly in mind.

❖ **Visual format:** Our expert series advisors have brought a wealth of knowledge about visual learning to help us to develop the books' visual format.

❖ **Tailored coverage:** Each book is tailored to the needs of your core curriculum course and presents all commonly taught topics.

❖ **Assessment-led revision:** Our authors are experienced teachers with an interest in how students learn, and they have structured each chapter around revision objectives that relate to the criteria you will be assessed on.

❖ **Assessment-led pedagogy:** The Aim Higher, Common Pitfalls, Up for Debate and Case precedent features used in these books are closely linked to common assessment criteria – showing you how to gain the best marks, avoid the worst, apply the law and think critically about it.

❖ **Putting it into practice:** Each chapter presents example essay or problem questions and template answers to show you how to apply what you have learned.

Routledge and the Optimize team wish you the very best of luck in your exams and essays!

Preface

We hope that the lively design of this book will make your revision less tedious and that the simple, to the point explanations and carefully designed diagrams will help you to remember the key areas of law. The 'putting it into practice' sessions will provide a useful self-test to enable you to check whether you have understood how the key facts are applied to a factual situation. Good Luck!

Tracey Hough
Kathrin Kühnel-Fitchen

Guide to Using the Book and the Companion Website

The Routledge *Optimize* revision series is designed to provide students with a clear overview of the core topics in their course, and to contextualise this overview within a narrative that offers straightforward, practical advice relating to assessment.

Revision objectives

A brief introduction to the core themes and issues you will encounter in each chapter.

Chapter Topic Maps

Visually link all of the key topics in each chapter to tie together understanding of key issues.

Illustrative diagrams

A series of diagrams and tables are used to help facilitate the understanding of concepts and interrelationships within key topics.

Up for Debate

Up for Debate helps you to critique current law and reflect on how and in which direction it may develop in the future.

Case precedent boxes

A variety of landmark cases are highlighted in text boxes for ease of reference. The facts, principle and application for the case are presented to help understand how these courses are used in legal problems.

Aim Higher and Common Pitfalls

These assessment-focused sections show students how to get the best marks, and avoid the most common mistakes.

Table of key cases

Drawing together the key cases from each chapter.

Companion Website

www.routledge.com/revision

Visit the Law Revision website to discover a comprehensive range of resources designed to enhance your learning experience.

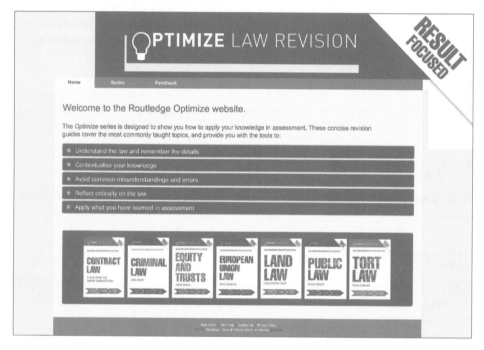

Resources for Optimize Law revision

- ❖ Revision tips podcasts
- ❖ Topic overview podcasts
- ❖ Subject maps for each topic
- ❖ Downloadable versions of chapter maps and other diagrams
- ❖ Flashcard Glossary
- ❖ MCQ questions

Table of Cases and Statutes

■ Cases

■ Statutes

1

Offer and Acceptance

Revision objectives

Understand the law
- Can you:
- Outline the difference between an offer and an invitation to treat?
- Classify the methods by which an offer can be revoked?
- Distinguish between an acceptance and a counter-offer?
- Outline the rules associated with effective acceptance?
- What is meant by an intention to create legal relations?

Remember the details
- Can you:
- Explain with examples and caselaw how different types of selling methods are likely to be construed? ie offer or invitation to treat?
- Explain with caselaw examples, the legal distinction between a counter-offer and a request for further information?
- Provide caselaw examples to illustrate the distinction between social and commercial agreements?

Reflect critically on areas of debate
- Can you:
- Identify where policy has played a part in the development of the law in contract creation?
- Highlight the overriding factors involved in deciding whether an intention to create legal relations exists in a contractual agreement?
- Offer an opinion upon whether the law on acceptance by instantaneous communication provides clear guidance on contracts created through modern day electronic communication?

Contextualise
- Do you:
- Understand the implications of a breakdown in the initial stages of contract formation upon the enforceability of a contract?
- Appreciate that the time and place that an agreement is secured will dictate which of the party's terms prevail?
- Understand the practical reasons for being able to determine between an invitation to treat and an offer in a commercial environment?

Apply your skills and knowledge
- Can you:
- Analyse a set of facts and arrive at a reasoned conclusion as to whether an agreement has been formed, and if so, on whose terms?
- Can you answer the question at the end of this chapter?

Chapter Map

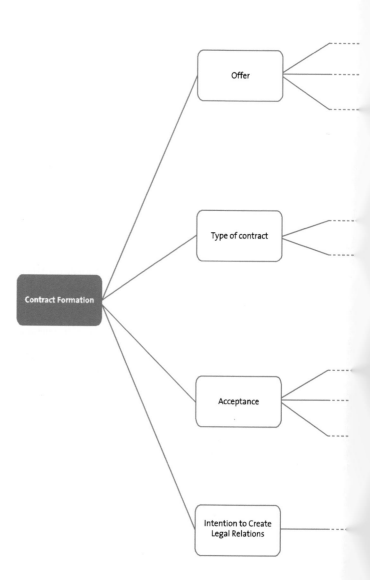

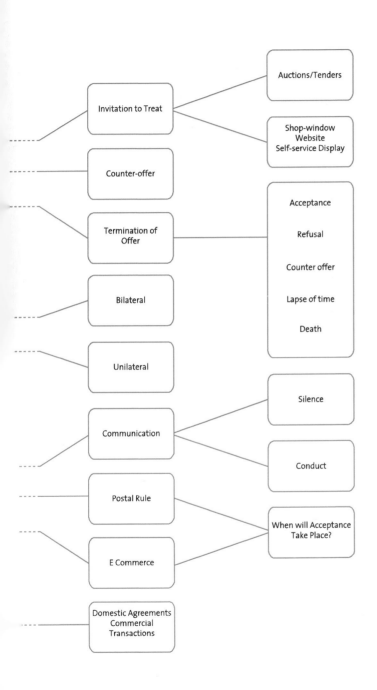

Invitation to Treat

Auctions/Tenders

Shop-window
Website
Self-service Display

Counter-offer

Termination of Offer

Acceptance

Refusal

Counter offer

Lapse of time

Death

Bilateral

Unilateral

Communication

Silence

Conduct

Postal Rule

When will Acceptance Take Place?

E Commerce

Domestic Agreements
Commercial
Transactions

The main part of this chapter is devoted to offer and acceptance but intention to create legal relations will be covered briefly towards the end.

Contract formation

A contract will not come into existence until an agreement has been reached.

The test for whether an agreement has been reached is an objective one. Based on external evidence, the court will consider at what point the reasonable man would conclude that an agreement has been reached and a contract created. The subjective intentions of the parties are not relevant.

> Lord Blackburn J in *Smith v Hughes* (1871) stated:
>
> '... if whatever a man's real intention may be, he so conducts himself that a reasonable man would believe he was assenting to the terms proposed by the other party, and that other party upon that belief enters into a contract with him, the man thus conducting himself would be equally bound as if he had intended to agree to the other party's terms.'

A contract is an exchange of promises that constitutes a legally binding agreement between two or more parties. Agreement is reached when an offer by one person, (the offeror) to another (the offeree) that indicates the offeror's willingness to enter into a contract on certain terms without further negotiations, is accepted by the offeree. The contracting parties can be individuals, groups or organisations.

Perhaps the best- known definition of an 'offer' is provided by Treitel:

> Treitel – Definition of offer
>
> 'an expression of willingness to contract on certain terms, made with the intention that it shall become binding as soon as it is accepted by the person to whom it is addressed'.
>
> G.H. Treitel, *The Law of Contract*, 10th edn

Types of contract

Bilateral contract

A contract can be bilateral or unilateral. A bilateral contract will occur when promises are made between two parties, e.g. Jack offers Melissa £10 for her

Optimize revision book. Melissa accepts the offer and promises to give the book to Jack for £10.

Unilateral contract

A unilateral contract is where only one party makes a promise. The promise does not have to be made to a specific person; indeed it can be to 'the whole world'. Acceptance is made when another party performs the promisor's request. For example, Bal lost his laptop on the university campus. He posts a notice on the student union website offering a reward of £100 payable to anyone who returns it to him. Winston finds the laptop and hands it back to Bal. Winston's act of finding and returning the laptop is acceptance of the offer and he is entitled to insist that the reward is paid.

Unilateral contracts are sometimes known as 'if' contracts, in that the offeror commits him/herself to do something, if the offeree does or gives something in return. For example, Sarah says that she will pay Jane £10 if she cleans her car. Jane has no obligation to fulfil the task, but if she does carry it out, she will have accepted the offer. Have a look at the following case:

Case precedent – *Carlill v Carbolic Smoke Ball Co* [1893] 1 QB 256

Facts: The Carbolic Smoke Ball Company advertised a 'smoke ball' claiming that it could cure influenza. The company stated that any person who used the smoke ball as directed and who subsequently caught influenza would receive a payment of £100. As an endorsement of their sincerity, the Smoke Ball Company deposited £1,000 with a named bank to settle any claims. Mrs Carlill purchased a smoke ball and used it as directed. She caught influenza and claimed £100.

Principle: The advertisement was an offer. An offer does not have to be made to a specific person; it can be made to the whole world. The manner in which the advert is termed can have the effect of waiving the need for acceptance. Fulfilment of the terms is sufficient to constitute acceptance. In this case, Mrs Carlill accepted the offer by purchasing and using the smoke ball in the prescribed manner. The court further determined that the bank deposit authenticated the terms of the advert.

Application: Where wording of an advertisement extends beyond the scope of a mere advertising slogan, it will constitute an offer.

In order to enforce this type of contract, the parties must show that all required contractual components are present. The components are set out in the diagram below:

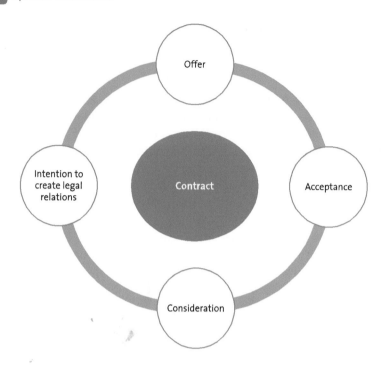

Provided that all components are present, a legally enforceable contract will exist.

A contract can be made orally, in writing, or by conduct, but in all cases, proof of a valid offer and acceptance must exist. A contract 'in writing' could encompass a variety of methods, such as e-mail, fax, or a website advertisement. An example of a contract by conduct would be eating a meal in a restaurant, or filling up one's car with diesel. In all circumstances, the offer must be made with the intention that it will be legally binding. The terms of the offer must be clear and unequivocal and there should be no external conditions attached to the offer that fall outside the agreement.

Invitation to treat

You must ensure that you can distinguish between an invitation to treat and an offer. An invitation to treat can be described as an invitation to enter into negotiations; a pre-offer communication, or an attempt to seek expressions of interest.

Example 1

I could ask if you were interested in buying my mountain bike. Such a statement would not be regarded as an offer. I could even give a suggestion as to the amount that I would like to receive for the bike, but again it would not constitute an offer; moreover, it would be an attempt on my part to see if any interest could be raised in the sale of my bike.

So, certain statements will fall short of an offer if they are not articulated in a way that a simple acceptance would suffice to cement the deal. When preliminary communications are opened, it is open to the person to whom the invitation is made to progress the negotiations by making a firm offer. The offer can then be either accepted or rejected. *Harvey v Facey* (1893) is a well-known case that illustrates this point well:

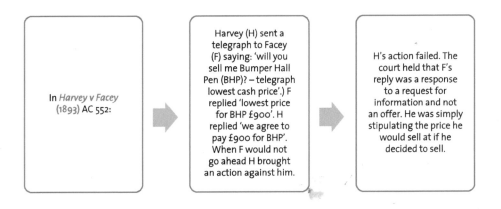

In *Harvey v Facey* (1893) AC 552:

Harvey (H) sent a telegraph to Facey (F) saying: 'will you sell me Bumper Hall Pen (BHP)? – telegraph lowest cash price'.) F replied 'lowest price for BHP £900'. H replied 'we agree to pay £900 for BHP'. When F would not go ahead H brought an action against him.

H's action failed. The court held that F's reply was a response to a request for information and not an offer. He was simply stipulating the price he would sell at if he decided to sell.

Example 2

Alex places a diamond ring in his shop window with a price tag of £999 on it. Victoria persuades her husband Martin to buy the ring for her and Martin enters the shop and offers Alex £999 for the ring. At this point Martin has made an offer. The display of the ring in the window is an invitation to treat. It is then up to Alex, the jeweller, either to accept or reject Martin's offer. At this stage he could refuse to sell the ring to Martin.

It is not always easy to draw the distinction between an offer and an invitation to treat. Sometimes the courts will determine that the language used reflects an invitation to treat rather than an offer. This was the situation in *Gibson v Manchester City Council* [1979], a case concerning the right to buy rented accommodation. Although a letter from the council appeared to contain all of the terms on which the council were willing to be bound, the HOL determined that the letter was an invitation to treat only. It was found to be insufficiently definite to constitute an offer.

Self-service displays

The law governing goods displayed for sale in a shop window and for self-service displays is now very clear. Let us consider the leading case on self-service displays:

Case precedent – *Pharmaceutical Society of Great Britain v Boots Cash Chemists* [1953] 1 ALL ER 482

Facts: Customers were able to take certain medicines from the shelf in a self-service store and pay for them at the till. Subsequently, Boots were charged under the Pharmacy and Poisons Act 1933 which stated that is was an offence to sell certain medicines unless they were under the supervision of a registered pharmacist. It was argued that the sale took place when the customer put the item(s) in their basket.

Principle: COA held that the sale was completed at the cash desk, where the customer made an offer to the cashier to buy the product. At this point a pharmacist would supervise the sale and could either accept or reject the offer. Thus no offence had been committed.

Application: The law is now very clear in this area. If you are asked a question about goods on self-service display, you can safely conclude that the display will constitute an invitation to treat. The offer will take place when the goods are handed over at the check-out desk.

Shop-window displays

It is pertinent to consider *Fisher and Bell* [1961] which concerned the display of a flickknife with a price label in a shop window. The defendant was charged under the Restriction of Offensive Weapons Act 1959 with offering a flickknife for sale. The House of Lords held that there had been no offence; Lord Parker was very clear in saying that the display of the knife in the window constituted an invitation to treat, not an offer.

Advertisements

The same pragmatic approach is taken with advertisements. An advertisement in a newspaper, a magazine, a website, or on TV will generally comprise an invitation to treat. In *Harris v Nickerson* (1873), following an advertisement announcing an auction, the plaintiff attended, only to discover that the item he had been interested in buying had been withdrawn from sale. On challenge for breach of contract, the advertisement for the auction was held to be an invitation to treat. Blackburn J observed that an advertiser would be liable to everyone who attended the auction if the advert were to constitute an offer, the prospect of which he described as a 'startling proposition'.

Let us consider *Partridge v Crittenden* [1968]:

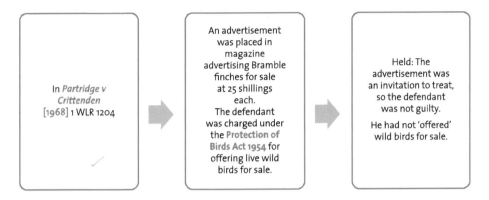

In *Partridge v Crittenden* [1968] 1 WLR 1204

An advertisement was placed in magazine advertising Bramble finches for sale at 25 shillings each.
The defendant was charged under the **Protection of Birds Act 1954** for offering live wild birds for sale.

Held: The advertisement was an invitation to treat, so the defendant was not guilty.

He had not 'offered' wild birds for sale.

This approach is both practical and logical. If the advertisement had been an offer, the consequential effect would have been that everyone who wanted to buy a bramble finch would have been entitled to one. The supply of the birds was clearly limited and an outcome of this nature would have created an untenable position in both the instant case and in the marketplace generally.

Consequently, in most cases an advertisement will be an invitation to treat. However, it is possible for an advertisement to constitute an offer if the wording and intention is very clear. For example, an advertisement reading: '100 Big Wheel 7 BMX bikes for sale at £99 to the first 100 customers' may well be treated as an offer. Indeed, it transpired in the American case of *Lefkowitz v Great Minneapolis Surplus Stores* (1957), where a newspaper advertisement stating: 'Saturday 9 am sharp; three brand new fur coats, worth $100, first come, first served, $1 each', that the advertisement was an offer.

The case of *Carlill v Carbolic Smoke Ball Co* (discussed above) is another instance where an advertisement was held to constitute an offer (i.e. a unilateral contract). In *Carlill*, the defendants had contended that their claim on the virtuosity of the smoke ball was not an offer in a contractual sense for three reasons:

❖ it was simply advertising 'puff',
❖ the advertisement was not directed at anyone specifically, hence could not be an offer,
❖ there had been no notification of acceptance.

The court rejected these arguments. Such statements could be regarded as an offer inasmuch as they could be accepted by anyone who fulfilled the conditions stated (analogous to reward cases). Acceptance occurs when a party performs the act specified in the advertisement. In *Carlill*, the advertisement was a unilateral offer to the whole world and the plaintiff accepted the offer by using the smoke ball as directed.

Offer

Communication of offer

An offer *must be communicated* to the other party. A person cannot accept an offer of which they are unaware. In *Williams v Carwardine* (1833) the court held that although the provision of information by the claimant was induced by other motives, and not the offer of a reward, she still knew about the offer and could claim the reward. Her reasons for giving the information were irrelevant. Alternatively, in the Australian case of *R v Clarke* (1927) a contract was not upheld, because it was unclear whether or not Clarke had the reward in mind when he provided information that led to the conviction of a murderer (see below). A person cannot accept an offer of which they are unaware.

> In *R v Clarke* (1927) 40 CLR 227, Higgins J stated:
>
> 'Clarke had seen the offer . . . but it was not present in his mind – he had forgotten it and gave no consideration to it in his intense excitement as to his own danger. There cannot be assent without knowledge of the offer; and ignorance of the other is the same thing, whether it is due to never hearing of it or to forgetting it after hearing.'

Tenders

An invitation to tender, where potential suppliers or servicers are invited to submit quotations will normally amount to an invitation to treat, as in *Spencer v Harding* (1870), where a circular offering stock for sale by tender was merely a notice to advertise that the defendants wished to receive offers for the purchase of goods. The situation differs if there is a statement saying, for example, that the lowest bid will be accepted. Such a statement will constitute an offer and the lowest bidder will be able to enforce the contract. This was highlighted in *Harvela Investments Ltd v Royal Trust of Canada Ltd* [1986], where the defendants had made it clear that they were going to accept the highest tender.

Auctions

An auctioneer's request for bids at an auction is an invitation to treat. The bidder makes an offer by placing a bid. Acceptance takes place when the auctioneer's hammer falls (now contained in s 57(2) Sale of Goods Act 1979). This was established in *Payne v Cave* (1789). A notice advertising an auction was held to be an invitation to treat in *Harris v Nickerson* (1873).

Warlow v Harrison (1859) is authority that an advertisement stating that goods at an auction will be sold without reserve is an offer to sell to the highest bidder. The offer is accepted by the person who makes the highest bid, in reliance on the offer. In

Heathcote Ball & Co (Commercial Auctions) Ltd v Barry [2000], where the auctioneer had undertaken to sell to the highest bidder, the court held that a collateral contract existed between the auctioneer and the highest bidder. By withdrawing the lot, the auctioneer was liable for breach of contract and had to pay the difference between the bid amount and the market price at the date of the auction.

Up for Debate

Nowadays, online auctions are growing in popularity through sites such as eBay. Applying what you have read so far, answer the following:

1. Is the advertisement an offer or an invitation to treat?
2. At what point is a contract formed?

Further reading: Rokiah Kadir, 'Rules of Advertisement in an Electronic Age', (2013) 55(1) *Int. J.L.M.* 42–54

Aim Higher

The ability to analyse a scenario, to pinpoint and apply the law to distinguish between an invitation to treat and an offer is a frequently tested area in contract law examinations.

Always take time to think carefully about the facts presented before reaching a conclusion. Sometimes you may need to explore more than one possible outcome. Have a look at the following scenario:

> Alex was aware that Masood wished to sell a plot of land, Sunnyside Ridge (SR). Alex emailed Masood saying, 'I have heard that you want to sell SR and I am interested in buying it. Would you be prepared to accept £250,000 for it?' Masood read the e-mail later that day and immediately replied saying: 'As you are aware, property prices have increased substantially over the last two years and SR is certainly worth more than the price suggested by you. I think £320,000 is more realistic.'

Alex replied by e-mail the same day saying, 'I agree to the price asked by you'. Masood received the e-mail but wishes to sell to someone else.

Does Masood have a contract with Alex? Your answer will depend upon your analysis of where the distinction between invitation to treat and offer lies. If you are not sure, return to the cases of *Harvey v Facey* and *Gibson v Manchester CC* and use the flowchart on the next page to aid your analysis and application.

You will have a further opportunity to practice this area of analysis in the 'Putting it into practice' section at the end of this chapter.

Summary – Offer or invitation to treat?

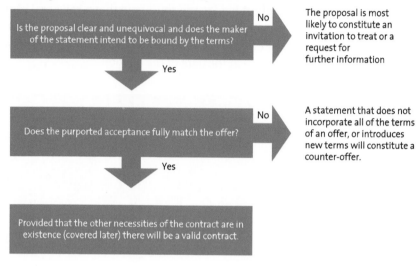

Is the proposal clear and unequivocal and does the maker of the statement intend to be bound by the terms? — **No** → The proposal is most likely to constitute an invitation to treat or a request for further information

Yes ↓

Does the purported acceptance fully match the offer? — **No** → A statement that does not incorporate all of the terms of an offer, or introduces new terms will constitute a counter-offer.

Yes ↓

Provided that the other necessities of the contract are in existence (covered later) there will be a valid contract.

Termination of offer

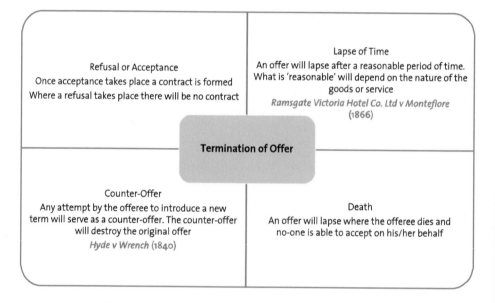

Refusal or Acceptance
Once acceptance takes place a contract is formed
Where a refusal takes place there will be no contract

Lapse of Time
An offer will lapse after a reasonable period of time. What is 'reasonable' will depend on the nature of the goods or service
Ramsgate Victoria Hotel Co. Ltd v Montefiore (1866)

Termination of Offer

Counter-Offer
Any attempt by the offeree to introduce a new term will serve as a counter-offer. The counter-offer will destroy the original offer
Hyde v Wrench (1840)

Death
An offer will lapse where the offeree dies and no-one is able to accept on his/her behalf

An offer that has been terminated cannot later be revived if the offeree changes his mind.

Revocation

Payne v Cave (1789) is authority that an offer can be revoked at any time before acceptance takes place. The rule applies even when the offeror has promised to keep the offer open for a particular period of time (*Routledge v Grant* (1828)).

In order to be effective, revocation of an offer must be communicated to the offeree.

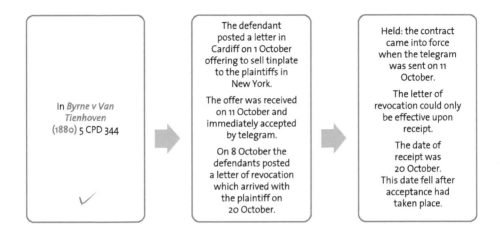

In *Byrne v Van Tienhoven* (1880) 5 CPD 344

✓

The defendant posted a letter in Cardiff on 1 October offering to sell tinplate to the plaintiffs in New York.

The offer was received on 11 October and immediately accepted by telegram.

On 8 October the defendants posted a letter of revocation which arrived with the plaintiff on 20 October.

Held: the contract came into force when the telegram was sent on 11 October.

The letter of revocation could only be effective upon receipt.

The date of receipt was 20 October. This date fell after acceptance had taken place.

Dickinson v Dodds (1876) is authority for the fact that revocation can be communicated by a reliable third party.

The rule that an offer can be revoked at any time before it is accepted can produce harsh results. Imagine a scenario where you have started to perform the terms of a unilateral contract. You have spent a considerable amount of time and money on performing the specified criteria, but have not quite completed the task. The offeror contacts you and revokes the contract.

Example

Fred offered Boris £500 to cycle from Leeds to Kent. Fred turned up when Boris was just five miles away from the border of Kent and told him that the offer was revoked. Would that be an effective revocation? Fred might argue that revocation has been communicated before acceptance.

Case law suggests that once a party has started to perform the contractual terms, revocation cannot take place. In *Errington v Errington* [1952] a father purchased a property for his son and daughter in law and told them that the house would be theirs if they paid off the mortgage. The couple started to pay the mortgage instalments, but when the father died, his widow sought possession of the house. The couple were successful in retaining the house, on the basis that once they had started to perform their side of the contract, the attempted revocation came too late.

Counter-offer

Once an offer has been established, it is necessary to ascertain whether valid acceptance has taken place. An acceptance must mirror the offer; otherwise it may fall short of the necessary consent to create an agreement. In most cases it is simple to determine, but in other cases, where protracted negotiations have taken place, it is not always easy to pinpoint when the agreement was finalised.

There may be a purported acceptance on slightly different terms; or the offeree may have requested further information. In either of these instances the dialogue must be carefully analysed to determine whether departure from the specified terms will amount to a counter-offer, or whether the statement is simply a request for further information.

A counter-offer will occur when the offeree attempts to vary the terms of the offer. For example, if Fred offers to sell his laptop to Ben for £75 and Ben says that he will take it for £60, Ben's response will be a counter-offer as he has changed the terms. Ben's counter-offer will destroy Fred's initial offer, so Ben cannot later insist upon Fred selling him the laptop for the original asking price of £75. It will be open to Fred to decide whether or not he wishes to accept Ben's counter-offer and if he does accept, an agreement will be formed.

Case precedent – *Hyde v Wrench* (1840) 49 ER 132

Facts: The defendant, Wrench (W) offered to sell his farm to the plaintiff, Hyde (H) for £1,000. H said that he would pay £950 but this was rejected by W. H later tried to accept the offer but W refused to go ahead.

Principle: The court held that H's counter-offer was a rejection of the initial (£1,000) offer. The initial offer had been destroyed by the counter-offer (£950), and could no longer be accepted. The counter-offer was a new offer which could either be accepted or rejected. W exercised his right to reject it.

Application: In answering a problem question a careful analysis of the words of exchange is required. If the purported acceptance does not mirror the terms of the offer, then the response may be treated as a counter-offer, which can be accepted or rejected.

Information requests

Simple requests for further information, such as: 'Can I pay by cheque?' or 'Will you accept my credit card?' will not amount to a counter-offer, since there is no attempt to change the terms of the contract. However, if the enquiry relates to the manner in which the contract will be performed, the enquiry will probably fall into the territory of a counter-offer, as in *Hyde v Wrench* (above). In *Stevenson, Jaques & Co v McLean* (1880), the defendant offered by telegram to sell some iron at a specified price and the offer was to be held open for a stated period of time. The plaintiff asked whether the defendant would accept an amount for delivery over two months, but if not, how long the defendant could give. The words were construed to constitute an enquiry only; not a counter-offer. The enquiry was simply an attempt to ascertain more information about the deal. In reality it can sometimes be difficult to assess whether something will be a request for information or a counter-offer.

Standard terms

The difficulty in distinguishing between a counter-offer and an acceptance is compounded by the fact that many businesses use pre-printed standard terms. The negotiations can often turn into a 'battle of the forms', where it is necessary to decipher who submitted the final set of terms.

In *Butler Machine Tool Co Ltd v Ex-Cell-O Corporation [England] Ltd* [1979] 1 WLR 401, Lord Denning summed up the position in his famous statement:

'... In some cases, the battle is won by the person who fires the last shot. He is the person who puts forward the latest term and conditions; and, if they are not objected to by the other party, he may be taken to have agreed with them.'

The *Butler Machine Tool* case exhibits the courts' observance of the traditional analysis to find a matching offer and acceptance. This approach was confirmed in *Tekdata Intercommunications v Amphenol Ltd* [2009].

Acceptance

Acceptance must be communicated and is only valid if it is communicated by a person with authority to do so (*Powell v Lee* (1908)). The offeree is responsible for ensuring that acceptance is communicated to the offeror.

In *Entores v Miles Far East Corporation* (1955), Lord Denning illustrated the principle by giving an example of two people standing on the opposite sides of the river.

A shouts across an offer but does not hear B's acceptance because of the noise of an aircraft flying overhead.

There is no contract between A and B because it is incumbent on B to repeat that acceptance so that it is communicated.

Similarly, if the acceptance is spoken into a telephone and the line goes dead, there is no contract because the offeror does not hear the acceptance.

If the acceptance is not heard through the fault of the offeror, he cannot deny the existence of the acceptance. Lord Denning: 'if the listener on the telephone line does not catch the words of the acceptance but nevertheless does not ask for the acceptance to be repeated ... the offeror cannot deny receipt of the acceptance if it is his own fault that he did not get it.'

To recap: Acceptance must be unconditional and correspond to the strict terms of an offer; anything less will amount to a counter-offer. It is always open to the offeror to express how s/he wishes acceptance to be made. If conditions are attached, then these must be fulfilled for an acceptance to be valid.

There are four important areas that need to be considered in relation to acceptance:

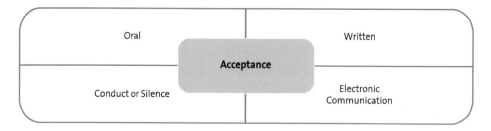

Oral	Written
Acceptance	
Conduct or Silence	Electronic Communication

Oral or in writing
Acceptance can be either oral or in writing and neither of these methods pose a problem per se. Written acceptances must fulfil the conditions of the postal rule.

Postal rule
Acceptance will occur instantaneously once a letter is placed into an authorised post box or handed to a person with authority to accept letters:

Case precedent – *Adams v Lindsell* (1818) 1 B & Ald 681

Facts: 2 September: the defendants (D) wrote to the plaintiffs (P) offering to sell them wool. The letter containing the offer was incorrectly addressed which caused a delay.

5 September: offer received. Letter of acceptance sent on same day.

9 September: acceptance letter received – two days after it could reasonably have been expected to have been received.

Having not received a reply when expected, D sold the wool to a third party (before the acceptance letter arrived). The issue was whether there was a contract between the D and P.

Principle: Acceptance occurred when the acceptance letter was posted. Thus the contract was formed **before** the wool was sold to the third party and D was liable to P for breach of contract.

Application: Note: the postal rule will govern postal acceptances only. It does not apply to other methods of acceptance or written revocations which are valid upon notification.

This postal rule was applied in *Household Fire and Carriage Accident Insurance Co v Grant* (1879), a case concerning an application and allocation of shares. A letter of allotment was posted but not received. A contract was formed when the letter was posted. The more recent case of *Brinkibon Ltd v Stahag Stahl und Stahlwarenhandelsgesellschaft GmbH* [1983] confirms that acceptance occurs when the written communication is placed in the control of the Post Office.

Henthorn v Fraser [1892] is authority that the postal rule will apply only when it is reasonable for the post to be used as a method of communication. Care should be taken here, for example, if there is an oral offer over the telephone, then acceptance by post, unless specifically agreed, many not constitute a reasonable mode of communication. *Quenerduaine v Cole* (1883), determined that acceptance by post to an offer made by telegram was not valid. *Holwell Securities Ltd v Hughes* [1974] is authority for the principle that where the offer specifically states that notice must be received, then such wording will effectively oust the postal rule, as the intentions of the offeror will have been made clear. Closely associated with this rule, if a specified method of acceptance is requested, it must be observed, as per *Manchester Diocesan Council for Education v Commercial and General Investments Ltd* [1969].

Conduct or silence

In unilateral contacts, acceptance will always take place by conduct.

Example

I have lost my cat and I offer a reward of £20 for her safe return. The person who returns my cat will have accepted my offer by his/her conduct in returning the cat.

Acceptance can also be by conduct in a bilateral contract, see *Brogden v Metropolitan Railway* (1877) below. In areas of dispute, the court will consider the conduct of the parties and whether it is reasonable to infer acceptance by conduct.

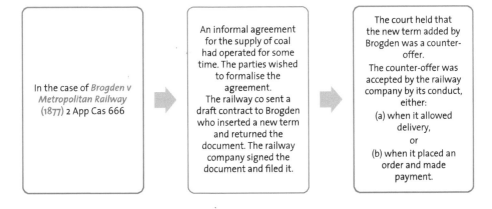

In the case of *Brogden v Metropolitan Railway* (1877) 2 App Cas 666

An informal agreement for the supply of coal had operated for some time. The parties wished to formalise the agreement. The railway co sent a draft contract to Brogden who inserted a new term and returned the document. The railway company signed the document and filed it.

The court held that the new term added by Brogden was a counter-offer. The counter-offer was accepted by the railway company by its conduct, either: (a) when it allowed delivery, or (b) when it placed an order and made payment.

Where a person purports to accept an offer, in most cases they must provide notification of their acceptance to the offeror. One notable exception is a unilateral contract. Here, the need to communicate acceptance is unnecessary as performance in line with the terms of the offer is sufficient. The situation with bilateral contracts is more complex. There must be some evidence to lead a reasonable person to the conclusion that an intention to accept exists. The general rule is that silence cannot amount to acceptance. The leading case in this area is *Felthouse v Brindley* (1862).

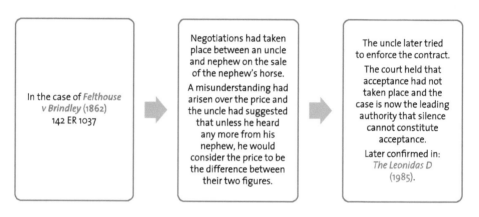

In the case of *Felthouse v Brindley* (1862) 142 ER 1037

Negotiations had taken place between an uncle and nephew on the sale of the nephew's horse. A misunderstanding had arisen over the price and the uncle had suggested that unless he heard any more from his nephew, he would consider the price to be the difference between their two figures.

The uncle later tried to enforce the contract. The court held that acceptance had not taken place and the case is now the leading authority that silence cannot constitute acceptance.

Later confirmed in: *The Leonidas D* (1985).

Note also that unsolicited goods sent to consumers become unconditional gifts with immediate effect (Consumer Protection (Distance Selling) Regulations 2000).

Electronic communication

In face-to-face communications, it is relatively simple to ascertain when acceptance takes place. Note the guidance provided in *Entores* (above). Clearly, if I accepted an offer during a telephone conversation with you, but unbeknown to me, you were not listening because at the same time you were watching an important football match on TV, it would be your fault that you had not heard the acceptance and my acceptance would be effective, i.e. *upon communication*.

Where electronic modes of communication are used, the rule that acceptance is effective upon communication will prevail. The postal rule does not apply. Examples of instantaneous electronic communications are telex, fax, telephone, e-mail and text. These modes of communication are generally accessible as soon as they are sent. This then raises the issue that such communications may arrive on a central server or similar domain instantaneously, but may not be accessed straight away.

Let us look at the cases that exist in this area:

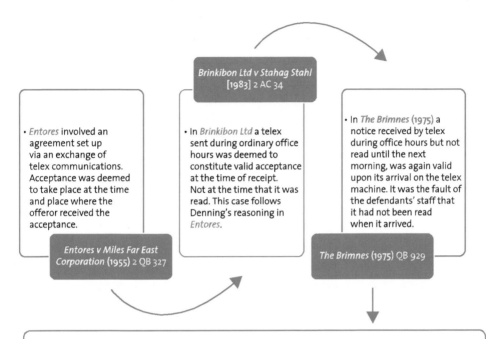

Brinkibon Ltd v Stahag Stahl [1983] 2 AC 34

• *Entores* involved an agreement set up via an exchange of telex communications. Acceptance was deemed to take place at the time and place where the offeror received the acceptance.

Entores v Miles Far East Corporation (1955) 2 QB 327

• In *Brinkibon Ltd* a telex sent during ordinary office hours was deemed to constitute valid acceptance at the time of receipt. Not at the time that it was read. This case follows Denning's reasoning in *Entores*.

• In *The Brimnes* (1975) a notice received by telex during office hours but not read until the next morning, was again valid upon its arrival on the telex machine. It was the fault of the defendants' staff that it had not been read when it arrived.

The Brimnes (1975) QB 929

In *The Brimnes*, the HOL declined to say whether the same outcome would apply in all circumstances. Lord Wilberforce did, however, indicate that the rule was not so rigid as to prevent account being taken of factors such as business practice and 'common sense' evaluation:

'No universal rule can cover all such cases: they must be resolved by reference to the intentions of the parties, by sound business practice and in some cases by a judgment where the risks should lie' Lord Wilberforce, *The Brimnes* (1975).

There is no conclusive answer on when an electronic communication will have been received. It is fairly clear that communications received during office hours and available to be read will be effective upon receipt. It seems to be accepted that a communication received outside office hours will be effective at a time when the offeror could reasonably have been expected to have read it. This was the approach taken in *Mondial Shipping and Chartering VB v Astarte Shipping Ltd* [1995]. With e-mail, this would mean that a correspondence could be deemed to be effective after a reasonable time for checking has passed; this may vary depending upon the organisation or individual. The courts may be persuaded to give consideration to past or usual business practice.

Online contracts

Electronic acceptances are now regulated by the Electronic Commerce (EC Directive) 2002. **Regulation 11** of the **Directive** is summarised in the table below:

Regulation 11(1)	
Where the recipient of a service places his order through technological means, a service provider shall do the following:	(a) acknowledge receipt of the order without delay (b) make available effective and accessible technical means to allow the recipient to make corrections prior to placing the order.

Regulation 11(2)
The order and the acknowledgment of receipt will be received when the buyer is able to access them.

Regulation 11(3)
The requirements of **Regulation 11(1)** will not apply to contracts concluded exclusively by exchange of e-mails.

Thus, under the regulations, the statutory assumption is that an order made by a customer will usually constitute the contractual offer and the supplier's acknowledgement will be the acceptance. The advertisement on the webpage is, in most circumstances, an invitation to treat.

The flowchart below provides a brief summary of the key characteristics of an acceptance:

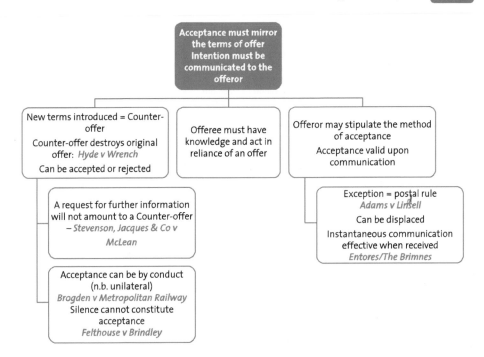

Intention to create legal relations

In addition to the usual contractual components, it should not be forgotten that a valid contract requires an intention on the part of the parties that the agreement is legally binding. In the absence of such an intention, a contract will not be enforceable. The ability to distinguish between social/domestic and commercial agreements is paramount.

Common Pitfall

This area of law is often included as part of a problem question and can be overlooked. Remember that valuable marks can be obtained for considering whether an intention to create legal relations is present in an agreement, particularly if the question mentions words such as 'his friend', or 'his mother', or 'his cousin' etc.

Social and domestic agreements

In social and domestic agreements, there is a presumption against legal relations but this can be rebutted by evidence to the contrary. The issue was considered in *Jones v Padavatton* [1969]:

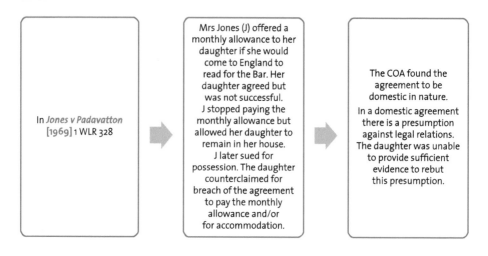

In *Jones v Padavatton* [1969] 1 WLR 328

Mrs Jones (J) offered a monthly allowance to her daughter if she would come to England to read for the Bar. Her daughter agreed but was not successful. J stopped paying the monthly allowance but allowed her daughter to remain in her house. J later sued for possession. The daughter counterclaimed for breach of the agreement to pay the monthly allowance and/or for accommodation.

The COA found the agreement to be domestic in nature.

In a domestic agreement there is a presumption against legal relations. The daughter was unable to provide sufficient evidence to rebut this presumption.

Compare and contrast two cases concerning an agreement between husband and wife. Note that in one case, an intention to create legal relations was found, but in the other it was not:

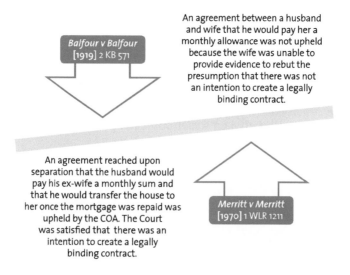

Balfour v Balfour [1919] 2 KB 571

An agreement between a husband and wife that he would pay her a monthly allowance was not upheld because the wife was unable to provide evidence to rebut the presumption that there was not an intention to create a legally binding contract.

An agreement reached upon separation that the husband would pay his ex-wife a monthly sum and that he would transfer the house to her once the mortgage was repaid was upheld by the COA. The Court was satisfied that there was an intention to create a legally binding contract.

Merritt v Merritt [1970] 1 WLR 1211

An example of the presumption against legal relations being rebutted in a domestic agreement can also be seen in *Simpkins v Pays* (1955), where a lodger and two other family members of the household engaged in a weekly competition. The entry was made out in just one of their names and each paid an equal amount to the stake. Upon winning the competition, the defendant argued that there was no intention to create legal relations and refused to share the winnings. The court held that although the agreement was domestic, there existed an intention amongst the parties to create legal relations and ordered that the money be shared.

Commercial transactions

In commercial and business transactions, there is a presumption that the parties intend to create legal relations. This presumption may be rebutted but the onus of proof is on the party seeking to exclude legal relations. This is illustrated in *Esso Petroleum v Customs and Excise Commissioners* [1976]:

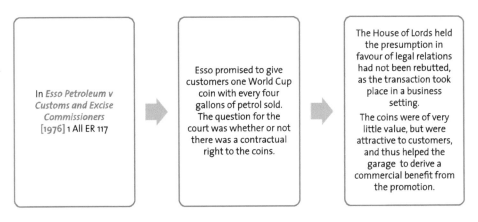

In *Esso Petroleum v Customs and Excise Commissioners* [1976] 1 All ER 117

Esso promised to give customers one World Cup coin with every four gallons of petrol sold. The question for the court was whether or not there was a contractual right to the coins.

The House of Lords held the presumption in favour of legal relations had not been rebutted, as the transaction took place in a business setting.

The coins were of very little value, but were attractive to customers, and thus helped the garage to derive a commercial benefit from the promotion.

Examples of Rebuttals

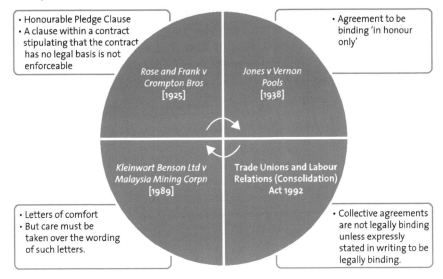

• Honourable Pledge Clause
• A clause within a contract stipulating that the contract has no legal basis is not enforceable

Rose and Frank v Crompton Bros [1925]

Jones v Vernon Pools [1938]

• Agreement to be binding 'in honour only'

Kleinwort Benson Ltd v Malaysia Mining Corpn [1989]

Trade Unions and Labour Relations (Consolidation) Act 1992

• Letters of comfort
• But care must be taken over the wording of such letters.

• Collective agreements are not legally binding unless expressly stated in writing to be legally binding.

Putting it into practice

Example problem question

Look at the scenario below, and then answer the following question:

Daisy is a collector of Victorian toys and has a large display of valuable dolls, some of which are rumoured to have belonged to the Queen herself. Recently, she has fallen on hard times and announced at the local village fete that she was thinking of selling off the collection to clear her debts. Having heard of the collection, Boris, a local antiques dealer telephoned Daisy and, as she did not pick up, left the following message on her answering machine: 'I am interested in buying your doll collection. Please telephone me and let me know how much you want for the dolls.'

Having never heard of Boris before, Daisy looked him up on the internet and found that he had an on-line business called 'Victorian Pastimes' which specialises in the restoration and sale of toys from the Victorian era. Satisfied that Boris appeared to be a legitimate buyer, Daisy e-mailed him through the website from her work e-mail address, at 3.15pm, stating: 'As I am interested in a quick sale, I would be prepared to accept £30,000'.

Unfortunately, Boris misread the price in the e-mail as £3,000. He was delighted with the response and immediately replied by e-mail stating: 'I agree to pay you £3,000 for your dolls.'

At 3.45 pm, Daisy received a call on her mobile phone from a national dealer Louisa, who asked if she could travel down from Liverpool that same evening and view the collection. Daisy agreed.

Three hours after his previous e-mail, having received no reply from Daisy, Boris discovered his error and sent another e-mail stating: 'I agree to pay your asking price of £30,000. I will assume that this is acceptable to you unless I hear from you in the next hour.' This e-mail reached Daisy's work e-mail address at 6:15 pm, but unfortunately, Daisy had gone home for the day and did not access her work e-mails again until the following morning.

Louisa arrived at Daisy's house at 7.00 pm that evening and inspected the collection. She was so keen to acquire it that she offered Daisy £32,000 for it. Daisy accepted her offer.

The next day, Boris was extremely frustrated to find that Daisy had sold the collection to Louisa. He claims to have a contract with Daisy for the sale of the collection to him for £30,000 and has threatened her with legal action.

Advise Daisy.

Outline answer – offer and acceptance

Identify subject area and define the legal principles

❖ *Boris's answering machine message – Offer or invitation to treat?*

- Such a question is unlikely to amount to an offer.
- Wording used has to be sufficiently certain for it to be held to be an offer (*Gibson v Manchester CC*).

- In *Harvey v Facey*, response to question from potential buyer to seller: 'What is the lowest price you'd be prepared to accept?' held not to be offer, but response to request for information. As no price proposed by B, then no offer here (although see SGA 1979, s. 8): Court can imply a reasonable price to remedy silence as to price in a sale of goods context).

❖ *D's e-mail to B – Need to cover two possibilities*:

- If B's answering machine message is not an offer, but is merely an invitation to treat or perhaps a request for information, then D's e-mail cannot be an acceptance or a counter-offer, but could maybe itself amount to an offer. However, *Harvey v Facey* is authority for the proposition that, in this context, a reply to a question from an interested potential buyer concerning the price is simply a response to a request for information and not an offer.
- Given that it is uncertain in its wording, it could conceivably be argued to be an offer.

❖ **B's first e-mail to D:** If the previous communications between the parties are correctly construed as a request for information and a response to that request, then this communication is sufficiently clear and certain to be an offer, even though the amount specified is inaccurate. The fact that the price specified is considerably lower than that suggested in D's response to B's request for information makes no difference. It is capable of acceptance by D. If, D's e-mail can be construed as an offer to B, then B's e-mail cannot amount to an acceptance, as acceptance must mirror the offer. This fails to do so, as in her e-mail, D specified figure of £30,000 and B's response specifies the price of £3,000. If B had intended to respond with a much lower price, this could be a counter-offer.

❖ **B's second e-mail to D**: At first sight, if D's e-mail amounts to an offer, this appears as if it could be an acceptance. On the other hand if D's e-mail was merely a response to a request for information, this could not amount to an acceptance, but could amount to an offer replacing B's earlier offer of £3,000.

Considering B's second e-mail as a potential acceptance, two issues arise:

- If B's first e-mail was a counter-offer, *Hyde v Wrench* is authority to the proposition that a counter-offer destroys the original offer, so that it becomes no longer capable of acceptance. By the same token, it can be said that B's offer of £3,000 had destroyed D's offer to sell the dolls for £30,000, and that therefore D was free to accept or reject B's fresh offer of £30,000.
- The second issue, looking at B's second e-mail as a potential acceptance, is that acceptance must be communicated. When using an instantaneous method of communication, such as e-mail, the acceptance has been held to be effective, as soon as the acceptance reaches the offeror's inbox (even if the offeror does not access it immediately), so long as, if the acceptance is sent to business premises, it is sent during office hours (*The Brimnes*).

❖ If the e-mail was received outside office hours, it would be deemed to be effective at the start of business on the next working day. Here, B's second e-mail was sent three hours after his initial one and this, in turn, was sent immediately after D's e-mail at 3:15 pm. B's second e-mail, therefore, was not sent until 6.15 pm and D did not see it because she had gone home for the day.

❖ If, on the other hand, D's e-mail is not an offer but a request for further information, then B's second e-mail is at best only an offer to buy D's collection for £30,000, which D is free to accept or reject. She does not accept it (because she does not see it before she enters into the contract with Louise), there is no contract between D and B, so D will not be in breach of contract.

❖ The answer is illustrated in diagrammatic form below:

Initial correspondence
• Offer?
• Invitation to Treat?
  • Analysis of case law
  • *Harvey v Facey*
  • *Gibson v Mancs CC*

B's e-mail to Daisy
Analyse on the basis that Daisy's e-mail was an offer.
Analyse on the basis that Daisy's e-mail was an invitation to treat.

B's e-mails
If Daisy's e-mail was an offer Boris's initial e-mail will be a counter-offer and destroy Daisy's offer. His second e-mail will amount to an offer which was never accepted.
Consider B's 2nd e-mail as potential acceptance.

B's attempted acceptance
Acceptance must be communicated. When using instantaneous method of communication, such as e-mail, the acceptance has been held to be effective, as soon as the acceptance reaches the offeror's inbox (even if the offeror does not access it immediately), so long as, if the acceptance is sent to business premises, it is sent during office hours (*The Brimnes*).

Conclude – If the e-mail received outside of office hours – effective at the start of business on the next working day. Here, B's second e-mail was sent three hours after his initial one, and this in turn was sent immediately after D's e-mail which was sent at 3:15 pm. B's second e-mail therefore was not sent until 6.15 p.m and D did not see it because she had gone home for the day.

If D's e-mail is not an offer but a request for further information – B's second e-mail is at best only an offer to buy D's collection for £30,000, which D can accept or reject. She does not accept it (because she does not see it before contracting with Louise), there is no contract between D and B, so D will not be in breach of contract.

Table of key cases referred to in this chapter

Key case	Area of law	Principle
Adams v Lindsell (1818) 1 B & Ald 681	Concerned a transaction for the sale of wool. Communications took place by post.	Established the postal rule. Where acceptance takes place by post and where postal acceptance is deemed to be reasonable, acceptance will be effective once the written communication has been placed within the safe custody of the postal service.
Balfour v Balfour [1919] 2 KB 571	Concerned an agreement between a husband and a wife that he would pay her an allowance. The agreement was not upheld as the presumption against legal relations was not rebutted.	In a social setting, where an agreement is made, there is a presumption against the creation of a legal relationship. Such a presumption can be rebutted.
Byrne v Van Tienhoven (1880) 5 CPD 344	Concerned written negotiations for the sale of tinplate. Revocation was communicated *after* the letter of acceptance had been posted.	Revocation of an offer will be effective when it has been communicated to the offeree.
Carlill v Carbolic Smoke Ball Co [1893] 1 QB 256	Concerned an advertisement for a smoke ball that was supposed to cure influenza.	Precedent on unilateral offers. An offer can be made to the world at large and communication of acceptance is not necessary.
Felthouse v Brindley (1862) 142 ER 1037	Concerned the sale of a horse. The uncle told his nephew that if he heard nothing he would assume a sale at a specified price.	Acceptance of an offer cannot be inferred from silence.

Key case	Area of law	Principle
Harvey v Facey [1893] AC 552	Concerned telegraph negotiations to buy a property.	Guidance on establishing where the distinction between an invitation to treat and an offer lies. Mere statements of information cannot constitute an offer.
Hyde v Wrench (1840) 49 ER 132	Concerned negotiations for the sale of a farm. An offer was made and the offeree responded by asking if the seller would accept a lower amount. This communication constituted a counter-offer.	Acceptance must match the terms of the offer. Anything less will amount to a counter-offer which will destroy the initial offer.
Merritt v Merritt [1970] 1 WLR 1211	Concerned a separation agreement between a husband and wife. He would pay her a monthly allowance and later transfer the house to her. The agreement was upheld.	A presumption against the creation of a legal relationship in a family setting can be rebutted by evidence showing a contrary intention.
Pharmaceutical Society of Great Britain v Boots Cash Chemists [1953] 1 All ER 482	Concerned a self-service display. Boots were charged for selling goods contrary to a statute that required certain drugs to be sold under the supervision of a registered pharmacist.	The display of goods in a shop will constitute an invitation to treat. The offer arises when the goods are handed over to a cashier. At this stage the offer can be either accepted or rejected.

@ **Visit the book's companion website to test your knowledge**

❖ Resources include a subject map, revision tip podcasts, downloadable diagrams, MCQ quizzes for each chapter, and a flashcard glossary

❖ www.routledge.com/cw/optimizelawrevision

2 Consideration

Revision objectives

Understand the law
- Can you explain the term 'consideration' in contract terms?
- Can you discuss the importance of consideration in a contract?
- Can you explain the circumstances, giving examples, where there will not be valid consideration?
- Can you explain how promissory estoppel can assist where an agreement may fail for lack of consideration?

Remember the details
- Can you align the relevant caselaw to specific principles within the doctrine of consideration?
- Can you explain the exceptions to the rule that past consideration cannot constitute good consideration?
- Can you recount the rules on the exceptions that part payment of a debt cannot constitute good consideration?
- Can you recall the criteria for a successful claim of promissory estoppel?

Reflect critically on areas of debate
- Following *Williams v Roffey*, why does the 'practical benefit' rule not apply to agreements relating to part payment of a debt?
- Has policy shaped the law in relation to the rules in respect of consideration sometimes being upheld in agreements relating to the performance of an existing contractual duty?

Contextualise
- Do you comprehend the importance of consideration in relation to enforceability of a contract?
- Can you think of practical examples where exceptions to the rule of past consideration will be upheld?
- Do you understand the practical benefits to commercial agreements in relation to the *Williams v Roffey* principles?
- Can you recognise when a claim for promissory estoppel is likely to be rejected?

Apply your skills and knowledge
- Can you analyse a set of facts and through careful analysis arrive at a reasoned conclusion on whether or not consideration is present within a given scenario?
- Can you answer the question at the end of this chapter?

Chapter Map

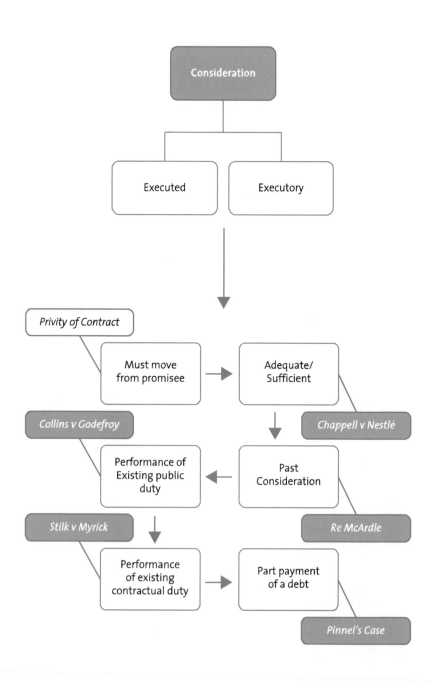

Consideration

Executed   Executory

Privity of Contract

Must move from promisee → Adequate/ Sufficient

Collins v Godefroy

Chappell v Nestlé

Performance of Existing public duty ← Past Consideration

Stilk v Myrick

Re McArdle

Performance of existing contractual duty → Part payment of a debt

Pinnel's Case

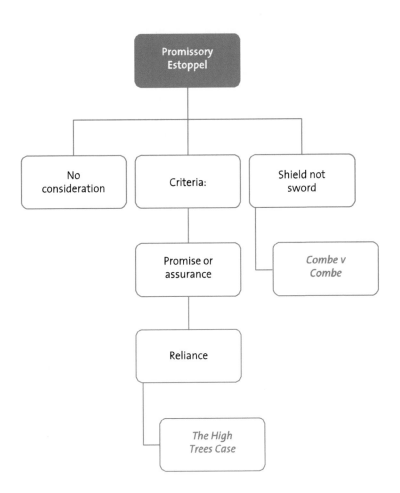

Consideration

Consideration is an essential ingredient within a contract. Quite simply, if there is no consideration, there is no contract. The law requires that, for an agreement to be binding, the promisee must provide some kind of payment for the promise they have received. Thus, a gratuitous promise is generally not enforceable. The term 'payment' is used widely here. Payment need not be of monetary value; whilst some 'detriment' on behalf of the promisee is required, the detriment can take the form of giving something up, for example, stopping smoking. The promisor need not receive any tangible part, so a promise made by the offeror to pay an overweight associate a sum of money upon losing a specified amount of weight would be enforceable.

Put simply, consideration is what one party is giving or promising, in exchange for what is being given or promised by the other party to the contact. The best-known definition originates from *Currie v Misa* (1875) LR 10 Ex 153:

DEF.

> *Corrie v Misa* (1875)
> Lush J
>
> 'a valuable consideration, in the sense of the law, may consist either in some right, interest, profit or benefit accruing to the one party or some forbearance, detriment, loss or responsibility, given, suffered or undertaken by the other.'

Example: If Jayne sells her iPad to Ellie for £240, Ellie will receive the benefit of the iPad and her detriment will be the surrender of £240 of her cash to Jayne.

There are two types of consideration:

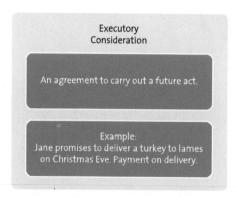

Executory Consideration

An agreement to carry out a future act.

Example:
Jane promises to deliver a turkey to James on Christmas Eve. Payment on delivery.

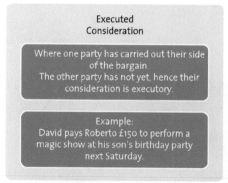

Executed Consideration

Where one party has carried out their side of the bargain. The other party has not yet, hence their consideration is executory.

Example:
David pays Roberto £150 to perform a magic show at his son's birthday party next Saturday.

The table below outlines four fundamental features of consideration:

Consideration must move from the promisee (but not essential that it moves to the promisor) *Tweddle v Atkinson* [1861]	Consideration need not be adequate but must be sufficient *Thomas v Thomas* (1842) *White v Bluett* (1853) *Ward v Byham* [1956] *Chappell v Nestle* (1960) ▪
Past consideration is not good consideration *Re McArdle* (1951) ▪ *Roscorla v Thomas* (1842) *Lampleigh v Braithwaite* (1615) *Re Casey's Patents* (1892) *Pao On v Lau Yiu Long* (1980) ▪	Performance of a pre-existing obligation cannot (usually) amount to consideration: Public duty imposed by law *Collins v Godefroy* (1831) · Contractual obligation *Stilk v Myrick* (1809) ˙ *Williams v Roffey Bros & Nicholls* (1990) ▪

The centre of the table is labelled **Consideration**.

Consideration must move from the promisee

The person who seeks to enforce the contract must show that they provided consideration; it is not enough to show that someone else provided it. The promisee must show that consideration was provided by, i.e. 'moved from' him but the consideration does not have to move to the promisor.

Example: If David (promisor) asks Robert (promisee) to pay Carole a sum of money as consideration for David's promise to Robert, that will be good consideration. However, if David (promisor) asks Carole to provide a payment as consideration for David's promise to Robert, that will not constitute good consideration (there is no detriment to David in such a case).

Consideration need not be adequate but must be sufficient

Consideration need not be adequate, i.e. the value to each of the parties need not be equal, but it must be legally sufficient.

Example: Rosie agrees to sell her horse to Jim for £10. In the eyes of the law, there is valid consideration. The agreement to pay £10 will be suffient consideration. The fact that it is not adequate does not matter, there is some economic value.

In *Thomas v Thomas* (1842), a promise made by the deceased, whereby his wife could remain in their house upon his death if she paid £1 per year in ground rent, was enforced. The amount of money involved, whilst disproportionate to the benefit gained, was nevertheless of some economic value and accorded good consideration. Similarly in *Ward v Byham* [1956], a promise to keep a child happy was held as good consideration. Conversely, in *White v Bluett* (1853), a promise made by a father to his son not to enforce a promissory note against his son if he stopped complaining was not enforceable as the son had not provided sufficient consideration.

Past consideration

Past consideration will not constitute good consideration:

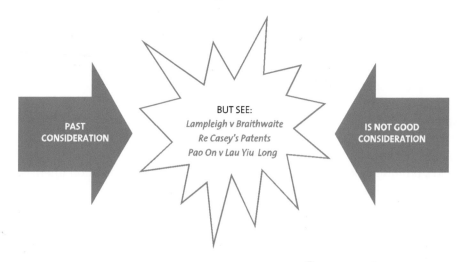

Consideration must arise at the time of the contract or after a contract has been agreed. Remember consideration is the price for the promise. Consideration provided before an agreement has been reached can never be regarded as part of the price for the promise and consequently will be construed as a gratuity or gift.

Scenario A below shows an example of good consideration. Here payment can be enforced. Scenario B is an example of past consideration. This payment is unenforceable.

Scenario A:	Scenario B:
Maureen agrees to pay her neighbour, Samuel, a sum of £100 to paint her house whilst she is on holiday. Samuel completes the task whilst Maureen is on holiday and leaves her an invoice for the agreed sum of £100. Samuel can enforce payment.	Samuel, a neighbour, decides to paint the outside of Maureen's house whilst she is on holiday. Maureen returns from her holiday and is delighted with Samuel's kind act. She promises to pay him £100. Maureen later refuses to pay Samuel. Samuel cannot enforce payment.
Good Consideration	**Past Consideration**

In scenario B above, the contract cannot be enforced because the promise was made after the work had been done.

In *Re McArdle* (1951) a father left his property to his adult children. Prior to the sale of the property one of the sons had been living in the property and had undertaken improvements. After the work had been carried out, his siblings agreed to contribute to the payment for the work out of their share of the proceeds of the property sale. The agreement was unenforceable as it was secured after the work had been carried out, thus amounting to past consideration. Again in *Roscorla v Thomas* (1842) the sale of a horse was negotiated. After agreement had been reached, the claimant was assured by the defendant that the horse was 'sound and free from vice'. This turned out to be false. The claimant was unsuccessful in his claim, again because the consideration was past.

Exception to the past consideration rule

The main exception to the rule was laid down in *Lampleigh v Braithwaite* (1615):

Case precedent – *Lampleigh v Braithwaite* (1615) 80 ER 255

Facts: Braithwaite had killed a man. He asked Lampleigh to obtain a King's pardon for him. Lampleigh secured the pardon and in recognition of his hard work and expenses, Braithwaite promised to pay him £100. He later refused to pay.

Principle: Whilst payment had not been discussed at the time of the request, it was clear that both of the parties would have anticipated payment for the activity. The court held that Braithwaite's request constituted an implied promise of payment.

Application: Three exceptions to the rule on past consideration flow from this case. In similar instances you should consider whether these conditions apply. If they do, it is likely that an exception to the general rule on past consideration will be upheld.

The three conditions that must be met for an exception to the past consideration rule to apply are:

❖ The act must have been carried out at the promisor's request.
❖ The parties must have understood that the act would be rewarded in some way.
❖ The payment must have been capable of legal enforcement had it been promised beforehand.

In *Re Casey's Patents* [1892] a manager was promised a one-third share in a patent that he had developed for his employers. He was able to enforce payment even though the promise came after he had undertaken the work on the premise that there had always been an implied promise that some reward would be provided.

The rules in *Lampleigh v Braithwaite* (1615) were later re-stated by Lord Scarman in *Pao On v Lau Yiu Long* [1979].

Aim Higher

Alex sees his neighbour Paul in the local pub. Alex is aware that Paul operates an airport shuttle service. Alex asks Paul if he can take him and his wife to the airport next Thursday. At the airport he promises to pay Paul £25 upon his return from Marbella. Can Paul enforce the payment?

Performance of an existing duty

We will now consider the question of whether performance of an existing duty can ever constitute consideration for a promise.

The main categories of existing duty are set out below:

Existing Duty – Public duty imposed by law	Existing Duty – Contractual obligation already owed to promisor
Performance of an existing public duty will not form good consideration. Exception – where performance is over and above the existing duty.	A promise to perform an obligation already owed to the other party cannot constitute good consideration. Exception – Practical benefit obtained.
Collins v Godefroy (1831) *Glasbrook Bros Ltd v Glamorgan CC* (1925) *Harris v Sheffield United FC* (1987)	*Stilk v Myrick* (1809) *Hartley v Ponsonby* (1957) *Williams v Roffey Bros & Nicholls* (1990)

Public duty imposed by law

Where a person is legally obliged to carry out a particular duty, it would be adverse to public policy to allow those individuals or bodies to make commercial agreements and profit from executing tasks that they are already bound to perform.

In *Collins v Godefroy* (1831) 109 ER 1040 → A witness was promised a payment for attending court. She was already already legally obliged to attend court. The payment could not be enforced. → Held: There was no consideration for the promise as the witness was bound by law to attend the court hearing.

If the promise goes beyond the existing legal duty, the courts can enforce payment. This was illustrated in *Glasbrook Bros v Glamorgan CC* [1925] which concerned an agreement between the mine owners and the police. The mine owners agreed to pay a sum of money for extra protection during a strike. The House of Lords confirmed that the police had provided services over and above their statutory requirement and payment was enforced. This approach was followed in *Harris v Sheffield United FC* [1987].

Aim Higher

If statute provided that every child in the borough of Greenfields was entitled to a free school meal and the school then attempted to charge each parent £1 towards the cost of its additional fuel bill to enable them to cook the extra food, would the payment be enforceable?

Contractual obligation already owed to promisor

The issue is whether or not a promise to perform something that a person is already contractually obliged to do can ever amount to good consideration.

Example: Donna's hairdresser Sarah agrees to put extensions in Donna's hair for £150 using a new technique. The consideration here is clear. The work is taking far longer than Sarah had anticipated but she promises to finish the extensions if Donna agrees to pay an extra £75. You will hopefully conclude that Sarah cannot enforce the additional payment as she is already contractually obliged to complete the hairdressing task.

The starting point here is that a promise to perform a contractual obligation already owed to another party will not amount to good consideration. The case of *Stilk v Myrick* (1809) is precedent for this point:

Case precedent – *Stilk v Myrick* (1809) 170 ER 1168

Facts: During a voyage, two crew members deserted their ship. The remaining crew were promised extra wages to staff the ship back to London. The captain later refused to pay the extra money.

Principle: The court held that there had been no consideration for the captain's promise of extra wages. The sailors had done no more than they had initially been contracted to do; i.e. to sail the ship for the complete voyage. No fresh consideration had been given for the promise.

Application: In problem scenarios, if an additional payment is promised for simply carrying out what the other party is already contracted to do and there is no additional benefit to the party receiving the work, then payment cannot be enforced.

A different approach was taken in *Hartley v Ponsonby* (1857) when around half of the crew deserted ship. The captain promised extra wages to the remaining crew. The outcome was different here, as the voyage was regarded as something altogether different to the original mission. Consequently, the agreement to pay extra wages was enforced on the basis that it was a fresh contract; the initial contract having become frustrated.

The position is more complex when we consider *Williams v Roffey Bros & Nicholls (Contractors)* (1990). The case concerned a contract to refurbish some flats. The contractor, Roffey, subcontracted the carpentry work to Williams at an agreed price.

Due to financial difficulties, it appeared unlikely that Williams would complete the work in time. There was a penalty clause in the main contract for late completion and to avoid this, Roffey agreed to pay an additional amount to Williams per flat completed. Roffey later refused to pay the additional sum for the completed flats. The issue for the Court of Appeal hinged upon whether there had been consideration for the promise of additional payments, on the basis that the subcontractor already owed an obligation to the contractor to complete the flats. It held that there was a contract and consideration had been provided. The new benefit achieved by the contractors was that they would avoid the detriment of being sued under the penalty clause for late completion and that they would not have to find new sub-contractors at short notice. In the words of Glidewell LJ, referring to the giving of a promise to the provider of the goods or services, 'as a result of giving his promise B obtains in practice a benefit, or obviates a disbenefit, and B's promise is not given as a result of economic duress or fraud … then the benefit to B is capable of being consideration for B's promise'.

A summary of the *Williams v Roffey* principles can be seen below:

Key Principles flowing from *Williams v Roffey Bros & Nicholls (Contractors) Ltd* [1990] 1 All ER 512 (1990)

Where party A and B have a contract for the provision of goods and services and it becomes apparent that the provider of the goods/services is unable to satisfy their commitment, an extra payment to complete the contract will be enforceable in the following instances:

1. Where the promise has not been gained through fraud or economic duress.

2. An extra benefit will be received by the recipient of the goods and services, or a detriment will be avoided as a result of the contract being completed.

Williams v Roffey (1990) represents a significant shift in the scope of the limits of consideration. A promise to perform an existing contractual duty can now constitute good consideration if it falls within the *Roffey* guidelines.

Common Pitfall

Consideration is a very popular exam topic and you will often come across a problem question that contains a variety of issues relating to whether or not there is valid consideration. Owing to the fact that there are a variety of principles to be aware of within the doctrine, students often grasp some of the issues but overlook others and do not gain the full range of marks available. Remember to carefully scrutinise the question and pinpoint all of the issues before putting pen to paper!

A recap of principles covered so far

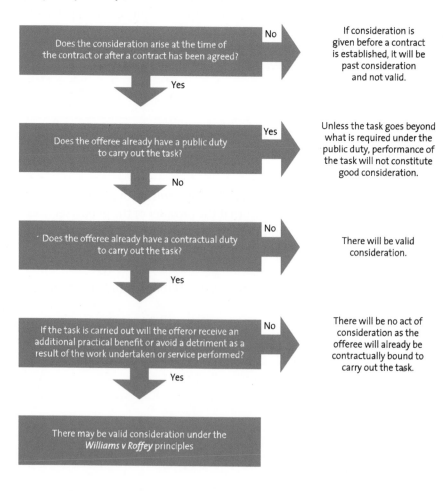

Does the consideration arise at the time of the contract or after a contract has been agreed?

No → If consideration is given before a contract is established, it will be past consideration and not valid.

Yes ↓

Does the offeree already have a public duty to carry out the task?

Yes → Unless the task goes beyond what is required under the public duty, performance of the task will not constitute good consideration.

No ↓

Does the offeree already have a contractual duty to carry out the task?

No → There will be valid consideration.

Yes ↓

If the task is carried out will the offeror receive an additional practical benefit or avoid a detriment as a result of the work undertaken or service performed?

No → There will be no act of consideration as the offeree will already be contractually bound to carry out the task.

Yes ↓

There may be valid consideration under the *Williams v Roffey* principles

Aim Higher

Using the flowchart above try to provide a reasoned solution to the following problem:

Ellie owned a 1926 Barker Salamanca Rolls Royce and, in order to raise a deposit for her new house, she decided to sell it to Sam, a mechanic, for £50,000. As part of the deal, Ellie agreed to have it restored for Sam. Ellie asked Richard, a vintage car restorer, to carry out the work within eight weeks for £8,000. One month later, Ellie was worried that Richard would not meet the deadline and, eventually offered him an extra £2,000 if the restoration was completed on time. Sam was anxious to have the car on time as he was going to sell it on and had a purchaser for it, so he offered to give Richard £500 for doing the work. Richard completed the restoration on time but Ellie has refused to pay him the extra £2,000, arguing that Richard was already obliged to complete the work for £8,000. Furthermore, Sam has told Richard that he can only give him £100, which Richard has reluctantly agreed to accept.

Can Richard insist on the full payments promised by Ellie and Sam?

Part payment of a debt

The rule in *Williams v Roffey* will not apply where an agreement concerns the discharge of a debt. When a loan is taken out, the debtor undertakes to repay the full debt, usually with interest. A promise by the creditor to accept part payment in settlement of the full debt cannot be enforced due to lack of consideration. The creditor will remain able to sue on the outstanding debt.

Example: David borrowed £1,000 from Masood last August. An agreement was made that David would pay the money back on 31 October. That date has now passed and David has significant financial problems. He promises to pay Masood £700 provided that he agrees to waive the remaining balance. Hopefully you will have applied the rule outlined above and concluded that Masood can pursue the remainder of the debt on the premise that a promise to make part-payment of a debt in settlement of the whole sum cannot constitute good consideration.

Exception to the rule

An exception to the rule was laid down in *Pinnel's Case* (1602) and later approved by the House of Lords in *Foakes v Beer* (1884). The rule in *Pinnel's Case* is that part payment of a debt on its due date will not discharge the full debt, unless it is supported by a new consideration or deed. The decision in *Foakes v Beer* (1884) illustrates the application of this rule:

| In *Foakes v Beer* (1884) 9 App Cas 605 | → | Beer had been awarded a sum of money against Dr Foakes.

Beer agreed that if Foakes paid £500 immediately and the outstanding balance by instalments she would take no further action.

Beer later sued Foakes for the interest payable on the instalments. | → | Held: Beer's promise was unenforceable due to lack of consideration.

Beer was entitled to the full amount outstanding plus interest. |

It is clear that a practical benefit could have been obtained by Beer, but the 'practical benefit' rule is not applicable in debt cases. The difference in approach is important and signifies that a different rule must be followed when dealing with agreements relating to debts (*Foakes v Beer* (1884)) and agreements relating to other types of contractual commitments (*Williams v Roffey* (1990)).

Again, in *Re Selectmove* [1995] a company made an agreement with the Inland Revenue to pay off its tax arrears by instalments. The agreement was unenforceable because the company had supplied no consideration for the instalment agreement. The argument that the agreement would be of practical benefit to the Inland Revenue did not persuade the COA in favour of the company. Also, to permit this line of argument would have been in direct conflict with the earlier House of Lords' decision in *Foakes v Beer* (1884).

As mentioned above, *Pinnel's Case* (1602) permits an exception to the rule where an agreement is supported by a 'new consideration or deed'. The diagram below outlines the accepted exceptions:

Creditor requests early payment and agrees to waive the remaining debt
Early payment

'the gift of a horse, hawk, or robe in satisfaction is good. For it shall be intended that a horse, hawk, or robe, might be more beneficial to the plaintiff than the money' *Pinnel's Case*.

Acceptance of something else towards the outstanding debt. For example, the creditor may accept the defendant's car in lieu of payment

Where several creditors are owed money by a debtor, they can accept a percentage of the full amount as full settlement of the whole amount owed

Composition agreements

Hirachand Punamchand v Temple (1911)

Part payment by third party

Privity of contract

Privity of contract is a small, yet important area on the contract law syllabus. It rarely appears on an exam paper as a full question, but often crops up as an issue within a larger themed problem, so you need to understand the key principles.

Case precedent – *Dunlop v Selfridge* [1915] AC 847

Facts: Dunlop sold tyres to a wholesaler, Dew & Co who expressly agreed in the contract that Dunlop could fix the minimum price for which the tyres could be sold and that they (Dew & Co) would not sell below that price. Dew & Co also agreed that the same terms would be replicated within customer contracts when they resold the tyres. Dew & Co sold some tyres to Selfridge under an agreement that incorporated the agreed terms on price, but Selfridge broke the agreement and re-sold the tyres for a price below the minimum amount. Dunlop sued Selfridge.

Principle: The court action against Selfridge failed. Dunlop had a contract with Dew & Co, but Selfridge was not a party to this contract.

Application: In problem scenarios be on your guard for questions that involve a third party attempt to enforce a contract. Of course, one of the exceptions to the common law rule may apply.

The basic common law rule on privity of contract is that only parties to a contract can sue, or be sued under an agreement. The rule can produce harsh results, particularly where a contract purports to confer a benefit on a third party. In *Tweddle v Atkinson* (1861) which concerned an agreement for marriage consideration, the claimant was unsuccessful in an action to claim a payment of £300, that had been agreed between his father and father-in-law, as he himself had provided no consideration. The fact that the contract had been made for his benefit was not relevant.

Over the years a number of exceptions to the rule have developed. See below:

Exceptions to the rule on privity of contract				
Statutory Exceptions	*Agency*	*Collateral Contracts*	*Trusts*	*Covenants in land law*
Contracts (Rights of Third Parties Act) 1999 Road Traffic Act 1988 – drivers must have third party insurance. s 56(1) Law of Property Act 1925 s 11 Married Women's Property Act 1882 – wife can claim on husband's life insurance policy. Bills of Exchange Act 1882 – third party can sue on a cheque.	The agent makes the contract on behalf of the Principal. He enters into a contract with the third party, but under the rules of Agency, there is no contract between the agent and third party.	A method to 'get around' the privity rule. A second contract can run alongside the initial contract, but the second contract can be with a third party and relate to the main contract. *Shanklin Pier v Detel Products Ltd* [1951]	An exception to the privity rule where one of the parties to a contract holds contractual rights in trust for a third party, whom the contract was intended to benefit. The third party interest must fall within the principles of trust law.	A restrictive covenant, in certain circumstances, can run with the land, and be enforced by a person who was not privvy to the initial agreement (e.g. not to run a business on some land). *Tulk v Moxhay* (1848)

Due to the issues with the strict rule of privity, and following the recognition of various exceptions to the rule, the Contracts (Rights of Third Parties) Act 1999 was introduced. See the diagram below for a summary of the main effects of the Act.

s 1(1)(a) Third party can enforce where the contract expressly states that he may, or

s 1(1)(b) where a term of the contract purports to confer a benefit on the third party.

> s 1(2) A benefit will not be conferred on the third party if it appears, upon construction of the contract, that the parties did not intend the term to be enforceable by the third party.
>
> > s 1(3) The third party must be expressly identified in the contract by name, as a member of a class or answering a particular description. The party need not exist when the contract is agreed.
> >
> > > Contracts (Rights of Third Parties) Act 1999 – rules governing when a third party can/cannot enforce a contract.

There are a few exceptions to the rules contained within the Act. The main exceptions are bills of exchange, promissory notes and negotiable instruments, contracts involving the carriage of goods by sea, certain partnership documents and contracts of employment.

A third party is entitled to any remedy that would have been available to him for breach of contract, if he had been a party to the contract.

Promissory estoppel

The equitable doctrine of promissory estoppel can sometimes be used to enforce an agreement that might otherwise fail due to a lack of consideration. In simple terms, estoppel prevents party A from withdrawing a promise made to party B, if party B has reasonably relied on that promise. See the definition in *Combe v Combe* (1951) below:

Lord Denning:

'Where one party has, by his words or conduct, made to the other a promise or assurance which was intended to affect the legal relations between them and to be acted on accordingly, then, once the other party has taken him at his word and acted upon it, the one who gave the promise or assurance cannot afterwards be allowed to revert to the previous legal relations as if no such promise or assurance had been made by him.'

Example: Jody hires a barge to Billy for a six-month period at a rent of £300 per week. Billy loses his job and Jody agrees to accept £100 for a set period of time, which is paid on time, each week by Billy. Jody could not later insist upon payment of the higher sum for the period of the agreement.

The doctrine was initially developed in the case of *Hughes v Metropolitan Railway Company* (1877):

In *Hughes v Metropolitan Railway Company* (1877) 2 App Cas 439	The landlord (H) served notice on the tenant (MRC), to perform repairs within six months, and if the repairs were not completed, the lease would be forfeited. In the period that followed, negotiations took place between the parties for the purchase of the demised premises. The negotiations broke down and the repairs had not been carried out after the expiry of the six-month period. H sought to evict MRC.	Held: House of Lords held that the conduct of H had led MRC to believe that H had suspended his legal rights under the lease whilst the discussions had been ongoing. It would be inequitable to permit the time to run against MRC during this period. Consequently the repairs were finished two months after the inital agreement and the House of Lords deemed this acceptable.

Perhaps the most famous case came 70 years later when Lord Denning revisited the doctrine in *Central London Property Trust Ltd v High Trees House Ltd* [1947]:

Case precedent – *Central London Property Trust Ltd v High Trees House Ltd* [1947] KB 130

Facts: The owners of a block of flats in London rented the block to the defendants for a sum per annum. As a result of the war, the defendants were unable to find sufficient tenants to populate the flats. The plaintiffs agreed to reduce the rent by 50%. The agreement continued until the end of the war. The plaintiffs then gave notice to revert to full rent and also queried whether they could claim the full rent for the war period as there had been no consideration for the promise for a lesser payment.

Principle: The plaintiffs were estopped from going back on their promise, but could revert back to the full rent after the war ended. Lord Denning drew on the equitable principle: 'A promise intended to be binding, intended to be acted upon, and in fact acted on, is binding so far as its terms properly apply.'

Application: In problem scenarios, where an agreement may fail due to an absence of consideration, examine whether the principles of estoppel may provide an alternative remedy.

Up For Debate

How can the decision in *High Trees* (1947), that effectively enforced an agreement for half payment of a rent, for no consideration, be reconciled with cases such as *Foakes v Beer* (1884), which held that part payment of a debt could never constitute good satisfaction for the whole?

The rather wide construction adopted by Lord Denning in the *High Trees* case has been narrowed somewhat in later decisions. The four main limitations to the rule are highlighted below:

Shield not a sword	❖ Promissory estoppel cannot form the basis of a cause of action ❖ It is available only as a defence ❖ *Combe v Combe* (1951)
Must be a legal relationship	❖ Doctrine is limited to the variation of existing legal agreements ❖ Doctrine will not create new obligations ❖ *High Trees* concerned modification of existing contractual obligations

Must be reliance
{ ❖ The party seeking to enforce a promise must have taken some action as a result of the promise }

Must be inequitable for the promisor to assert strict legal rights
{ ❖ There must be no undue pressure on the promisor
❖ *D and C Builders v Rees* [1966]
❖ *Collier v P & M J Wright (Holdings) Ltd* (2007) }

Scope of estoppel

In some circumstances promisory estoppel will be only suspensory. For example in *Hughes v Metropolitan Railway* (1877), the obligation to repair was reinstated after the sale negotiations broke down. Likewise in *High Trees*, the obligation to pay full rent was restored after the war. However, the effect of estoppel can extend to extinguish some rights altogether. Looking at *High Trees* again, we observe that the right to receive full rent during the war period was extinguished. To further illustrate this point let us review the case of *Tool Metal Manufacturing Co v Tungsten Electric Co* [1955]:

In *Tool Metal Manufacturing Co v Tungsten Electric Co* [1955] 1 WLR 761

The owner of a patent promised to suspend periodic payments during the war.

Held: The promise was binding for the duration of the war but the owners could, on giving reasonable notice at the end of the war, revert to their original legal entitlements.

Overall, the position as to whether or not promissory estoppel will extinguish or suspend rights hinges upon the nature of the promise and the circumstances of the agreement.

Summary

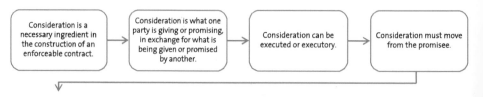

Consideration is a necessary ingredient in the construction of an enforceable contract.

Consideration is what one party is giving or promising, in exchange for what is being given or promised by another.

Consideration can be executed or executory.

Consideration must move from the promisee.

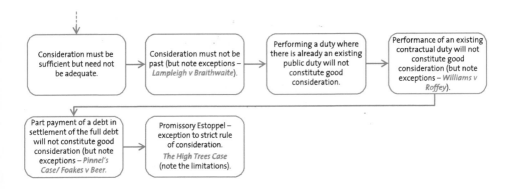

Putting it into practice

Example problem question:

Look at the scenario below, and then answer the following question:

Bob is a builder. Last year he renovated three cottages in his local village. The cottages are called 'Sunnyside', 'Cloverleaf' and 'Mistletoe'.

Bob lives next door to 'Sunnyside, which is owned by Ruth. Ruth has had problems with her wood burner and a few weeks ago she asked Bob to take a look. Bob called round and repaired the wood burner. Ruth was so impressed with Bob's work that she promised to give him £100 for the work he had done. She is now refusing to pay. *past consid.*

Jackie, an antique dealer, owed Bob £12,000 for fitting a new kitchen in 'Cloverleaf'. Unable to pay Bob the full amount by the date agreed, she consented at his request to pay him £7,000 and to give him an antique bronze statue of an African white rhinoceros. Bob has now decided that the bronze statue looks mismatched in his lounge and he wishes to receive the outstanding amount on the debt.

Bob renovated 'Mistletoe' for Sam last summer. Bob has recently received a letter from the Local Authority informing him that the joists within the roof are not of the required specification and are in breach of building regulations. The Local Authority has informed him that he has three months to remedy the defects. Sam who has had sleepless nights worrying about the roof collapsing agrees to pay Bob £800 to complete the work. Bob completed the work, but Sam is now refusing to pay.

Bob also owns some retail units in the nearby town of Padsville. Mohammed, one of the tenants occupying No 62 The Parade (the shop), is causing him immense aggravation. In April 2007, the shop had a long lease of twelve years left to run. The annual rent had become higher than the annual profits of the shop and there were onerous repairing covenants. Bob had told Mohammed, that if he would perform certain specified repairs, he would be satisfied with only half of the rent for the remainder of the lease and would further make Mohammed an interest-free loan of £4,000 so that he could install central heating. Mohammed duly performed the specified repairs and Bob accepted one-half of the rent.

In December 2012, Bob gave notice to Mohammed that he would require full rent in future, and he claimed repayment of the arrears from April 2007. He has consistently refused to make the promised loan of £4,000 for the central heating.

Bob is eager to recover as much money as he can from his customers and his tenant. Advise Bob on whether he can recover the money that he believes is owed him by Ruth, Jackie, Sam and Mohammed.

Define the law and apply to each character

Ruth

❖ Is Ruth under a legal obligation to pay Bob the £100 that she promised?
❖ Define 'consideration': it is the price for which the promise of the other is bought.
❖ Probably a case of past consideration. Ruth's promise comes after Bob's performance.
❖ Explain the rule against past consideration: past consideration is no consideration: see *Roscorla v Thomas* (1842), *Re McArdle* [1951].
❖ State and explain the exception: where there is an implied promise to pay: see *Re Casey's Patents* [1892], *Lampleigh v Braithwaite* (1615).
❖ Exception may apply here – discuss.

Jackie

❖ Issue – will Bob succeed in an action to recover the £5,000 he believes Jackie still owes him?
❖ Identify the issue as part-payment of debt. State and explain the rule in *Pinnel's Case* (1602): part-payment of a debt is not satisfaction for the whole debt even if the creditor accepts the part-payment. The creditor may still recover the balance of the debt.
❖ Identify and explain the relevant exception to the rule in *Pinnel's Case*: provision of some other consideration by the debtor, at the request of the creditor, will prevent the creditor from recovering the balance: see *Pinnel's Case*.

❖ Apply the law to the facts of the problem. Jackie has agreed, at Bob's request, part-payment of the debt together with an antique statue.
❖ The court will look to form not value: consideration need not be adequate (*Chappell v Nestlé* [1960]). Jackie will not fail on that point. The issue, however, is: Is this sufficient consideration for valid part payment? The additional consideration was provided at the request of Bob. See *Pinnel's Case* – the rule here is that part payment of a debt on its due date will not discharge the full debt, unless it is supported by a new consideration or deed. The bronze statue will constitute new consideration so Bob will be unable to recover the balance of money owing.

Sam

❖ Issue – whether consideration has been provided for the promise. Sam offered to pay Bob to remedy the defects. A contract had already been agreed in the previous year for the renovation of 'Mistletoe'.
❖ It appears that the defects are in breach of building regulations. It is likely that Bob already has an existing legal duty to remedy the defects as his previous work is in breach of building regulations.
❖ Where a legal duty exists, an agreement to carry out the same activity for reward cannot constitute good consideration (*Collins v Godefroy* (1831)). It is unlikely that Bob will be able to enforce the payment of £800 against Sam.

Mohammed

Bob has promised:

❖ That he will be satisfied with half rent if Mohammed performs specified parts of repairing covenants- Bob is claiming arrears of rent and future rent payments; that he will lend Mohammed £4,000 if he performs specified parts of repairing covenants. Is this promise binding regarding the arrears? Has Mohammed given any consideration? NO – he has covenanted to do the repairs – in doing any of them, he is performing existing contractual obligations (*Stilk v Myrick* (1809)) – no consideration.
❖ Can Mohammed rely on the doctrine of promissory estoppel: State criteria and apply:
❖ Existing contractual relationship between the parties? Yes. There must be a clear and unequivocal promise that the promisor will not insist on his strict legal rights – Yes, Bob has promised. It must be inequitable to allow the promisor go back on his promise. Yes – Mohammed has performed all of Bob's requests. Defendant must have acted in reliance on promise – Mohammed has relied upon the promise. Case law – *High Trees* (1947), *v MRB* (1877), *Combe v Combe* (1951) – formulated requirements. If Bo'

claim repayment of arrears, Mohammed can use promissory estoppel as defence – will probably be successful. How about future full rent? – may be able to claim estoppel – but note, can be suspensory in nature – *Tool Metal Manufacturing Co v Tungsten Electric Co* (1955). Central heating loan of £4,000? – Mohammed has given no consideration for loan – can he rely on estoppel to claim it? Note – estoppel can only be used as shield, not sword (*Combe v Combe* (1951)) – Mohammed cannot enforce the loan as he has given no consideration, he cannot rely on estoppel as a cause of action.

The answer can be shown diagrammatically. This is a useful way to plan answers:

Ruth	Jackie
Define consideration	Issue – Part Payment of Debt not good consideration – *Pinnel's case* (1602)
Past consideration	Exceptions to rule
Re McArdle [1951]	Statue – fresh consideration at creditor's request
Exceptions: *Lampleigh v Braithwaite* [1615]	Consideration = sufficient – *Chappell v Nestle* [1960]
Likely to recover	Bob unikely to recover the monetary balance

Bob's claim

Sam	Mohammed
Promise to provide something where a legal duty already exists = not good consideration – *Collins v Godefroy* (1831)	Can Mohammed rely upon estoppel?
	Criteria for estoppel:
	Existing contractual relationship – Yes
Bob in breach of building regulations – statutory duty to carry out work to certain standard – not performed	Clear and unequivocal promise that the promisor will not insist on his strict legal rights – Yes
Bob cannot charge Sam as he already has existing duty to perform this act	Must be inequitable to allow the promisor go back on his promise – Yes
	Defendant must have acted in reliance on promise – Yes
	Caselaw: *High Trees*; *Hughes v MRB*
	Shield not sword? Yes, but not for loan

Table of key cases referred to in this chapter

Key case	Area of law	Principle
Chappel & Co Ltd v Nestlé Co Ltd [1960] AC 87	Concerned an argument as to whether chocolate wrappers could form consideration within a contract.	Consideration must be sufficient but need not be adequate.
Central London Property Trust Ltd v High Trees House Ltd [1947] KB 130	Concerned an agreement between a landlord and tenant of a block of flats. The landlord agreed to accept half-rent due to difficulties in letting the flats during the war. After the war had ended, the landlord sued for payment of the full rent.	The rent was increased after the war, but not for the war period. The doctrine of estoppel prevents a party from withdrawing a promise made to another party, if the other party has reasonably relied on that promise to his detriment.
Dunlop v Selfridge [1915] AC 847	Concerned an attempt by Dunlop to enforce a contract against a third party who had not been party to the agreement.	A contract can only be enforced by the parties who are privy to the agreement (although some exceptions now apply).
Lampleigh v Braithwaite (1615) 80 ER 255	Concerned a request from Braithwaite to Lampleigh to obtain a King's pardon, for killing someone.	Past consideration can be enforced where there is an implied promise that payment will be made.
Pinnel's Case (1602) 5 Co Rep 117a	Concerned an agreement to discharge a debt. Cole owed Pinnel a sum of money, and at Pinnel's request, to discharge the debt in full, Cole paid part of the debt a month early.	Payment of a lesser sum when it is due cannot provide satisfaction of the full debt, unless some additional consideration is provided.
Stilk v Myrick (1809) 170 ER 1168	Concerned a promise by the captain of a ship to pay extra wages to the crew when two crew members abandoned the voyage.	An agreement to carry out a task that a party already has a contractual duty to perform cannot constitute good consideration.
Tool Metal Manufacturing Co v Tungsten Electric Co [1955] 1 WLR 761	Concerned a promise to suspend periodic payments on a patent for the duration of the war.	The promise was upheld. Estoppel will temporarily suspend rights, it will not necessarily extinguish them.

Key case	Area of law	Principle
Williams v Roffey Bros & Nicholls (Contractors) Ltd [1990] 1 All ER 512	Concerned a building contract, where some of the work had been sub-contracted. The sub-contractors were unlikely to finish their work on time, which meant that the head contractors would endure a penalty under their contract terms. The contractors agreed to pay the sub-contractors extra to complete on time.	An additional payment to perform a party's existing obligations can constitute good consideration where a practical benefit can be obtained, or a detriment can be avoided.

@ **Visit the book's companion website to test your knowledge**

❖ Resources include a subject map, revision tip podcasts, downloadable diagrams, MCQ quizzes for each chapter, and a flashcard glossary

❖ www.routledge.com/cw/optimizelawrevision

3

Terms

Revision objectives

Understand the law
- Can you outline the differences between a term and a representation?
- Can you classify the different types of terms?
- Can you explain what is meant by incorporation and interpretation of terms?
- Can you outline what is meant by implication and exemption of terms?

Remember the details
- Can you explain the different ways in which a term might be incorporated into a contract and outline the different cases which illustrate these different methods of incorporation?
- Can you explain the so-called parol evidence rule and its effects?
- Can you explain the different ways in which a term might be implied into a contract and outline the cases which illustrate these different methods of implication?
- Can you explain how the Unfair Contract Terms Act 1977 and the Unfair Terms in Consumer Contracts Regulations 1999 work?

Reflect critically on areas of debate
- Do you understand the subtleties in relation to incorporation of a term by a course of previous dealings as exemplified by the cases of *Hollier v Rambler Motors (AMC) Ltd* [1972] and *British Crane Hire Corp Ltd v Ipswich Plant Hire* [1975]?
- Do the principles of contractual interpretation as developed by the courts mean that, effectively, the courts are rewriting the contracting parties' bargain?

Contextualise
- Do you understand the importance of terms in relation to the question of the enforceability of a contract?
- Do you understand the differences in the remedial effects between a term and a (mis)representation?

Apply your skills and knowledge
- Can you answer the question at the end of this chapter?

Chapter Map

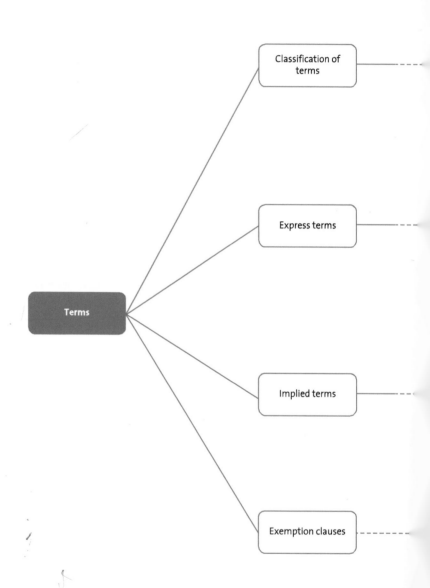

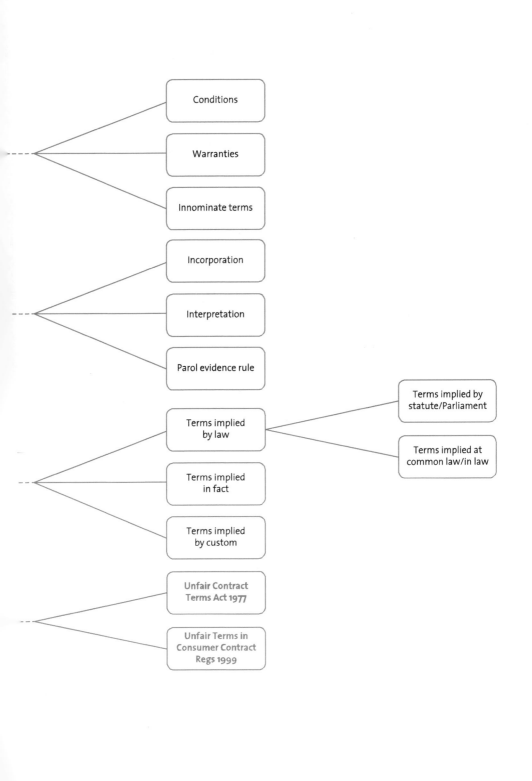

Introduction

Whilst offer, acceptance and consideration might be described as the basic requirements for a contract, terms might probably be best described as the 'ingredients' of the contract: they tell us what each party to the contract is expected to do under the contractual agreement. Terms thus identify the respective obligations of each party under the contract: they amount to contractual promises. Contractual terms are, therefore, to be distinguished from mere puffs or representations which are non-promissory in nature and do not amount to terms: a puff is an advertising statement which praises the advertised goods in such vague/ boastful terms that the statement made cannot be taken seriously; a representation is a statement which induces one party to enter the contract but which does not form part of the contract, i.e. which does not amount to a contractual term. This distinction is important as only the breach of a contractual obligation/term will give rise to liability for damages for breach of contract – if a puff is broken/false, no liability is incurred for this; if a representation is broken/false, the remedies, if any, are those for misrepresentation (see Chapter 4 on Misrepresentation).

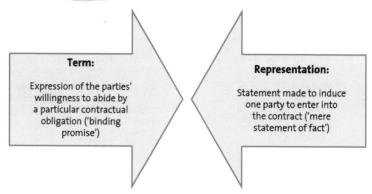

Term:
Expression of the parties' willingness to abide by a particular contractual obligation ('binding promise')

Representation:
Statement made to induce one party to enter into the contract ('mere statement of fact')

Classification of terms

Contractual terms can be classified in different ways: either according to their source (i.e. where they originate from – express agreement between the parties or implication of a term into the contract) or according to their remedial effect (i.e. what remedy they give rise to in case of a breach).

Condition

* Essential term of the contract, i.e. one which is so important that it goes 'to the root' of the contract.
* Important quote: '[Conditions] go so directly to the substance of the contract or, in other words, are so essential to its very nature that their non-performance may fairly be considered by the other party as a substantial failure to perform the contract at all.'
   (*L Schuler AG v Wickman Machine Tool Sales Ltd* [1973]).

❖ A breach of a condition entitles the innocent party *not only* to sue for damages *but also* to terminate the contract, i.e. to treat his contractual obligations as being at an end. The innocent party may, however, also choose to affirm the contract and merely claim damages.

Warranty

❖ Minor term of the contract, i.e. one which is of lesser importance as it is merely collateral or ancillary to the main purpose of the contract.
❖ Important quote: 'obligations which, though they must be performed, are not so vital that a failure to perform them goes to the substance of the contract.' (*L Schuler AG v Wickman Machine Tool Sales Ltd* [1973]).
❖ A breach of a warranty entitles the innocent party to sue for damages only but does not give rise to the right to treat the contract as repudiated. If no loss was suffered, the innocent party can only recover nominal damages.

Innominate/intermediate term

❖ Contractual term which is classed neither as a condition nor as a warranty at the time the contract was formed but whose classification depends upon the effects of its breach.
❖ Important quote: 'There are [. . .] many contractual undertakings of a more complex character which cannot be categorised as being "conditions" or "warranties" [. . .]. Of such undertakings all that can be predicated is that some breaches will and others will not give rise to an event which will deprive the party not in default of substantially the whole benefit which it was intended he should obtain from the contract; and the legal consequences of a breach of such undertaking, unless provided for expressly in the contract, depend upon the nature of the event to which the breach gives rise and do not follow automatically from a prior classification of the undertaking, as a "condition" or a "warranty".'(see *Hongkong Fir Shipping Co Ltd v Kawasaki Kisen Kaisha Ltd (The Hongkong Fir)* [1961]).
❖ The availability of remedies depends upon the seriousness of the breach: if the innocent party has been substantially deprived of the benefits of the contract by means of the breach, then the courts will treat this as a breach of a condition (➪ damages and right to terminate the contract). If the breach is less serious, then it will be treated as a breach of warranty (➪ damages only).

Express terms

Express terms are those which have been expressly agreed upon by the contracting parties. This may be orally, in writing or both. It is however important to remember that not everything said by the parties during negotiations subsequently becomes a term of the contract: only the breach of a term will afford the innocent party a right to sue for breach of contract. It is therefore necessary to be able to distinguish between those (pre-contractual) statements which have become part of the contract and those which have not. This is a question of evidence; naturally, it is more difficult to discern whether a statement has become a contractual term when dealing with an oral contract than in the case of a written contract.

In differentiating between representations and terms, the courts are looking *objectively* for the (presumed) intention of the parties by asking the question: 'What would a reasonable man conclude was the intention of the parties with regard to a particular statement in view of the circumstances of the case at hand?' (*Heilbut Symons & Co v Buckleton* [1913]). The courts have developed several pointers which assist them in their task of determining whether a statement is a representation or a term.

Pointers developed by the courts in order to distinguish between representations and terms				
Lapse of time: The greater the lapse of time between a statement being made and the contract being entered into, the greater the presumption that the statement is a REPRESENTATION; *Bannerman v White* (1861) and *Routledge v McKay* [1954].	**Reduction of the contract into writing:** If an orally made statement is not included into the written contract, then the presumption drawn from this 'exclusion' is that the oral statement is a REPRESENTATION; *Routledge v McKay* [1954].	**Importance of statement:** If the person to whom the statement was made attached such importance to it that he would otherwise not have entered the contract and the maker of the statement realised (or even knew) that this statement was important to the other party, then the presumption is that it is a TERM; *Bannerman v White* (1861) and *Couchman v Hill* [1947].	**Special knowledge or skill:** If the person making the statement has special knowledge or skills regarding the subject matter which places him in a stronger position than the person to whom the statement is made, then it is more likely that the courts will regard this statement as a TERM; *Dick Bentley Productions Ltd v Harold Smith (Motors) Ltd* [1965]; *Esso Petroleum Co Ltd v Mardon* [1976].	**'Guaranteeing the truth of the statement':** If the party making the statement is basically assuming responsibility for the truth of the statement, then it is more likely that the statement is a TERM; *Schawel v Reade* [1913].

Incorporation

> **Common Pitfall**
>
> Textbooks often mention the topic of incorporation only in the context of exemption clauses. It is however important to remember that incorporation is not confined to these types of contract terms: incorporation issues arise in relation to any contract term and, indeed, for a contractual term to be effective, it is necessary that the term has been properly incorporated into the contract.

In the context of express terms, after having identified that a statement is, in fact, a term and not merely a representation, the next important issue to consider is the question of whether or not it has been incorporated into the contract: a term will only be effective (i.e. bind the parties) if it has been properly incorporated into the contractual agreement. There are three primary methods by which a term can be incorporated into a contract:

Incorporation by signature

A party who signs a contractual document will be bound by the terms contained in that document, regardless of whether or not they have actually read the document in question. The operation of this common law rule and its requirements are illustrated by the cases of *Curtis v Chemical Cleaning & Dyeing Co* [1951] and *L'Estrange v Graucob* [1934], the latter of which also shows that the strict application of this rule may lead to rather harsh results.

Incorporation by notice

Irrespective of signature, a party may be bound by the terms of the contract if reasonably sufficient notice of those terms is brought to the party's attention. This requires the following: first, as illustrated by *Olley v Marlborough Court Ltd* [1949] the reasonable notice must be given before or at the time the contract is made. Second, as illustrated by *Chapelton v Barry UDC* [1940] the term(s) must have been contained or referred to in a contractual document, i.e. a document which is intended to have contractual effect. Finally, 'reasonably sufficient' notice does *not* mean actual notice; rather, as illustrated by *Parker v South Eastern Railway* [1877], it is required that the party trying to introduce the term(s) in question took reasonable steps to make the other party aware of the existence of the term(s). This question of what is a reasonable step has to be approached objectively, i.e. would a reasonable person have taken notice of the existence of the term(s)?

If these three conditions are fulfilled, then it is irrelevant whether or not that party is aware of the actual content of the term(s) in question: the term(s) will be incorporated into the contract.

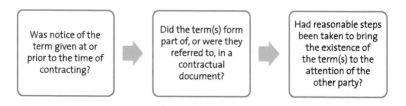

Was notice of the term given at or prior to the time of contracting? ➡ Did the term(s) form part of, or were they referred to, in a contractual document? ➡ Had reasonable steps been taken to bring the existence of the term(s) to the attention of the other party?

Common Pitfall

While 'reasonably sufficient notice' does not mean actual notice, you should however remember that the *objective* test laid down in *Parker v South Eastern Railway Co* has nonetheless to be applied *within in the facts of the particular case*. Have a look at *Thompson v London Midland and Scottish Railway Co* [1930] for a good example of how this test is applied in practice.

Incorporation by previous course of dealings

Terms may also be incorporated by a previous course of dealings: this means that, although there may not have been notice of the terms in question in relation to a particular contract, the term(s) may be incorporated into the contract as a result of a previous course of dealings between the parties. In order for this to take place, two requirements must be satisfied. There must be:

❖ sufficient notice of the term AND
❖ consistency in the previous dealings.

If both requirements are met, then it is irrelevant whether or not the party to whom the term(s) is/are 'presented' actually knows about the term(s) in question in relation to a particular contract; rather, based on the use of the term(s) in previous contractual transactions between the two parties, knowledge of the term(s) in question in relation to the contract at hand is inferred from the use of the term(s) in previous contracts between the parties. The operation of this principle and its requirements are illustrated by the cases of *McCutcheon v David MacBrayne Ltd* [1964] and *Spurling v Bradshaw* [1956].

Aim Higher

The cases mentioned above show that it is difficult to predict what the courts will regard as sufficient in terms of consistency (i.e. frequency and uniformity) of dealings in order to incorporate a term by a previous course of dealings into the contract; it might also be difficult to show/establish a sufficient regularity of dealings between the contractual parties, especially if the contract at hand is a business-to-consumer contract (see e.g. *Hollier v Rambler Motors (AMC) Ltd*

[1972]). However, in cases where the contractual transaction is between two businesses/commercial entities, be aware that the courts appear to apply the requirement of regular and consistent dealings between the parties in a less stringent way as illustrated by the case of *British Crane Hire Corp Ltd v Ipswich Plant Hire* [1975].

What will the courts consider when deciding if previous dealings were sufficiently frequent?

British Crane Hire Corp Ltd v Ipswich Plant Hire

Lord Denning, MR: '[. . .] here the parties were both in the trade and were of equal bargaining power. Each was a firm of plant hirers who hired out plant. The defendants themselves knew that firms in the plant-hiring trade always imposed conditions in regard to the hiring of plant: and that their conditions were on much the same lines [. . .] From that evidence it is clear that both parties knew quite well that conditions were habitually imposed by the supplier of these machines: and both parties knew the substance of those conditions. In particular that if the crane sank in soft ground it was the hirer's job to recover it: and that there was an indemnity clause. In these circumstances, I think the conditions on the form should be regarded as incorporated into the contract. I would not put it so much on the course of dealing, but rather on the common understanding which is to be derived from the conduct of the parties, namely, that the hiring was to be on the terms of the plaintiffs' usual conditions.'

Hollier v Rambler Motors (AMC) Ltd

Salmon LJ: '[Counsel said] that there was a course of dealing which constituted the three or four occasions over five years – that is, on an average, not quite one dealing a year – from which it is to be implied that what he called "the condition" at the bottom of the contract should be imported into the oral agreement made in the middle of March 1970. I am bound to say that, for my part, I do not know of any other case in which it has been decided or even argued that a term could be implied into an oral contract on the strength of a course of dealing (if it can be so called) which consisted at the most of three or four transactions over a period of five years.'

Interpretation

Interpretation (also referred to as 'construction') denotes the process by which courts establish the meaning and legal effect of contractual terms which have been incorporated into the contract. This process applies in relation to all types of terms, i.e. written, oral, express and implied terms. At university level, the emphasis is usually on the interpretation of written terms, therefore, the following revision notes focus on the interpretation of written terms. However, many of the points made here also apply with regard to oral terms.

Common Pitfall

In problem questions, the question of interpretation of a contractual term usually (i.e. unless the question tells you otherwise) arises if the term has been incorporated into the contract at hand. This means (a) that you need to analyse the issue of incorporation of a term BEFORE trying to interpret/construe the meaning of this particular term; and (b) that the interpretation of a term is no substitute for the incorporation of a term. In other words, by establishing the meaning of a term you *cannot* also establish that the term has been successfully incorporated into the contract: both are separate and distinct legal issues which require separate analysis.

The aim of interpreting the terms of a written agreement is to establish the meaning of the contractual term(s) as intended by the parties; sometimes, this is referred to as establishing the common or mutual intention of the parties. As summarised by Lord Hoffmann in *Investors Compensation Scheme Ltd v West Bromwich Building Society* [1998] (see below), the intention of the parties is to be established *objectively* which means that the question to be asked *is not* what one or other of the parties meant or understood by the words used *but rather* what a reasonable person in the position of, and with the knowledge of all the background information reasonably available to, the parties would have understood the words to mean at the time of making the contract.

Aim Higher

The so-called *contra proferentum* rule states that, if a term is ambiguous, it is interpreted in the way which is least favourable to the party trying to rely upon it, i.e. the ambiguity is resolved ('construed') against the party who is proffering the ambiguous term. Although this rule is of particular interest and importance in relation to the interpretation of exclusion clauses (see below), it should be noted that it applies to contract terms generally and not just in the context of exclusion clauses (*Tam Wing Chuen v Bank of Credit and Commerce Hong Kong Ltd (in liq)* [1996] and *Vaswani v Italian Motor Cars Ltd* [1996]).

Lord Hoffmann, in *Investors Compensation Scheme Ltd v West Bromwich Building Society* [1998] sets out five principles of contractual interpretation.

1
> Interpretation is the ascertainment of the meaning which the document would convey to a reasonable person having all the background knowledge which would reasonably have been available to the parties in the situation in which they were at the time of the contract.

2
> The background was famously referred to by Lord Wilberforce as the 'matrix of fact,' but this phrase is, if anything, an understated description of what the background may include. Subject to the requirement that it should have been reasonably available to the parties and to the exception to be mentioned next, it includes absolutely anything which would have affected the way in which the language of the document would have been understood by a reasonable man.

3
> The law excludes from the admissible background the previous negotiations of the parties and their declarations of subjective intent. [...] The law makes this distinction for reasons of practical policy and, in this respect only, legal interpretation differs from the way we would interpret utterances in ordinary life. The boundaries of this exception are in some respects unclear.

4
> The meaning which a document (or any other utterance) would convey to a reasonable man is not the same thing as the meaning of its words. The meaning of words is a matter of dictionaries and grammars; the meaning of the document is what the parties using those words against the relevant background would reasonably have been understood to mean.

5
> The 'rule' that words should be given their 'natural and ordinary meaning' reflects the common sense proposition that we do not easily accept that people have made linguistic mistakes, particularly in formal documents. On the other hand, if one would nevertheless conclude from the background that something must have gone wrong with the language, the law does not require judges to attribute to the parties an intention which they plainly could not have had.

It should however be noted that the *ICS* principles of interpretation, while allowing for a more flexible and less rigidly semantic style of construction of contractual terms, do *not* necessarily mean that the court is free to reformulate/rewrite the contract (*Charter Reinsurance Co Ltd v Fagan* [1996] and *Rainy Sky SA v Kookmin Bank* [2011]). Janet O'Sullivan (2012) 'Absurdity and ambiguity – making sense of contractual construction', *Cambridge Law Journal* 71(1), 34–37.

Up for Debate

Charter Reinsurance Co Ltd v Fagan [1996] and *Rainy Sky SA v Kookmin Bank* [2011] (see quotes below) both held that, generally speaking, the courts are restricted in their ability to rewrite the parties' bargain as outlined in the contractual document. Despite this apparent overall agreement, however, there are subtle differences in the respective approaches taken in either case. Can you spot these differences? Do you (dis)agree with their Lordships' reasoning; and if so, why?

Charter Reinsurance Co Ltd v Fagan

Lord Mustill: 'There comes a point at which the court should remind itself that the task is to discover what the parties meant from what they have said, and that to force upon the words a meaning which they cannot fairly bear is to substitute for the bargain actually made one which the court believes could better have been made. This is an illegitimate role for a court. Particularly in the field of commerce, where the parties need to know what they must do and what they can insist on not doing, it is essential for them to be confident that they can rely on the court to enforce their contract according to its terms. [...] In the end, however, the parties must be held to their bargain.'

Rainy Sky SA v Kookmin Bank

Lord Clarke: 'It is not [...] necessary to conclude that, unless the most natural meaning of the words produces a result so extreme as to suggest that it was unintended, the court must give effect to that meaning. The language used by the parties will often have more than one potential meaning. [...] the exercise of construction is essentially one unitary exercise in which the court must consider the language used and ascertain what a reasonable person, that is a person who has all the background knowledge which would reasonably have been available to the parties in the situation in which they were at the time of the contract, would have understood the parties to have meant. In doing so, the court must have regard to all the relevant surrounding circumstances. If there are two possible constructions, the court is entitled to prefer the construction which is consistent with business common sense and to reject the other. [...] Where the parties have used unambiguous language, the court must apply it.'

How to approach the interpretation of a contractual term

The starting point for the interpretation of a contractual term is the contractual document itself.

The words actually used in the document are to be given their natural and ordinary meaning where possible.

If a strict interpretation gives the words used a meaning which is contrary to business commonsense, then one can/should look beyond the words themselves ('the available background' or 'the factual matrix').

However, pre-contractual negotiations are still excluded from being admissible background information, *Prenn v Simmonds* [1971] and *Chartbrook Ltd v Persimmon Homes Ltd* [2009].

The parol evidence rule

The so-called 'parol evidence' rule concerns a special instance in relation to the interpretation of written contracts: when dealing with a bargain between parties which has been reduced into writing, i.e. embodied in a written contractual document, the question might arise whether it is possible to admit evidence which is not contained in the written contract to change, vary, contradict or add to the content of the written contract. The parol evidence rule states that, in cases where the contract is wholly contained in writing, evidence other than that which is embodied in the written document cannot be relied upon in order to change the written contractual terms (*Jacobs v Batavia and General Plantations Trust* [1924]).

Three additional points are worth making: first, it should be noted that the term 'parol evidence' is slightly misleading insofar that – as 'parol' means 'oral' – this rule not only applies to oral statements but also to any other extrinsic evidence (i.e. evidence not contained in the written contract itself) such as draft contracts, preliminary agreements, letters of negotiation and correspondence. Second, the parol evidence rule does not apply in relation to a contract which is partly in writing and partly oral as this is not considered to be a written contract, see *Law Commission, The Law of Contract: The Parol Evidence Rule* (Law Commission Report No. 154). Third, as the previous point suggests, the parol evidence rule is subject to a number of exceptions and is thus much narrower in scope than it might first appear. For example, extrinsic evidence will be admissible in the following (non-exhaustive) situations:

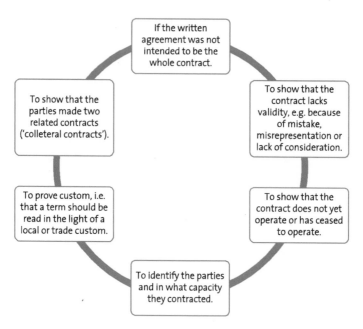

If the written agreement was not intended to be the whole contract.

To show that the contract lacks validity, e.g. because of mistake, misrepresentation or lack of consideration.

To show that the parties made two related contracts ('colleteral contracts').

To prove custom, i.e. that a term should be read in the light of a local or trade custom.

To show that the contract does not yet operate or has ceased to operate.

To identify the parties and in what capacity they contracted.

(See also Edwin Peel (ed.), Treitel, *The Law of Contract*, 13th edn 2011, paras. 6-013–6-030.)

Implied terms

Although in many occasions express terms will make up the whole of the contract, i.e. outline the obligations of the parties, this is not always the case as it is also possible that the parties have either failed to include a particular obligation and thus not expressed it in the contract or, in fact, failed to provide for every contingency which may arise in relation to the execution of the contract. This is where implied terms come into play: implied terms are those terms which have not been expressly agreed between the parties but which may, or in some certain circumstances must, be read ('implied') into the contract to supplement the expressly agreed obligations outlined in the contract and which thereby make up for the (deliberate or accidental) omissions of the parties.

Implied terms can be differentiated into four groups:

* Terms implied by statute (sometimes also called 'Terms implied by Parliament').
* Terms implied at common law (sometimes also called 'Terms implied in law').
* Terms implied in fact.
* Terms implied by custom/trade usage.

Categories of implied terms			
Terms implied by statute/Parliament: Terms which are implied into a particular type of contract regardless of the parties' intentions by operation of statute.	Terms implied at common law: Terms which are implied irrespective of the intentions of the parties as the implication is based on the type of contract.	Terms implied in fact: Terms which are imputed from the intentions of the parties, i.e. it is assumed that the parties would have intended to include such a term if they had thought about it.	Terms implied by custom/trade usage: Terms which are implied into a contract from the usage or custom of the industry or market in which the parties transact.

Terms implied by statute/Parliament

Terms implied by statute (sometimes also called 'terms implied by Parliament') are those terms which, usually regardless of the parties' intentions (see 'Exemption of terms' below), are implied into a particular type of contract as a result of legislative intervention by means of a statutory provision, i.e. Parliament has decided that certain terms should be implied into all contracts of a particular type: for example, certain terms are – by virtue of the Sale of Goods Act 1979 – implied into a contract for the sale of goods which gives the buyer important rights against the seller and which can only be excluded or limited if certain strict requirements are fulfilled. Terms implied by statute are often – but not always – the result of codification of common law principles.

In contract law, the most commonly encountered terms implied by statute are those inserted by the Sale of Goods Act 1979 and the Supply of Goods and Services Act 1982 and which concern the following types of contract:

When studying contract law, the most commonly encountered statutory provisions which imply terms into a contract are those contained in the Sale of Goods Act 1979:

Similar provisions implying terms – with necessary modifications – can be found in ss 13–15 of the Supply of Goods and Services Act 1982 (concerning contracts for the supply of services), ss 2–5 of the Supply of Goods and Services Act 1982 (concerning contracts for work and material) and ss 7–10 of the Supply of Goods and Services Act 1982 (concerning contracts for hire of goods).

Common Pitfall

Note that, with regard to the above contracts, terms relating to the quality or fitness for purpose will *only* be implied if the seller deals 'in the course of a business'. As to the meaning of 'in the course of a business' in this context (and in contrast to the narrower meaning of the same phrase in relation to the **Unfair Contract Terms Act 1977**), see *Stevenson v Rogers* [1999].

Stevenson v Rogers		
Rogers, a fisherman for some 20 years, sold his boat 'Jelle' to Stevenson. Rogers had previously bought another boat and subsequently sold another fishing vessel. He also bought another fishing boat as a replacement for the Jelle. Stevenson claimed that the Jelle was of unsatisfactory quality and sought to rely on s 14(2) of the Sale of Goods Act 1979 whose application requires that the sale is made 'in the course of business'. Rogers argued that his business was not selling and buying boats.	Court of Appeal held that the sale was made 'in the course of a business' even though the sale was incidental to his business.	Note the difference between the meaning of 'in the course of a business' under the Sale of Goods Act 1979 and UCTA 1977 – a sale which is merely incidental to the actual business of the seller is enough to 'trigger' s 14 of the Sale of Goods Act 1979.

Terms implied at common law/in law

Terms implied at common law (also called 'terms implied in law' but *not* to be confused with 'terms implied by statute') are those terms which may be implied by the court to impose a particular obligation onto one or both parties and which arise as a consequence of type of contract at hand, e.g. a contract of sale of goods or a tenancy agreement.

The difference between terms implied *in fact* and terms implied *by (common) law*.
per Steyn LJ, *Society of Lloyds v Clementson* [1995]

| 'Terms *implied in fact* are individualised gap-fillers, depending on the terms and circumstances of a particular contract.' | 'Terms *implied by law* are in reality incidents attached to standardised contractual relationships, or, perhaps more illuminatingly, such terms can in modern United States legal terminology be described as standardised default rules.' |

(See also Lord Steyn, *Equitable Life Assurance Society v Hyman* [2002]).

Consequently, the implication of a term at common law is neither based upon the particular contract between, say, Tom and Jerry nor is it based on the contracting parties' intention in relation to the contract at hand. Instead, the implication of a term at common law can be said to be dependent upon the fulfilment of two requirements (*El Awadi v Bank of Credit and Commerce International SA Ltd* [1989]):

❖ The contract at hand should be of a defined type; AND
❖ The implication of the term should be necessary (sometimes also referred to as 'reasonable').

Aim Higher

Showing an awareness of the different requirements needed for implying a term in law and for implying a term in fact, especially with reference to quotes from key cases (see below) which emphasise these differences, is a good way of demonstrating a thorough understanding and thus likely to gain higher marks.

What is needed for implication in law and implication in fact?

Term implied in law?

Liverpool City Council v Irwin [1977]	Scally v Southern Health and Social Services Board [1991]
Lord Cross: 'When it implies a term in a contract the court is sometimes laying down a general rule that in all contracts of a certain type – sale of goods, master and servant, landlord and tenant and so on – some provision is to be implied unless the parties have expressly excluded it. In deciding whether or not to lay down such a prima facie rule the court will naturally ask itself whether in the general run of such cases the term in question would be one which it would be reasonable to insert. Sometimes, however, there is no question of laying down any prima facie rule applicable to all cases of a defined type but what the court is being in effect asked to do is to rectify a particular – often a very detailed – contract by inserting in it a term which the parties have not expressed. Here it is not enough for the court to say that the suggested term is a reasonable one the presence of which would make the contract a better or fairer one; it must be able to say that the insertion of the term is necessary to give – as it is put – 'business efficacy' to the contract and that if its absence had been pointed out at the time both parties – assuming them to have been reasonable men – would have agreed without hesitation to its insertion.'	Lord Bridge: 'A clear distinction is drawn [...] between the search for an implied term necessary to give business efficacy to a particular contract and the search, based on wider considerations, for a term which the law will imply as a necessary incident of a definable category of contractual relationship. [...] I fully appreciate that the criterion to justify an implication of this kind is necessity, not reasonableness. But I take the view that it is not merely reasonable, but necessary, in the circumstances postulated, to imply an obligation on the employer to take reasonable steps to bring the term of the contract in question to the employee's attention, so that he may be in a position to enjoy its benefit.'

Term implied in fact?

(See also *Malik v BCCI* [1997] which provides a useful example of how, in practice, courts imply a term in law.)

Common Pitfall

The requirement that the implication of a term should be 'necessary' as a matter of law (i.e. a term implied in law) should not be confused with the necessity test as applied in relation to terms implied in fact (i.e. 'implication necessary to make contract work', see below). 'Necessity' in the context of terms implied in law means that specified duties ought to be attached to the particular type of contractual relationship (e.g. contract of sale, tenancy agreement) in question; the cases mentioned above all serve as useful illustrations of this difference.

Terms implied in fact

Terms implied in fact are those terms which might be implied by the court to fill the gaps in the particular contract between the parties (as opposed to a particular *type* of contract, see above) if the court is satisfied that the parties must have intended to include such a term had they thought about it. In order to decide what the intention of the parties was, the courts have developed several methods to decide whether or not a certain term ought to be implied into the contract at hand, the two most important of which are the 'officious bystander' test (*Shirlaw v Southern Foundries (1926) Limited* [1939]) and the 'business efficacy' test (*The Moorcock* (1889)). Both tests are, to some extent, overlapping.

The 'business efficacy' test: The Moorcock

Bowen LJ.: 'In business transactions such as this, what the law desires to effect by the implication is to give such business efficacy to the transaction as must have been intended at all events by both parties who are business men; not to impose on one side all the perils of the transaction, or to emancipate one side from all the chances of failure, but to make each party promise in law as much, at all events, as it must have been in the contemplation of both parties that he should be responsible for in respect of those perils or chances.'

The 'officious bystander' test: Shirlaw v Southern Foundries

MacKinnon LJ.: 'Prima facie that which in any contract is left to be implied and need not be expressed is something so obvious that it goes without saying; so that, if, while the parties were making their bargain, an officious bystander were to suggest some express provision for it in their agreement, they would testily suppress him with a common "Oh, of course!" '

Implication of term necessary in order **to make the contract work**

Implication of term necessary in order **to give effect to the parties' intentions**

Common Pitfall

Don't be fooled into thinking that both tests need to be satisfied in order for a court to imply a term in fact. Case law (*Greene Wood & McClean LLP v Templeton Insurance Ltd* [2009]) suggests that, while both test might be (and often are) used together, satisfying either the criteria of the 'business efficacy' test or those of the 'officious bystander' test will suffice for the implication of a term in fact as both tests are 'but a route to the presumed intention of the parties' (*Richco International v Alfred C. Toepfer International* [1991]).

Terms implied by custom/trade usage

Terms implied by custom or trade usage are those terms which might be implied by the court in order to incorporate a particular term which is the result of an established, invariable, reasonable and certain custom or trade usage of the market, industry or locality in which the parties transact (*Hutton v Warren* (1836)). However, implication by custom or trade usage will not take place if the custom or trade usage is inconsistent with, or contrary to, the express or necessarily implied terms of the contract at hand (*Les Affréteurs Réunis SA v Leopold (London) Ltd* [1919]).

When will a term be implied on the basis of a custom or trade usage?

Term implied by usage →

Cunliffe-Owen v Teather & Greenwood [1967]

Ungoed-Thomas J: ' "Usage" as a practice which the court will recognise is a mixed question of fact and law. For the practice to amount to such a recognised usage, it must be certain, in the sense that the practice is clearly established; it must be notorious, in the sense that it is so well known, in the market in which it is alleged to exist, that those who conduct business in that market contract with the usage as an implied term; and it must be reasonable. The burden lies on those alleging "usage" to establish it [. . .]. The practice that has to be established consists of a continuity of acts, and those acts have to be established by persons familiar with them, although [. . .] they may be sufficiently established by such persons without a detailed recital of instances. Practice is not a matter of opinion, of even the most highly qualified expert, as to what it is desirable that the practice should be. However, evidence of those versed in a market [. . .] may be admissible and valuable in identifying those features of any transaction that attract usage and in discounting other features which for such purpose are merely incidental [. . .].'

Kum and Another v Wah Tat Bank Ltd [1971]

Lord Devlin: 'Universality, as a requirement of custom, raises not a question of law but a question of fact. There must be proof in the first place that the custom is generally accepted by those who habitually do business in the trade or market concerned. Moreover, the custom must be so generally known that an outsider who makes reasonable enquiries could not fail to be made aware of it. The size of the market or the extent of the trade affected is neither here nor there. [. . .] the question whether the alleged custom, if proved in fact [. . .], is good in law must be determined in accordance with the requirements of the English common law. These are that the custom should be certain, reasonable and not repugnant. It would be repugnant if it were inconsistent with any express term in any document it affects, whether that document be regarded as a contract or as a document of title.'

Term implied by custom ↓

Exemption clauses

Parties to a contract may sometimes seek to exempt themselves from liability for certain breaches of contract, i.e. they either attempt to avoid liability completely for certain breaches of contract or attempt to restrict/limit their liability for a breach of contract by introducing terms ('clauses') to this effect into the contract. Clauses seeking to exclude all liability for a breach of contract are called 'exclusion clauses' and clauses seeking to limit/restrict liability for a breach of contract (usually in financial terms) are called 'limitation clauses'. The term 'exemption clause' is the generic term which is commonly used to describe both types of clauses without directly differentiating whether the term at hand attempts to 'merely' limit liability for a breach of contract or whether the term in question seeks to completely exclude all liability for a breach of contract (see e.g. the use of the term 'exemption clauses' in the heading of s 13 of the Unfair Contract Terms Act 1977).

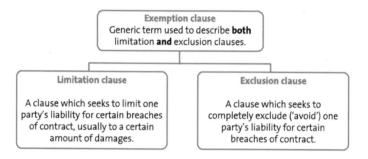

However, the law does not always allow exemption clauses contained in the actual contract to come into force. Sometimes, it recognises that there are situations where it might unreasonable to give effect to the terms of the contract and thus aims to control the operation (and thereby, ultimately, also the effectiveness) of exemption clauses. While the need to control the operation of (potentially unfair) exemption clauses might be greater in relation to business-to-consumer contracts, i.e. situations in which a consumer of goods or services enters into a contract with an entity whose business it is to provide goods or services, this need also exists in relation to business-to-business contracts. In either case, the courts exercise this control (which can essentially be described as the courts' trying to establish whether or not a particular clause is effective) by a combination of both common law rules and statutory provisions. The process to control the effectiveness of exemption clauses used by the courts can be broken down into three essential steps:

(1) Incorporation	(2) Construction/Interpretation	(3) Statuory provisions
Has the exemption clause been incorporated into the contract, i.e. has it become a term of the contract?	Does the exemption clause cover the breach, i.e. is it appropriately worded to cover what has occurred?	Is the exemption clause affected by statutory provisions (UCTA 1977 or UTCCR 1999), i.e. is the clause in question subject to legislation?

The first two steps are subject to the common law rules outlined above under the headings of 'Incorporation' and 'Interpretation'.

Aim Higher

As stated above under 'Interpretation', the common law rules regarding the question how terms are to be construed/interpreted are generally applicable to all types of terms and are not limited to exemption clauses. However, it should be noted that the courts have taken a stricter approach towards the interpretation of exemption clauses than in relation to the interpretation of other types of contractual terms. Of particular importance in this context is the so-called *contra proferentem* rule (see above under 'Interpretation') and the '*Canada Steamship* test' regarding the attempt to exclude liability for negligence (see below). Showing an awareness of this stricter approach to interpretation in the context of exemption clauses and, where relevant, being able to explain and apply the principles laid down in *Canada Steamship* is likely to gain you a higher mark as it demonstrates that your understanding is not just 'skin-deep'.

The test laid down in *Canada Steamship Lines Ltd v The King* [1952] AC 192, per Lord Morton

'(1) If the clause contains language which expressly exempts the person in whose favour it is made (hereafter called "the proferens") from the consequence of the negligence of his own servants, effect must be given to that provision. [...]'

Meaning : if the clause expressly refers to (exemption of) negligence or synonyms thereof, then the court will give effect to this clause.

'(2) If there is no express reference to negligence, the court must consider whether the words used are wide enough, in their ordinary meaning, to cover negligence on the part of the servants of the proferens. If a doubt arises at this point, it must be resolved against the proferens [. . .].'

Meaning : if negligence is not expressly mentioned, but the ordinary meaning of the words is wide enough to cover negligence, then the clause will be effective if it only *limits* liability for negligence. If the clause is wide enough to cover the *total exclusion* of negligence, then the court will also look at point 3 below.

'(3) If the words used are wide enough for the above purpose, the court must then consider whether "the head of damage may be based on some ground other than that of negligence," to quote again Lord Greene in the *Alderslade* case [1945] KB 189] . The "other ground" must not be so fanciful or remote that the proferens cannot be supposed to have desired protection against it; but subject to this qualification, which is no doubt to be implied from Lord Greene's words, the existence of a possible head of damage other than that of negligence is fatal to the proferens even if the words used are prima facie wide enough to cover negligence on the part of his servants.'

Meaning : if the clause is wide enough to cover total exclusion of liability for negligence, the court will consider the question if the exemption clause can be read to also cover liability other than negligence. If the answer to this question is no, then the exemption clause is effective to exclude liability for negligence.

It should be noted however that the '*Canada Steamship* test' pre-dates the enactment of the Unfair Contract Terms Act 1977 which means that many exemption clauses covering liability for negligence will now be subject to s 2 of UCTA 1977 and might, in certain cases, also be affected by the Unfair Terms in Consumer Contracts Regulations 1999 (see below). As cases such as *Shell Chemical v P&O Tankers* [1995] 1 Lloyd's Rep 297 and *Monarch Airlines Ltd v London Luton Airport Ltd* [1997] CLC 698 show, the courts still regularly make reference to this test, especially in non-consumer cases.

Statutory control of exemption clauses

If the two common law steps of incorporation and interpretation have both been satisfied, it is then necessary to consider, where applicable, the requirements and effects of the relevant legislation, e.g. UCTA 1977 and the UTCCR 1999, as even an incorporated and appropriately worded exemption clause might be rendered ineffective by the operation of legislation. In this respect, it might even be said that the most important and most effective means of controlling exemption clauses is nowadays provided by statute, rather than by common law alone.

Control of exemption clauses by means of common law rules and statutory provisions

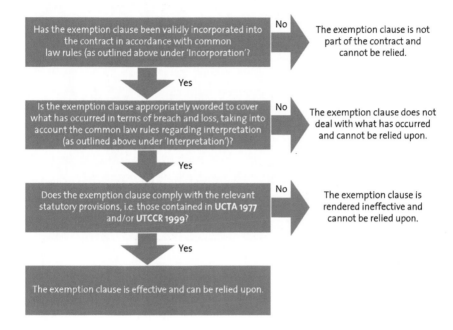

In any case, the existence and importance of statutory provisions such as those contained in UCTA 1977 and the UTCCR 1999 (to name but a few) means for you that, after having considered the issues of incorporation and interpretation of terms, you will regularly have to examine the question whether the exemption clause at hand is affected by either piece of legislation.

The differences in applicability between UCTA 1977 and the UTCCR 1999

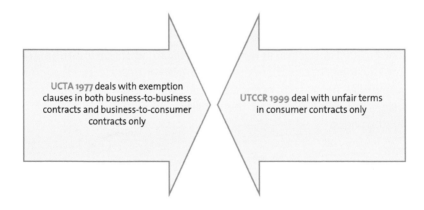

Unfair Contract Terms Act 1977 (UCTA 1977)

> ## Common Pitfall
>
> Don't be fooled into thinking that the **Unfair Contract Terms Act 1977** applies to ALL types of contract terms: the title 'Unfair Contract Terms Act 1977' is misleading insofar that this Act *only* deals with exemption clauses *but not* with contract terms in general. Equally, don't assume that **UCTA 1977** applies to ALL types of contractual transactions: whilst it applies to both business-to-business contracts and business-to-consumer contracts, it does *generally* NOT apply to private transactions, i.e. consumer-to-consumer contracts. Note, in this context, however the exceptions in e.g. ss 6(4) and 8 of **UCTA 1977** which means that there are some limited situations in which **UCTA 1977** might also apply in purely private transactions. Finally, don't be fooled into thinking that **UCTA 1977** applies to ALL TYPES of contracts. Schedule 1 contains a list of those contracts which are excluded from its scope, e.g. insurance contracts.

Scope of UCTA 1977

In general terms and the exceptions mentioned above aside, UCTA 1977 deals with 'business liability' which is defined in s 1(3) as liability for breach of obligations or duties arising:

(a) from things done or to be done in the course of a business (whether his own business or another's); or

(b) from the occupation of premises used for business purposes of the occupier.

This means that UCTA 1977 usually only applies to contracts in which at least one party is not a consumer but a business and where this non-consumer party attempts to limit or exclude its liability for breach of its obligations or duties. 'Business' is defined in s 14 as including 'a profession and the activities of any government department or local or public authority'. Two things should be kept in mind in this context: first, case law suggests that the words 'in the course of a business' require that the thing done or to be done is either an integral part of the business carried on or that the type of transaction at hand is at least carried out on a sufficiently regular basis (*R & B Customs Brokers Co Ltd v United Dominions Trust Ltd* [1988]; *Air Transworld Ltd v Bombardier Inc* [2012]). Second, it would appear that the words 'whether his own business or another's' cover the activities of an agent in the course of his principal's business.

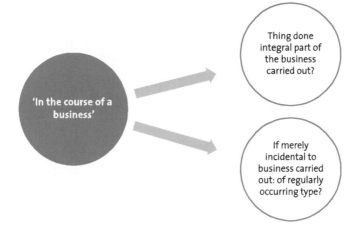

In addition, many of the provisions contained in UCTA 1977 only apply where one of the contracting parties (i.e. in most cases the one against whom the exemption clause is being used) is 'dealing as consumer'. For a party to be 'dealing as consumer' s 12 of UCTA 1977 requires:

(a) that the party in question neither makes the contract in the course of a business nor holds himself out as doing so; and
(b) that the other party does make the contract in the course of a business.

However, it should be noted that the mere fact that a party is itself a business does not necessarily mean that it is prevented from 'dealing as a consumer' for the purposes of UCTA 1977. This was clarified by the Court of Appeal in *R&B Customs Brokers Co Ltd v United Dominions Trust Ltd* [1988]:

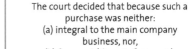

The claimant wished to defeat exclusion clauses in a contract concerning a defective Mitsubishi Shogun, bought as a company car, by arguing that though themselves a business (dealing in road haulage and Heavy Goods Vehicles) they had not purchased the car 'in the course of that business' within the meaning of UCTA 1977 and should therefore be treated as 'consumers' and protected by the statute.

The court decided that because such a purchase was neither:
(a) integral to the main company business, nor,
(b) frequent (three in five years),
the business had truly bought as a consumer and had the full benefit of the protection enjoyed by a consumer under UCTA 1977 in relation to statutory implied terms.

Aim Higher

This approach (which differs from the approach taken in relation to the issue of 'in the course of a business' in the context of terms implied by statute (see *Stevenson v Rogers* [1999]) was also followed in *Feldaroll Foundary plc v Hermes Leasing (London) Ltd* [2004] and *Air Transworld Ltd v Bombardier Inc* [2012]. Being able to refer to the way in which legal principles have been applied (and how a particular principle has developed) in more recent cases demonstrates a knowledge which goes beyond pure textbook knowledge and is likely to gain you a higher mark.

Sections in UCTA 1977 which affect the validity of exemption clauses

The following table provides an overview of the most important sections in UCTA 1977 which have a bearing upon the validity of exemption clauses. It contains the most important 'active sections', i.e. several of those provisions which EITHER render some exemption clauses *automatically ineffective* OR state that a clause is effective *only if* the exemption clause in question *satisfies the requirement of 'reasonableness'* as per s 11 of UCTA 1977.

Section	Scope	Effect
s 2(1)	Deals with liability for death or personal injury resulting from negligence	Clause automatically ineffective
s 2(2)	Deals with liability for loss or damage other than death or personal injury resulting from negligence	Clause effective only if 'reasonable', s 11
s 3	Deals with contracts where one party 'deals as consumer' or on the other's 'written standard terms of business'	Clause effective only if 'reasonable', s 11
s 4	Deals with indemnity clause regarding liability for negligence or breach of contract in relation to consumer	Clause effective only if 'reasonable', s 11
s 5(1)	Deals with clause attempting to exempt liability for loss or damage arising from goods proving defective whilst in consumer use by reference to manufacturer's guarantee	Clause automatically ineffective

s 6(1)	Deals with liability for breach of implied terms regarding passing of possession or ownership in relation to sale or hire purchase of goods	Clause automatically ineffective
s 6(2)	Deals with liability for breach of the obligations arising from ss 13, 14 or 15 of the Sale of Goods Act 1979 or ss 9, 10 or 11 of the Supply of Goods (Implied Terms) Act 1973 as against a consumer	Clause automatically ineffective
s 6(3)	Deals with same situation as s 6(2) but in non-consumer context	Clause effective only if 'reasonable', s 11
s 7(2)	Deals with business liability for breach of an implied obligation in a contract where the possession or ownership of the goods passes under or in pursuance of the contract (other than a contract governed by the law of sale of goods or hire-purchase) against a consumer	Clause automatically ineffective
s 7(3)	Deals with same situation as s 7(2) but in non-consumer context	Clause effective only if 'reasonable', s 11
s 7(4)	Deals with exemption terms in other contracts regarding liability in respect of the right to transfer ownership of the goods or give possession, or the assurance of quiet possession to a person taking goods in pursuance of the contract	Clause effective only if 'reasonable', s 11
s 8	Deals with term attempting to exempt liability for misrepresentation	Clause effective only if 'reasonable', s 11

The requirement of reasonableness, s 11 UCTA 1977

If the relevant section in UCTA 1977 provides that the exemption clause will only be effective if it satisfies the requirement of reasonableness, then s 11 of UCTA 1977 needs to be considered, which details what is meant by this requirement.

Common Pitfall

Don't apply the requirement of reasonableness 'across the board', i.e. regardless of whether or not the relevant active section in **UCTA** requires the satisfaction of this requirement for the exemption clause to be effective. Remember: you only need to examine the reasonableness of an exemption clause if the relevant active section in **UCTA** declares that the clause's effectiveness depends upon the satisfaction of this requirement.

Relevant points to be considered in the context of assessing the reasonableness of an exemption clause include the following:

❖ Section 11(1) of UCTA 1977 states that the requirement of reasonableness for the purposes of the relevant provisions in UCTA 1977 (and of s 3 of the Misrepresentation Act 1967) is that 'the term shall have been a fair and reasonable one to be included having regard to the circumstances which were or ought reasonably to have been, known to or in the contemplation of the parties when the contract was made'.

❖ Section 11(2) of UCTA 1977 further specifies what is meant by this somewhat circular 'definition' of reasonableness and refers to the five guidelines regarding the application of the reasonableness 'test' in Schedule 2. These guidelines are:

(a) the strength of the bargaining positions of the parties relative to each other, taking into account (among other things) alternative means by which the customer's requirements could have been met;

(b) whether the customer received an inducement to agree to the term, or in accepting it had an opportunity of entering into a similar contract with other persons, but without having a similar term;

(c) whether the customer knew or ought reasonably to have known of the existence and the extent of the term (having regard, among other things, to any custom of the trade and any previous course of dealing between the parties);

(d) where the term excludes or restricts any relevant liability if some condition was not complied with, whether it was reasonable at the time of the contract to expect that compliance with that condition would be practicable; and

(e) whether the goods were manufactured, processed or adapted to the special order of the customer.

❖ Section 11(1) of UCTA 1977 provides that, in relation to assessing the reasonableness of *limitation* clauses, regard is to be had to a) the resources which the party putting forward the term could expect to be available to it for the purpose of meeting the liability should it arise; and b) how far it was open to this party to cover himself by insurance.

❖ Section 11(1) of UCTA 1977 provides that the burden of proof to show that an exemption clause satisfies the requirement of reasonableness is on the party who wishes to rely on the term in question.

Common Pitfall

Don't assume that the guidelines provided in Schedule 2 are exhaustive. Case law (*Overseas Medical Supplies Ltd v Orient Transport Services Ltd* [1999]) has provided at least seven further factors which might be considered in assessing the reasonableness of an exemption clause. There might well be more.

How to use UCTA 1977

> Does the contract at hand fall within the scope of UCTA 1977 ?

> Which (if any) section in UCTA 1977 deals with the exemption clause in question?

> What does this section 'do' to the exemption clause, i.e. is the clause rendered automatically ineffective or subject to the requirement of reasonableness?

> ONLY IF EXPRESSLY STATED IN RELEVANT SECTION OF UCTA 1977 : consider requirement of reasonableness in s 11 in order to determine if clause at hand is effective.

Unfair Terms in Consumer Contracts Regulations 1999 (UTCCR 1999)

The Unfair Terms in Consumer Contracts Regulations 1999 are another important piece of legislation which might come into play when assessing the effectiveness of exemption clauses.

Scope of the UTCCR 1999

Unlike UCTA 1977 which has domestic origins, the UTCCR 1999 owe their existence to the EC Directive on Unfair Terms in Consumer Contracts (93/13/EC, initially implemented in the UK by means of the Unfair Terms in Consumer Contracts Regulations 1994 (SI 1994/3159)) but which have subsequently been completely repealed and replaced by the Unfair Terms in Consumer Contracts Regulations 1999

(SI 1999/2083) which came into force on 1 October 1999. Despite proposals for reform in relation to both consumer rights and unfair contract terms, the UTCCR 1999 still form the current legal regime. Note that the origin of the UTCCR 1999 as an EC Directive must be borne in mind when interpreting the UTCCR 1999 so that effect is given to the Directive.

Common Pitfall

The UTCCR 1999 in places differ quite considerably from their predecessor (e.g. in relation to enforcement), the UTCCR 1994 ; in fact, the language employed in the 1999 Regulations is much closer to the EC Directive than the 1994 Regulations. These changes might not only potentially cause confusion in terms of understanding when reading judgments (such as *Director General of Fair Trading v First National Bank* [2001] 3 WLR 1297 (HL)) which refer to the old 1994 Regulations but also, and more importantly, might result in incorrectly stating the law.

Like UCTA 1977 however, the UTCCR 1999 can be, and indeed are, used to control the effectiveness of exemption clauses. It should therefore come as no surprise that there are certain overlaps between both pieces of legislation and that, as a consequence of these overlaps, there are situations in which an exemption clause might be subject to both UCTA 1977 and the UTCCR 1999.

Yet despite these overlaps, there are certain differences between UCTA 1977 and the UTCCR 1999 which should be remembered when assessing the effectiveness of an exemption clause:

The UTCCR 1999 only apply to consumer contracts, i.e. business-to-consumer contracts only. More importantly, reg 3(1) defines consumer as 'any natural person who, in contracts covered by these Regulations, is acting for purposes which are outside his trade, business or profession.'	This makes the scope of the UTCCR 1999 in terms of the parties falling within its ambit much narrower than that of UCTA 1977.	Consequently, companies will not able to rely on the UTCCR 1999 as they do not fall within the UTCCR 1999 definition of consumer (unlike the situation under UCTA 1977, see above).
The UTCCR 1999 apply to all types of (unfair) contract terms generally and are not, like UCTA 1977, restricted to exemption clauses only.	This makes the scope of the UTCCR 1999 in terms of the types of clauses within its ambit much wider than that of UCTA 1977.	Consequently, the UTCCR 1999 are not restricted to assessing the effectiveness of exemption clauses but might, in fact, also be of relevance in relation to other types of clauses.

In addition, the following qualifications regarding the scope of the UTCCR 1999 should be taken into account:

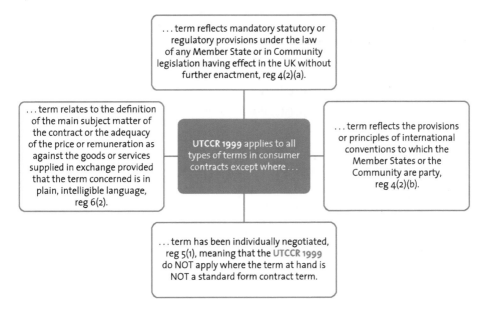

... term reflects mandatory statutory or regulatory provisions under the law of any Member State or in Community legislation having effect in the UK without further enactment, reg 4(2)(a).

... term relates to the definition of the main subject matter of the contract or the adequacy of the price or remuneration as against the goods or services supplied in exchange provided that the term concerned is in plain, intelligible language, reg 6(2).

UTCCR 1999 applies to all types of terms in consumer contracts except where ...

... term reflects the provisions or principles of international conventions to which the Member States or the Community are party, reg 4(2)(b).

... term has been individually negotiated, reg 5(1), meaning that the UTCCR 1999 do NOT apply where the term at hand is NOT a standard form contract term.

Terms which pass these 'hurdles' will be deemed to fall within the scope of the UTCCR 1999.

Assessing the effectiveness of a term under the UTCCR 1999

If a contract term in a consumer contract has been found to fall within the ambit of the UTCCR 1999, it will be subject to at least one, if not two, requirement(s) for it to be effective:

(a) that the term should be 'fair' (see reg 5(1)); and
(b) that, when in writing, the term should be written in 'plain, intelligible language'(see reg 7(1)).

The 'fairness test'

The basic framework for the 'fairness test' is provided by regs 5(1) and 6(1) which state:

'A contractual term which has not been individually negotiated shall be regarded as unfair if, contrary to the requirement of good faith, it causes a significant imbalance in the parties' rights and obligations arising under the contract, to the detriment of the consumer.' (reg 5(1))

'Without prejudice to regulation 12, the unfairness of a contractual term shall be assessed, taking into account the nature of the goods or services for which the contract was concluded and by referring, at the time of conclusion of the contract, to all the circumstances attending the conclusion of the contract and to all the other terms of the contract or of another contract on which it is dependent.' (reg 6(1))

In addition, reg 5(5) refers to an indicative and non-exhaustive list of the terms contained in **Schedule 2** of the UTCCR 1999 which may be regarded as unfair.

These provisions indicate that the assessment of the (un)fairness of a term under the UTCCR 1999 principally consists of two elements:

(1) the factor 'fairness' itself as outlined in reg 5(1), i.e. the question if it is contrary to the requirement of good faith and causes a significant imbalance in the parties' rights and obligations to the consumer's detriment; and
(2) the non-exhaustive 'indicative' or 'grey list' of terms found in Schedule 2 of the UTCCR 1999 which may be regarded as unfair.

Subsequently, the meaning of 'good faith' and 'significant imbalance' was clarified in *Director General of Fair Trading v First National Bank* [2002]:

Significant Imbalance: 'The requirement of significant imbalance is met if a term is so weighted in favour of the supplier as to tilt the parties' rights and obligations under the contract significantly in his favour. This may be by the granting to the supplier of a beneficial option or discretion or power, or by the imposing on the consumer of a disadvantageous burden or risk or duty. The illustrative terms set out in Schedule 3 to the [1994] Regulations [now Sch.2 of the UTCCR 1999] provide very good examples of terms which may be regarded as unfair; whether a given term is or is not to be so regarded depends on whether it causes a significant imbalance in the parties' rights and obligations under the contract. This involves looking at the contract as a whole. But the imbalance must be to the detriment of the consumer; a significant imbalance to the detriment of the supplier, assumed to be the stronger party, is not a mischief which the Regulations seek to address.'

UNFAIRNESS

Good Faith: 'The requirement of good faith in this context is one of fair and open dealing. Openness requires that the terms should be expressed fully, clearly and legibly, containing no concealed pitfalls or traps. Appropriate prominence should be given to terms which might operate disadvantageously to the customer. Fair dealing requires that a supplier should not, whether deliberately or unconsciously, take advantage of the consumer's necessity, indigence, lack of experience, unfamiliarity with the subject matter of the contract, weak bargaining position or any other factor listed in or analogous to those listed in Schedule 2 to the [1994] Regulations [note: these criteria have not been reproduced in the UTCCR 1999 but are likely to be of continuing importance in relation to assessing 'good faith']. Good faith in this context is not an artificial or technical concept; nor, since Lord Mansfield was its champion, is it a concept wholly unfamiliar to British lawyers. It looks to good standards of commercial morality and practice. Regulation 4(1) [now reg.5(1)] lays down a composite test, covering both the making and the substance of the contract, and must be applied bearing clearly in mind the objective which the Regulations are designed to promote.'

Effect of the fairness test

If the term in question is found to be 'unfair' under the above 'fairness test', reg 8(1) of the UTCCR 1999 provides that it shall not be binding on the consumer.

How to use the UTCCR 1999

Does the (unfair) term fall within reg 4(1)?

Look at (and apply) the definitions of 'consumer' and 'seller/supplier' in reg 3(1)

If the definitions are satisfied: does the term relate to core subject matter (reg 6(2))?

If the term in question does not relate to core subject matter, is it one which has NOT been individually negotiated (reg 5)?

If the term is a standard form contract term (i.e has NOT been individually negotiated), does it satisfy the 'fairness test' (regs 5(1), 6(1) and Schedule 2)?

If the term satisfies the 'fairness test', then it will be effective and can be relied upon. (Note however the potentially important requirement that, when in writing, the term should be written in 'plain, intelligible language', reg 7(1).)

If the term does NOT satisfy the 'fairness test', then it will not be effective and cannot be relied upon.

Putting it into practice

Nasrin is a professional baker who runs her own baking business 'Beautiful Bakes Ltd', specialising in very elaborate cakes for weddings and other special occasions. The bakery operates from a spare room in Nasrin's home where she has installed a professional oven and which also houses all the necessary tools she uses for her business. As the oven needed replacing, Nasrin went to Barry's shop 'Baking Supplies' to buy a new oven for her baking business. (The oven had been replaced on one previous occasion and is also sometimes used by Nasrin for some personal baking.) Barry's shop had been recommended to her by another baker; Nasrin had never done business with Barry before. In Barry's shop, 'Beautiful Bakes Ltd' bought a new oven. Nasrin is severely short-sighted and, consequently, she did not read the sign above the till in Barry's shop which states:

> 'Liability for any breach of any of the terms implied by sections 13–15 of the Sale of Goods Act 1979 is limited to the price of the goods purchased.'

In breach of the terms implied by s 14 of the Sale of Goods Act 1979, the oven proved to be seriously defective. As a consequence of this defect, 'Beautiful Bakes Ltd' was not only unable to properly perform an order for a five-tiered wedding cake but the defective oven also led to 'Beautiful Bakes Ltd' losing an unusually valuable contract for wedding cakes for the wedding of triplet sisters.

Advise 'Beautiful Bakes Ltd' as to whether Barry can rely upon the limitation clause.

Example feedback

The question requires you to advise 'Beautiful Bakes Ltd' in relation to the effectiveness of the limitation clause over the till in Barry's shop as Barry will only be able to rely upon this clause if it is effective. However, the fact that you are asked to advise 'Beautiful Bakes Ltd' does not mean that you should only include the points which are favourable to it. Rather, you should aim for a balanced analysis of all relevant legal points.

The introduction should set out the basic points which need to be considered to answer the question set, i.e. you should introduce those issues which are relevant to the task of advising 'Beautiful Bakes Ltd'. These are, as you are asked about the effectiveness of a limitation clause, the issues of incorporation, interpretation and statutory control of exemption clauses. These three issues should then be addressed in the relevant order as outlined in this chapter.

Therefore, the first point to be addressed is that of incorporation:

Was the clause properly incorporated into the contract between 'Beautiful Bakes Ltd' and Barry? Here, this needs consideration of the question when and how a clause is incorporated by means of a notice (the sign in Barry's shop): was there reasonably sufficient notice of the term?

This requires that

(a) reasonable notice must be given before or at the time the contract is made (*Olley v Marlborough Court Ltd*);
(b) the term must have been contained or referred to in a document which is intended to have contractual effect (*Chapelton v Barry UDC*); and
(c) the party trying to introduce the term in question has taken reasonable steps to make the other party aware of the existence of the term (*Parker v South Eastern Railway* – this means that you need to ask the question whether an ordinary person would have taken notice of the existence of the term)?

In this context, a particular point to note is Nasrin's severe short-sightedness: Does this matter? In all likelihood not, as the test regarding 'reasonably sufficient notice' is objective in nature (see *Thompson v London Midland and Scottish Railway Co* which indicated that the claimant's illiteracy was irrelevant in this respect).

If the conclusion is reached that the clause has been incorporated then the next point to consider is interpretation (construction): Is the clause in question appropriately worded to cover what has happened? Here, the clause is clearly addressing the issue of a breach of terms implied by ss 13–15 of the Sale of Goods Act 1979 ; the facts tell us that the oven is in breach of the term implied by s 14 of the Sale of Goods Act 1979. Hence, the clause is appropriately worded to cover what has happened. (NB: if it is clear that a clause is appropriately worded to cover what has happened, do not spend too much time discussing the issue; remember that relevancy is one important assessment factor: do not waste your and your examiner's time by lengthily describing things which are clear.)

If the conclusion is reached that the clause is appropriately worded to cover the breach then the effect of relevant legislation must be considered, i.e. you need to ask the question if the clause in question is affected by e.g. UCTA 1977 and/or the UTCCR 1999. (NB: When analysing the effectiveness of an exemption clause, it is usually not a bad idea to start with UCTA 1977 rather than with the UTCCR 1999 as UCTA 1977 is not limited to exemption clauses in consumer contracts but also covers such clauses in relation to business-to-business contracts. Furthermore, when considering the applicability of a statute, be sure to use the specific language used in that statute, e.g. with regard to UCTA 1977 'dealing as consumer' and not just 'consumer' or 'requirement of reasonableness' instead of merely 'reasonableness'. This is because accuracy is an important assessment factor: your accurate use of these phrases/definitions not only demonstrates knowledge but also a good understanding of how to use a statute, both of which are likely to gain you a higher mark.)

❖ Does UCTA 1977 apply? This requires the consideration of the following steps:

❖ Does the contract between 'Beautiful Bakes Ltd' and Barry fall within the scope of UCTA 1977 ? Answer: yes, the sale of goods contract between 'Beautiful Bakes Ltd' and Barry lies within the basic scope of UCTA 1977.

❖ Which, if any, section(s) in UCTA 1977 deal(s) with the limitation clause which is at issue here? Answer: s 6(2) or s 6(3) of UCTA 1977 might be applicable here as the limitation clause relates to Barry's liability for breach of the obligations arising from ss 13–15 of the Sale of Goods Act 1977. If 'Beautiful Bakes Ltd' dealt as consumer, then s 6(2) of UCTA 1977 would render the limitation clause on the sign in Barry's shop automatically ineffective; if 'Beautiful Bakes Ltd' did not deal as consumer, then the limitation clause will, according to s 6(3) of

UCTA 1977, be effective only if it satisfies the requirement of reasonableness (s 11 UCTA 1977).

Consequently, the question to be asked is 'Did 'Beautiful Bakes Ltd' deal as consumer?' This requires the consideration of whether or not 'Beautiful Bakes Ltd' contracted in the course of a business. Look at s.12 UCTA 1977 and *R & B Customs Brokers Co Ltd v United Dominions Trust Ltd*: Nasrin's personal use of the oven would appear not to be relevant as the question to be asked in this context is 'was the transaction an integral part to the business or was it one which occurred with sufficient regularity?'. With regard to the latter, Nasrin had replaced the oven only once before, so it cannot be said that the transaction at hand was one which occurred with sufficient regularity. With regard to the former, it would appear that the transaction between Barry and 'Beautiful Bakes Ltd' is not one which is integral to business carried out by 'Beautiful Bakes Ltd' as the business is not selling and buying ovens but baking cakes.

It would therefore seem that 'Beautiful Bakes Ltd' dealt as consumer within the meaning of s 12 UCTA 1977.

Consequently, it would appear that Barry will not be able to rely on the limitation clause against 'Beautiful Bakes Ltd' as s 6(2) UCTA renders this clause automatically ineffective.

(NB: Given that 'Beautiful Bakes Ltd' can be said to have dealt as consumer within the meaning of UCTA 1977, it might also be asked if the UTCCR 1999 are applicable here. However the answer is no, as the UTCCR 1999 only apply between sellers/ suppliers and consumers and the definition of consumer is limited to natural persons only. 'Beautiful Bakes Ltd' is NOT a natural person.)

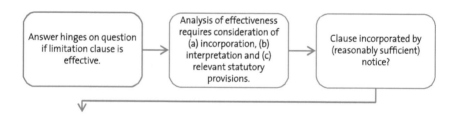

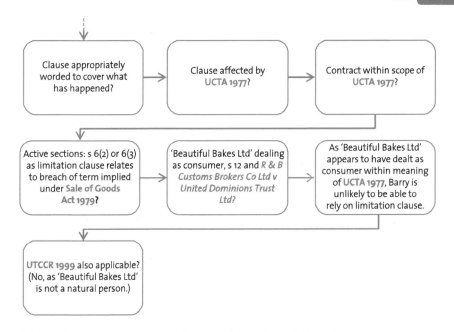

Table of key cases referred to in this chapter

Key case	Area of law	Principle
Chapelton v Barry UDC [1940] 1 KB 52	Incorporation of terms by written notice: the form of the notice.	The written notice must be contained in a document which would be expected and understood to contain contractual terms.
Chartbrook Ltd v Persimmon Homes Ltd [2009] UKHL 38	Interpreting the meaning of the provisions of a final contractual document.	Pre-contractual negotiations are not admissible to assist a court with construing such a contract.
Curtis v Chemical Cleaning & Dyeing Co [1951] 1 KB 805	Effect of misrepresentation on incorporation of terms by signature.	A misrepresentation as to the nature of the contract terms may defeat the attempt to incorporate terms by signature.
Hutton v Warren (1836) 1 M&W 466	How and when may terms be implied by custom?	Evidence of custom or usage may be admitted as evidence (if the contract is silent upon such customs or usages) and may thereby modify such a contract.

Key case	Area of law	Principle
Les Affréteurs Réunis SA v Leopold (London) Ltd [1919] AC 801	When may terms NOT be implied by custom?	There can be no implication of a term based on a custom which is either expressly varied by the contract or which is generally of inconsistent application.
Malik v BCCI [1998] AC 20	What terms may be implied into an individual employment contract?	A term that an employer would not conduct a corrupt and dishonest business was implied into the contract.
Routledge v McKay [1954] 1 WLR 615	Status of oral statement prior to a *written* contract.	The absence of an oral statement from a later written contract shows that the statement was not a contract term but only a representation.
Shirlaw v Southern Foundries (1926) Limited [1939] 2 KB 206	How and when may terms be implied into a written contract which is silent on a matter?	To fill a gap accidentally left by the contract parties which they would BOTH have envisaged should be so filled when agreeing the contract.
Spurling v Bradshaw [1956] 1 WLR 461	When will onerous exclusions be deemed incorporated by notice?	If written standard terms are particularly unreasonable to the other party they require positive indication to be effectively incorporated.

@ **Visit the book's companion website to test your knowledge**

❖ Resources include a subject map, revision tip podcasts, downloadable diagrams, MCQ quizzes for each chapter, and a flashcard glossary

❖ www.routledge.com/cw/optimizelawrevision

4 Misrepresentation

Revision objectives

Understand the law
- Can you outline the key characteristics of misrepresentation?
- Can you identify the characteristics of the different types of misrepresentation discussed in this chapter?
- What is the effect of a finding of misrepresentation on the contract?

Remember the details
- Can you remember the names of the principal supporting cases that highlight the key features of misrepresentation?
- Can you remember the key characteristics of each type of misrepresentation and the associated case law?
- Can you relay the remedies available for each type of misrepresentation?

Reflect critically on areas of debate
- Are you able to discuss the rationale for the different heads of misrepresentation and advise on which would provide the most effective remedy in a given scenario?

Contextualise
- Can you understand the difference between a 'term' of a contract and a 'representation'? Are you able to advise on the most beneficial route of action within the context of a contract where inaccurate information has been given?

Apply your skills and knowledge
- Can you complete the problem question at the end of the chapter?

Chapter Map

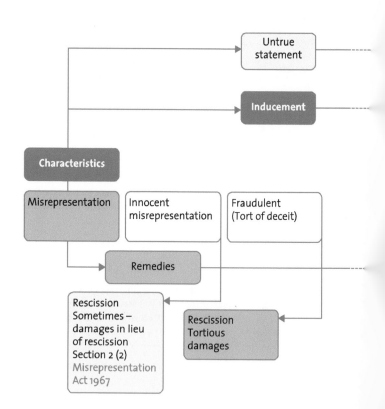

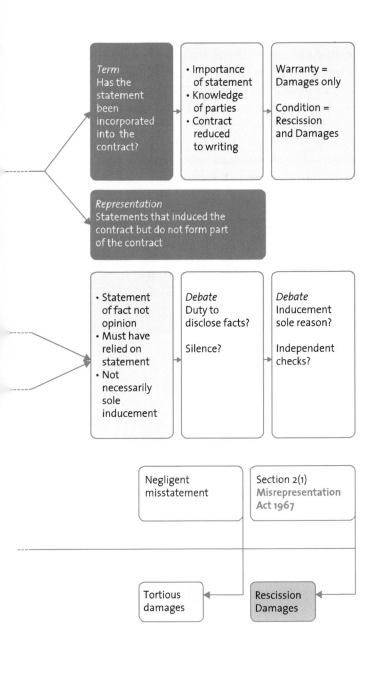

Term
Has the statement been incorporated into the contract?

- Importance of statement
- Knowledge of parties
- Contract reduced to writing

Warranty = Damages only

Condition = Rescission and Damages

Representation
Statements that induced the contract but do not form part of the contract

- Statement of fact not opinion
- Must have relied on statement
- Not necessarily sole inducement

Debate
Duty to disclose facts?

Silence?

Debate
Inducement sole reason?

Independent checks?

Negligent misstatement

Section 2(1)
Misrepresentation
Act 1967

Tortious damages

Rescission
Damages

Introduction

During the course of negotiations leading to the formation of a contract, statements made will constitute either terms of the contract, or representations. Representations are statements that helped to induce the contract. The latter, if untrue, will be actionable as misrepresentations. Certain core ingredients must be present for a successful claim in misrepresentation and if misrepresentation is proven the contract will be voidable. Once the criteria have been met, it is also necessary to determine the relevant category of misrepresentation. The type of misrepresentation will determine which remedies are available to the claimant.

Aim Higher

As you progress through this chapter, think about how the remedies available would differ if the 'representation' at issue had been incorporated into the contract and had formed a 'term' of the contract. How would the remedies differ, and would a claim for breach of contract be **more** or **less** advantageous than a claim under misrepresentation?

Definition of misrepresentation

An untrue statement of fact made by one party to another which induces the other party to enter into the contract

The characteristics of misrepresentation can be broken down into three key areas:

Essential Characteristics of Misrepresentation		
Untrue statement of fact	An active representation	Inducement

Untrue statement of fact

A misrepresentation must be a false statement of *fact*. A fact must be distinguished from other types of statement made about the substance of the contract. Other types of statement may include:

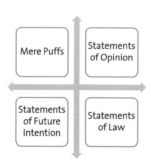

Mere puffs

A mere puff is a statement which is intended to draw attention to a particular product or brand to encourage sales. It is too vague to constitute a statement of fact, for example an advertisement outside a tea shop saying: 'probably the best cream teas in Devon!'

Statements of opinion

A genuinely held opinion cannot amount to a statement of fact. It is essential to establish whether or not the opinion was genuine at the time that the contract was made. What was the state of mind of the person making the statement? *Bissett v Wilkinson* [1927] explained below shows us why a statement made by a person selling a sheep farm could not constitute a statement of fact.

| In *Bissett v Wilkinson* [1927] AC 177 | The vendor told the purchaser that in his opinion the land would support 2,000 sheep. The vendor did not know its true capacity as the land had not previously been used for this purpose. | The action against the vendor failed. The statement was regarded as no more than an honest statement of opinion. |

If it can be shown that a reasonable person having the same knowledge as the representor could not have *honestly held* such an opinion, then a statement of opinion *can* be challenged for misrepresentation. For example, in *Smith v Land & House Property Corporation* (1884), when the vendor described his property as being let to 'a most desirable tenant', the court found the statement to be one of fact and an actionable misrepresentation. It transpired that, at the time of sale, the vendor had failed to disclose that the tenant was in arrears with his rent and the vendor knew the true facts of the situation. The position was later affirmed in *Esso Petroleum Co. Ltd v Mardon* [1976]:

| In *Esso Petroleum Co. Ltd v Mardon* [1976] 2 All ER 5 | The vendor told a prospective purchaser that the petrol station (under constuction) could achieve possible sales of 200,000 gallons per annum. Planning permission was refused which resulted in the relocation of the pumps in a less accessible position – the vendor said that the sales would be unaffected. | The sales output was far less than represented. The owner defaulted on its loan to Esso and Esso sought possession. The owner claimed misrepresentation. Esso's contention that the output statment was merely an opinion was rejected. Esso had skill in forecasting potential sales in locations of this type and had failed to take reasonable care in relation to the output advice given. |

Statement of future intention

A statement of intention that induces a person to enter into a contract can be actionable as a misrepresentation of fact if it can be proven that the representor knew that the promise would not be carried out. A good illustration of the rule extends from *Edgington v Fitzmaurice* (1885). Here, the company directors had issued a prospectus encouraging subscriptions for debentures. The prospectus stated that the money raised would be utilised to complete alterations to the company's premises and to expand the business. The company's real intention was to clear its debts. This was held to be a fraudulent misrepresentation.

Statements of law

Since the case of *Kleinwort Benson v Lincoln City Council* [1998] statements of law are now actionable; this line was also taken in *Pankhania v Hackney LBC* [2002]. There remains some uncertainty in this area as, prior to these cases; statements of law had not been actionable.

Representation and conduct

Whilst a statement is normally made orally or in writing, it can also be made by conduct. See *Spice Girls Ltd v Aprilla World Services* [2000] below:

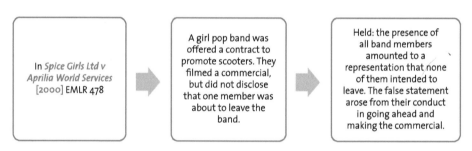

In *Spice Girls Ltd v Aprilia World Services* [2000] EMLR 478 → A girl pop band was offered a contract to promote scooters. They filmed a commercial, but did not disclose that one member was about to leave the band. → Held: the presence of all band members amounted to a representation that none of them intended to leave. The false statement arose from their conduct in going ahead and making the commercial.

Silence as a misrepresentation

Silence will not usually constitute a misrepresentation. There is no obligation to provide information that has not been requested. There are, however, three important areas where an exception will apply:

Half truths → Change of circumstances → Confidential/fiduciary (*uberrimae fidei*)

Half truths

Where certain facts are omitted, reducing the statements provided to only 'half-truths'. For example in *Dimmock v Hallett* (1866), the vendor of land stated that the land was let out to tenants, but he failed to disclose that the tenants were in the process of terminating the lease, which would result in a fall in income.

In this instance the non-disclosure was sufficiently significant to distort the picture and amount to a misrepresentation.

Change of circumstances

Where an original representation has been made, and circumstances later change, the representor has a duty to provide an update on the revised position. This was highlighted in *With v O'Flanagan* [1936] when an initial value of a doctor's practice was provided during the negotiations for sale of the business. Later, the doctor became ill and at the time the practice changed hands, most of the patients had relocated. Failure to disclose the substantial decline in the value of the business amounted to a misrepresentation.

Contracts uberrimae fidei (Confidential/Fiduciary Relationships)

Contracts *uberrimae fidei* (i.e. of utmost good faith) are an exception to the rule of non-disclosure. Insurance contracts fall under this head. For this type of contract all material facts must be disclosed, on the basis that the facts are used by the insurer to decide whether to accept/decline the business and to fix the level of premiums.

Time of representation

The representation must be made either before or at the time that the contract is agreed. If made after the agreement is concluded, the representation will not be actionable as a misrepresentation as it will not have induced the representee to enter into the contract

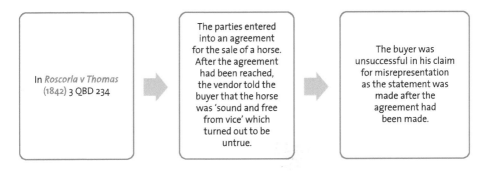

In *Roscorla v Thomas* (1842) 3 QBD 234 → The parties entered into an agreement for the sale of a horse. After the agreement had been reached, the vendor told the buyer that the horse was 'sound and free from vice' which turned out to be untrue. → The buyer was unsuccessful in his claim for misrepresentation as the statement was made after the agreement had been made.

Inducement

The representation must have induced the representee to enter into the contract. The test is an objective one. The representation must have been of material significance to the contract to be actionable as a misrepresentation (*Downs v Chappel* [1996]) and the claimant must be *aware* of the representation (*Horsfall v Thomas* (1862)).

Provided that the representation was *one* of the inducements, it need not have been the *sole* inducement.

Where the representee does not take up an opportunity to check a statement, he will not be stopped later from taking an action in misrepresentation:

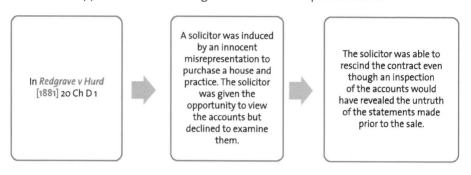

In *Redgrave v Hurd* [1881] 20 Ch D 1

A solicitor was induced by an innocent misrepresentation to purchase a house and practice. The solicitor was given the opportunity to view the accounts but declined to examine them.

The solicitor was able to rescind the contract even though an inspection of the accounts would have revealed the untruth of the statements made prior to the sale.

However, if the representee makes his own enquiries and relies upon his findings rather than the statements of the representor, a claim for misrepresentation cannot be made:

Case precedent – *Attwood v Small* (1838) 7 ER 684

Facts: The contract involved the purchase of a mine and premises. The purchaser was given information on the capacity of the mine and the information was confirmed by his own mining engineers. Later, it transpired that the information provided by the former owners was inaccurate but an action in misrepresentation failed because the purchasers had relied upon their own mining reports and not the information provided by the vendor.

Principle: The misrepresentation must have been relied upon.

Application: In problem questions check whether the claimant has sought independent information or advice on the central areas of the dispute. If he has, it is unlikely that he will have a claim.

Where it can be shown that the representee did not rely on a false statement and that he would have still entered into the contract if the false statement had not been made, the vital element of reliance is absent and the contract cannot be rescinded, see below:

Case precedent – *JEB Fasteners Ltd v Marks, Bloom & Co* [1983] 1 All ER 583

Facts: During negotiations for the takeover of another company, the claimant relied on the company's accounts which had been negligently compiled. The real reason for the takeover was to secure the services of two of the directors of the other company. The claim for misrepresentation failed.

Principle: A misrepresentation must have been of material significance to the contract for it to be actionable.

Application: In problem questions, you need to consider what material factors induced the representee to enter into the contract. Was the misstatement:

(a) not relied upon; or
(b) insignificant to the consent of the representee; or
(c) immaterial because there is evidence to show that the representee would have entered into the contract regardless of the statement.

If so, any claim for misrepresentation will be unsuccessful.

Categories of misrepresentation and remedies

Misrepresentation can be classified under three distinct heads:

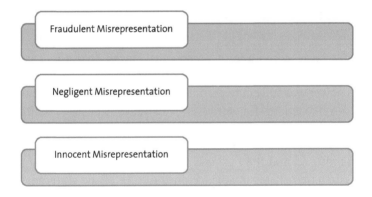

Fraudulent Misrepresentation

Negligent Misrepresentation

Innocent Misrepresentation

A misrepresentation can be an inaccurate statement made by a person who is unaware that the statement is wrong. The representor could have relied upon information passed on to him by a third party; perhaps within a log book or manual, or another source that he had considered to be reliable. Alternatively, the statement could be a conscious untruth, made with the intention of misleading the other party to the contract. Falling somewhere in between these positions, a representation may have been made carelessly. Perhaps the representor has not checked his information properly, or has assumed certain information without proper knowledge of the facts. It is important to classify the misrepresentation correctly as this dictates which remedies are available to the victim of the misrepresentation.

Fraudulent misrepresentation

> *Derry v Peek* (1889):
>
> 'A false statement made knowingly or without belief in its truth or recklessly careless whether it be true or false'
> Lord Herschell

Where fraudulent misrepresentation is found, damages are available through the *tort of deceit*. In *Derry v Peek* (1889) a clear distinction was drawn between fraud and negligence. In order to establish *fraud* it must be shown that a defendant knows that a statement is untrue, has no belief in its truth, or is reckless as to whether it is true or false.

Case precedent – *Derry v Peek* (1889) 14 App Cas 337

Facts: A Tramway corporation's prospectus stated that the company had permission to use steam power instead of horse power. However, the right to use steam power was subject to permission being granted by the Board of Trade. The company had applied for permission and honestly believed that they would be given permission, based on their understanding that permission was a mere formality. After the claimant had purchased shares, permission to use steam power was refused and the business went into liquidation. The shareholders, who had purchased shares in reliance on the truth of the statements made in the prospectus, took an action in deceit against the company directors.

Principle: The House of Lords held that there was insufficient proof of fraud. To establish fraud, the claimant must prove that the makers of the statement did not hold a genuine belief in the truth of the statement.

Application: In a problem question, in order to establish fraud, you must prove one of three things:

1. Did the representor know that the statement was false?
2. Did the representor act without belief in the statement?
3. Was the representor reckless or careless as to whether the statement was accurate or inaccurate?

Unless one of the above three criteria can be proven a claim will not succeed under the tort of deceit.

To summarise, to succeed under fraudulent misrepresentation, the claimant must show:

Up for Debate

Fraudulent misrepresentation is the most serious of the three categories of misrepresentation. It is also the most difficult to prove. Demonstrating someone's 'intent' is an arduous task. It is often asserted that the requirements to establish fraud are so restrictive there is little point in trying to pursue a claim under this remedy.

❖ Why is it difficult to prove someone's intent?

❖ Why is it no longer as important to succeed in a claim for fraudulent misrepresentation? Is there an alternative?

Negligent misrepresentation

Prior to the case of *Hedley Byrne & Co Ltd v Heller & Partners Ltd* [1964] all non-fraudulent misrepresentations were treated as innocent misrepresentations. Since *Hedley Byrne*, the common law tort of negligence has been extended to cover negligent misstatements where the claimant has suffered a loss.

In *Hedley Byrne & Co. Ltd v Heller & Partners Ltd* (1964) AC 465	Hedley Byrne (HB) received a large order from a customer, Easipower (EP). HB wanted to check EP's financial position, and creditworthiness, before executing the order and providing credit. HB asked EP's bank for a report, and the bank (H & P) responded with a positive reference, but excluded any liability for the reference. Later, EP went into liquidation and HB lost a substantive sum on contracts. HB sued H & P for negligence, claiming that their information was negligent and misleading. H & P contended that there was no duty of care owed regarding the statements and, regardless of this fact, they had disclaimed liability for their reference.	The action failed due to the disclaimer. However, in its judgment, the House of Lords stated, *obiter dicta* that such an action would be possible where a relationship between parties is 'sufficiently proximate' as to create a duty of care. Where it is reasonable for a party to have known that the information that they had given would likely have been relied upon for contractual relations, this can give rise to a 'special relationship' in which the defendant would have to take sufficient care in giving advice to avoid liability in negligence.

In summary, under *Hedley Byrne* principles, negligent misstatement can be established if the misrepresentee can show:

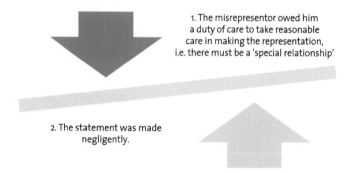

1. The misrepresentor owed him a duty of care to take reasonable care in making the representation, i.e. there must be a 'special relationship'

2. The statement was made negligently.

Later cases have refined the criteria and added additional requirements that must be established to succeed in a claim of negligent misstatement. Clarity has also been provided on the '*special relationship*' requirement and the extent of the '*degree of proximity*'.

Caparo Industries plc v Dickman [1990] established that, in order to be liable, the misrepresentor must have known, or ought to have known, the reasons for which the advice was being sought. A special relationship will normally exist in relationships between professional persons, particularly if the profession involves giving advice to clients, e.g. solicitors, barristers, agents. However, following *Esso Petroleum Co Ltd v Mardon* [1976] it is clear that a special relationship will also exist in commercial transactions where the representor has greater wisdom and experience than the representee and where it is reasonable to expect the representee to rely upon the statements. Liability is unlikely to occur where it can be shown that it would have been reasonable for the representor to have expected the representee to seek advice from their own experts or advisers.

In summary, the representee must show:

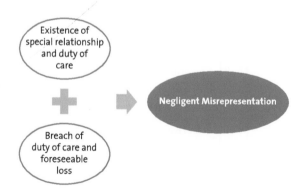

Existence of special relationship and duty of care

+

Breach of duty of care and foreseeable loss

Negligent Misrepresentation

The Misrepresentation Act 1967

Section 2(1) of the Misrepresentation Act 1967 introduced a statutory remedy for negligent misrepresentation. This remedy is important because the requirements are far less stringent than for fraudulent misrepresentation. Under this head, the claimant need prove no more than would be required to prove an innocent misrepresentation. Section 2(1) is clear and easy to follow:

> **Section 2(1)** Misrepresentation Act 1967
> 'Where a person has entered into a contract after a misrepresentation has been made to him by another party thereto and as a result thererof he has suffered loss, then if the person making the misrepresentation would be liable to damages in respect thereof had the misrepresentation been made fraudulently, that person shall be so liable notwithstanding that the misrepresentation was not made fraudulently unless he proves that he had reasonable grounds to believe and did believe up to the time the contract was made that the facts represented were true.'

To summarise:

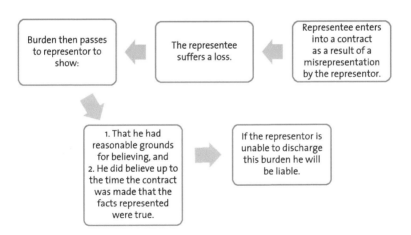

Thus an action under the Misrepresentation Act is far easier to pursue than an action in fraudulent misrepresentation, as the representee needs only to prove that the statement at issue was untrue. The burden then passes to the representor to show that he had reasonable grounds for believing that the statement was true. The fact that this is a heavy burden to discharge is illustrated in the case below:

Case precedent – *Howard Marine & Dredging v Ogden & Sons (Excavations)* [1978] QB 574

Facts: A barge hire company provided inaccurate information on carrying capacity to the hirer of two of their barges. The hire company had taken its information from Lloyds register, generally regarded as an accurate source of information, but had not checked the actual shipping register (which listed the accurate figures). The company was unable to discharge the burden of showing that it had reasonable grounds for believing that its statement was true.

Principle: The burden of proving that a party had reasonable grounds for making an inaccurate statement is extremely difficult to discharge.

Application: Careful checks should be made to find out how the representor acquired his knowledge. If there are alternative avenues for obtaining the information and the findings contradict the source of the representor's knowledge and these avenues were within the remit of the representor to pursue and find out the true picture, then he is unlikely to be able to discharge the burden of proving that he had reasonable grounds for his belief.

Innocent misrepresentation

This category of misrepresentation is restricted to wholly innocent misrepresentations. It can also be used where an action fails under the Misrepresentation Act, where the defendant has succeeded under the defence that he had reasonable grounds for his belief.

Remedies for misrepresentation

Remedies available will depend upon the type of misrepresentation. Rescission is available for all types of misrepresentation, but damages are available only for fraudulent and negligent misrepresentation. Sometimes rescission will be unavailable if the right to rescind has been lost (see later).

Rescission

The effect of misrepresentation is to render a contract voidable. Note: a contract will remain in force until the representee takes action to set it aside. The representee may rescind by informing the other party that he no longer intends to be bound by the contract. Under this action, the representee must not delay with rescission or he may be deemed to have affirmed the contract (see bars to rescission below). If the representor cannot be contacted, the representee can rescind by informing another third-party authoritative source (*Car and Universal Finance Co Ltd v Caldwell* [1964]).

Rescission can also be used as a defence for non-performance of a contract where the defendant is arguing that a contract is void for misrepresentation.

Bars to rescission
The remedy of rescission is subject to certain limits or 'bars':

Affirmation
Where a misrepresentation has occurred, the representee may wish to affirm the contract, i.e., continue with the contract and make a claim for damages to compensate his loss. He must take action quickly; otherwise it may be found that he has affirmed the contract. This can happen where the value of goods fluctuates frequently or the goods are of a perishable nature. Affirmation may be express or implied by conduct.

Lapse of time
Where a fraudulent misrepresentation has occurred, time will start to run from the time of detection of the fraud. For all other types of misrepresentation, rescission must take place within a reasonable time, even where it can be shown that there was no intention on the part of the representee to affirm the contract.

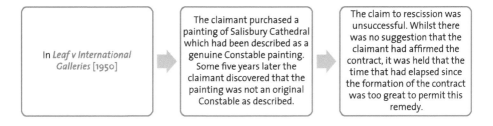

Restitution not possible
Restitution underpins the remedy of rescission. Under restitution, all that has been given and received under a contract must be returned. Where the parties cannot be returned to their pre-contractual positions, rescission cannot take place. For example, goods may have been consumed, expended, damaged or declined in value.

For example, a case of wine represented to be a rare six-year-old Claret that later transpires to be cheap mass-produced unbranded table wine, could have been ordered for and consumed at a party arranged by the buyer.

Acquisition of third-party rights

The representee cannot claim the return of property from a third party who has acquired a **good title** from the representor. Time is of the essence in these circumstances. Provided that rescission has taken place before the goods pass to a third party, then a claim in rescission will be upheld and any goods must be returned to the representee. If the goods have passed *before* rescission has taken place, the third party will have acquired good title to the goods and rescission will be barred.

Case precedent – *Car and Universal Finance Co Ltd v Caldwell* [1965] 1 QB 525

Facts: A cheque used by a fraudster to pay for a car was dishonoured. The fraudster could not be traced. In an attempt to recover his car, the seller notified the police and the Automobile Association. A third party later purchased the car in good faith. It was held that informing the police and the Automobile Association was sufficient action to demonstrate the representee's intention to rescind. Consequently, the rogue did not have good title to the car to pass on to a third party and the car was returned to its owner.

Principle: Timing of rescission is of significant importance. If rescission is effected before a third party acquires rights, it will prevent any rights being acquired. Also where the representor cannot be traced, rescission will be effected when the representee openly makes his intention to rescind clear, i.e. in cases of fraud – notifying the police.

Application: In problem questions you should ascertain exactly when rescission was effected. If this is before the acquisition of the goods by a third party, the goods must be returned to the representee. If rescission came after the goods had passed to a third party, then the third party will have acquired good title.

Aim Higher

Where a party (representee) has been deceived by a person pretending to be somebody else, the contract will be voidable at the option of the representee. This means that if goods have passed to an innocent third party *after* the representee has rescinded the contract, the innocent party must hand back the goods. If the representee rescinds the contract before the goods pass to an innocent third party. *Is it right that an innocent party who purchases in good faith must hand back goods obtained in such circumstances?*

Damages in lieu of rescission

The right of rescission is sometimes lost where the court exercises its discretion under s 2(2) of the Misrepresentation Act 1967 to award damages in lieu of rescission. The discretion of the court is never exercised in cases of fraudulent misrepresentation. The discretion is used where the effects of the misrepresentation are insignificant and the court considers that damages will provide a satisfactory remedy. The discretion can be used in innocent misrepresentation in appropriate cases where the award of damages in not usually available, but cannot be exercised where a claim to rescission has been barred (see above – bars to rescission).

Categories of damages

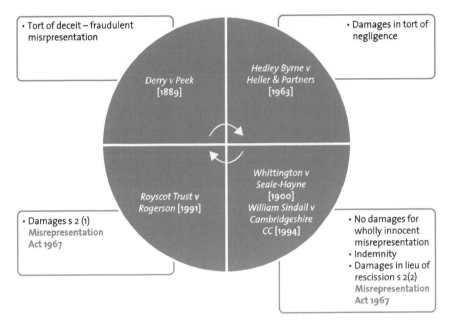

Damages for fraudulent misrepresentation

Damages for fraudulent misrepresentation are claimed under the tort of deceit and calculated on the *reliance basis*. The overall aim is to return the claimant to the position he was in before the tort was committed. Damages in fraud do not have to be reasonably foreseeable, although there must be a causative link. Thus all losses flowing from the fraudulent statement (including consequestial losses), are recoverable (*Doyle v Olby (Ironmongers) Ltd* [1969] and *Smith New Court v Scrimgeour Vickers* (1996)).

Damages for negligent misrepresentation

Damages for negligent misrepresentation at common law are assessed using a tortious measure. They are subject to the remoteness of damages test, i.e., damages are linked to those that are foreseeable.

Section 2(1) of the Misrepresentation Act 1967

Damages under the Act are assessed according to the tort measure on the *reliance basis*. This provides authority for the fact that all losses can be recovered whether or not they were foreseeable, provided that they are not too remote. Doubts about this approach were expressed in *Smith New Court Securities Ltd v Scrimgeour Vickers (Asset Management) Ltd* [1996] but, to date, the rules in *Royscot* remain applicable. It is far easier to succeed in a claim under s 2(1) than to prove the 'intent' of a party, which is necessary under a claim for fraudulent misrepresentation.

Aim Higher

Taking on board the measure of damages available under the tort of deceit and for negligent misrepresentation, what motivation is there for a claimant to pursue an action in fraudulent misrepresentation?

Damages for innocent misrepresentation

Damages cannot be recovered for innocent misrepresentation. As mentioned above, the court can exercise its discretion and award damages in lieu of rescission under s 2(2) of the Misrepresentation Act 1967 where rescission would be available. In *William Sindall v Cambridgeshire CC* [1994], Lord Hoffmann stated that in order to exercise discretion under s 2(2) of the Act, three factors needed to be considered to decide what is 'equitable'.

| Lord Hoffmann

Three factors for consideration under s2(2) | 1. Nature of misrepresentation. | 2. The loss caused to the representee if contract is upheld. To prevent unfair oppression for an innocent misrepresentation. | 3. The hardship caused to misrepresentor if contract rescinded. |

Indemnity

Whilst damages cannot be awarded for an innocent misrepresentation, an indemnity can be granted to allow the recovery of any expenses incurred by the representee, as a result of entering into the contract. An indemnity award should not be confused with damages:

Case precedent – *Whittington v Seale-Hayne* [1900] 82 LT 49

Facts: A poultry breeder took on a lease of a farm, induced by the owner's representation that the premises were in a sanitary condition. The representation turned out to be untrue. The water was contaminated; the manager became ill and some poultry died. The claimant was entitled to rescission and an indemnity to represent costs such as rent and rates, but was not entitled to damages as the misrepresentation was not fraudulent.

Principle: Where a claimant has incurred losses through wasted expenditure as a victim of an innocent misrepresentation, he can be awarded an indemnity. Note: the remedy is one of restitution rather than compensation.

Application: In problem questions note that there is no right to damages unless a misrepresentation is either fraudulent or negligent. The remedy will always be rescission but the court can grant an ancillary order of indemnity where wasted expenditure has been incurred by the claimant.

Common Pitfall

Candidates often fare very well in analysing a problem scenario on misrepresentation and reaching an accurate conclusion. However, valuable marks are often lost by not seeing the answer through to a final conclusion. Following a correct classification of the 'type' of misrepresentation, candidates often forget to discuss what damages are available for the stated category.

Summary

Fraudulent Misrepresentation (Tort of deceit)	Negligent Misrepresentation	Innocent Misrepresentation
Characteristics: A statement made: knowingly, without belief in its truth, or recklessly Defence: An honest belief that the statement is true	Characteristics: Negligent mis-statement Special relationship giving rise to a duty of care Defendant aware of reliance Characteristics: S 2(1) Misrepresentation Act Negligent statement Defence: An honest belief that the statement is true	Characteristics: An untrue statement that is neither fraudulent nor negligent
Remedies: Damages – tort of deceit All losses flowing from the fraud Rescission	Remedies: Misstatement: Damages – tort measure Rescission Remedies: S 2(1) Misrepresentation Act Damages – tort measure Rescission	Remedies: No right to damages Damages in lieu of rescission may be awarded under s 2(2) Misrepresentation Act 1967 Indemnity Rescission

Putting it into practice

Look at the scenario below, and then answer the following question:

On 15 January, Mohammed, a collector of antiques, saw a carved ebony crocodile in an antique shop in the high street. George, the owner of the shop told him that, in his opinion, it was a rare work of art from the Renaissance period (sixteenth century). He also said that he was sure that the crocodile's eyes were made from emeralds.

Mohammed did not buy the crocodile, but said he would think about it. The next day he went to see his friend Josie in her office. Josie specialises in sixteenth-century art. Mohammed asked her to examine the crocodile for him. Josie carefully examined the crocodile and assured Mohammed that it was a genuine sixteenth-century Renaissance creation. Whilst certain about the age of the crocodile, Josie was unable to confirm whether or not the eyes were real emeralds. On 25 January, Mohammed purchased the crocodile for £2,000.

Two months later, Mohammed took the crocodile to be valued by an auctioneer. The auctioneer told him correctly that it was nineteenth-century reproduction and the eyes were not made from emeralds. The auctioneer valued it at around £120.

Advise Mohammed on his rights and remedies (if any) against George and Josie.

Example feedback
In all problem questions always remember to:

1. Identify the relevant area of law.
2. Define the relevant law.
3. Explain the relevant law.
4. Apply the relevant law.

When looking at this scenario, it is important to first break down the information, and then consider each of the possible occurrences in turn, as follows:

❖ Is there a contract? Yes – all contractual elements are all present.
❖ Is the statement a term or a representation? Whether a statement is a term or a representation is an *objective test*. There are various guidelines to help the court. The statements were not made immediately before the sale as Mohammed bought the crocodile over a week later. This timing suggests the statements are just representations – *Routledge v McKay* [1954]. Consider which party has special skill and knowledge. If the maker of the statement has special skill and knowledge this suggests the statement is a term of the contract – *Dick Bentley v Harold Smith Motors* [1965] – whereas if the other party has special skill and knowledge it is more likely to be a representation – *Oscar Chess v Williams* [1957].
❖ Here George only has a local high street antique shop and Mohammed is a collector and may have greater skill and knowledge. Also George said that, in his opinion, the crocodile was sixteenth century. If he had encouraged Mohammed to check, this would suggest the statements were representations – *Ecay v Godfrey* (1947), but no such encouragements were made. Overall, it seems more likely that the statements are representations and not terms.
❖ Now consider whether there has been a misrepresentation. Let us look at George's statements first:
❖ Define misrepresentation. A false statement of fact made by one party to the other which induces the other party to enter into the contract. The burden of establishing misrepresentation will be on the representee, Mohammed.

❖ Work through the definition to ascertain whether it is satisfied. *Mohammed v George* – To be a misrepresentation the statements must be statements of fact and not opinion – *Bissett v Wilkinson* [1927], *Smith v Land and House Property Corporation* (1884). George's statement about the crocodile being sixteenth century appears to be given as an opinion and so cannot amount to a misrepresentation. George's statement about the eyes is more likely to be a statement of fact. If either statement is a statement of fact, to constitute a misrepresentation it must also have induced him to enter into the contract. It appears that Mohammed relied on what Josie said about the age of the crocodile and on what George said about the eyes. Remember, it is not necessary for George's statement to be the *sole* inducement for entitlement to misrepresentation to exist.

❖ Remedies: Misrepresentation makes the contract voidable so Mohammed can rescind the contract by notifying George. The aim of restitution is to restore the parties to their pre-contractual position so Mohammed will return the crocodile and George will return the money. However, Mohammed has delayed for two months – possible bar to rescission? – *Leaf v International Galleries* [1950]. If this is so he will not be able to return the crocodile. Notwithstanding any possible bar to rescission, Mohammed can still claim damages which can be awarded regardless of whether the contract is rescinded. There is no suggestion that George's misrepresentation was fraudulent or that he was aware that what he was saying was untrue. If Mohammed were to pursue this option, he would have the burden of proving fraud and this is often difficult to do. It is easier for Mohammed to claim under s 2 (1) of the Misrepresentation Act 1967. George will be liable under s 2 (1) unless he can show he had reasonable grounds to believe that the statements were true. This is very difficult to do – *Howard Marine and Dredging v Ogden* [1978].

❖ Under the Misrepresentation Act, damages are awarded in the same way as for fraudulent misrepresentation – *Royscot Trust Ltd v Maidenhead Honda Centre* [1991]. Aim of the court will be to return Mohammed to the position he was in before the misrepresentation was made and he can recover all direct loss. He will recover the amount he paid less the value of the crocodile.

❖ If George can show reasonable grounds for believing what he said was true then he will have made an innocent misrepresentation. Damages are not available as of right for innocent misrepresentation, but the court may award damages in lieu of rescission under s 2(2) of the Misrepresentation Act 1967.

❖ Finally, consider whether Mohammed can make a claim against Josie. Under *Hedley Byrne & Co Ltd v Heller & Partners* [1964] and *Caparo Industries v Dickman* [1990], Mohammed will have to establish both that Josie owed him a duty of care and that a special relationship existed.

❖ Josie communicated the statement directly to Mohammed and she knew the purpose for which her advice was required. Mohammed must also establish that Josie knew he would be very likely to rely on her advice in deciding whether to buy the crocodile and it must have been reasonable for him to do so. Liability can depend on the context in which the advice is given and a duty can be owed even where advice is given by a friend (*Chaudry v Prabhakar (1989)*).

❖ Although Josie is Mohammed's friend, he did go to see her in her office and she is a specialist in sixteenth-century history, although we do not know the exact nature of her knowledge or expertise. It may be that she did owe Mohammed a duty of care and will be liable to him in tort for negligent misstatement.

❖ This can be shown diagrammatically, and is a useful way to plan your answers when answering a scenario or problem question within an exam:

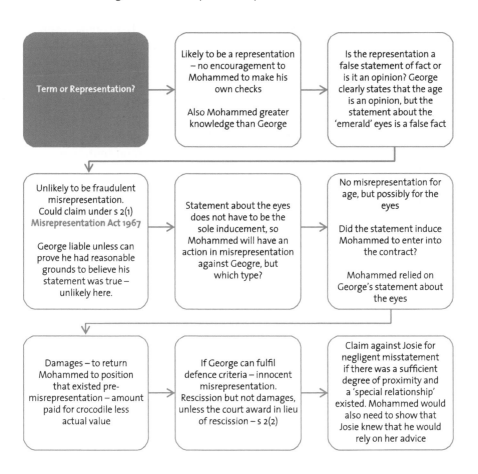

Term or Representation?

→ Likely to be a representation – no encouragement to Mohammed to make his own checks

Also Mohammed greater knowledge than George

→ Is the representation a false statement of fact or is it an opinion? George clearly states that the age is an opinion, but the statement about the 'emerald' eyes is a false fact

Unlikely to be fraudulent misrepresentation. Could claim under s 2(1) Misrepresentation Act 1967

George liable unless can prove he had reasonable grounds to believe his statement was true – unlikely here.

→ Statement about the eyes does not have to be the sole inducement, so Mohammed will have an action in misrepresentation against Geogre, but which type?

→ No misrepresentation for age, but possibly for the eyes

Did the statement induce Mohammed to enter into the contract?

Mohammed relied on George's statement about the eyes

Damages – to return Mohammed to position that existed pre-misrepresentation – amount paid for crocodile less actual value

→ If George can fulfil defence criteria – innocent misrepresentation. Rescission but not damages, unless the court award in lieu of rescission – s 2(2)

→ Claim against Josie for negligent misstatement if there was a sufficient degree of proximity and a 'special relationship' existed. Mohammed would also need to show that Josie knew that he would rely on her advice

Table of key cases referred to in this chapter

Key case	Area of law	Principle
Attwood v Small (1838) 7 ER 684	Concerned the purchase of a mine. Information was provided on the mine's capacity. The buyers also commissioned their own report. Their report confirmed the information provided by the vendors.	A claim for misrepresentation was unsuccessful as, although the capacity information was inaccurate, the buyers had relied upon their own independent report.
Bissett v Wilkinson [1927] AC 177	Concerned a contract to buy a farm; the seller cited an opinion on the capacity of the farm.	Where a statement is clearly an opinion only, it will not be actionable as a misrepresentation.
Dimmock v Hallett (1866) LR 2 Ch App 21	Concerned the position of 'half-truths'. Here the vendor told a purchaser that the land was let, but failed to mention that notice to quit had been given.	Where a non-disclosure distorts the picture significantly enough it can amount to a misrepresentation.
Hedley Byrne & Co Ltd v Heller & Partners Ltd [1964] AC 465	Concerned an action against a bank for the provision of negligent information on the creditworthiness of a company to which the claimants had provided a service on credit terms.	The common law tort of negligence can be used to claim against negligent misstatements that cause loss.
Howard Marine & Dredging Co Ltd v Ogden & Sons (Excavations) Ltd [1978] QB 574	Concerned information provided on the carrying capacity of a barge. The information had been taken from a source that usually reliable, but was on this occasion was inaccurate. The correct information was available on the Shipping Register.	To disprove negligence a defendant must demonstrate reasonable grounds for belief in the truth of the statement that is under challenge (s 2(1) of the Misrepresentation Act 1967).

Redgrave v Hurd [1881] 20 ChD 1	Concerned the purchase of a business. The claimant was offered the opportunity to look at business accounts to verify statements made by the vendor, but declined.	Where an opportunity to verify information is provided and not taken, a future action in misrepresentation will not usually be barred.
Roscorla v Thomas (1842) 3 QBD 234	Concerned the sale of a horse. The seller stated after the sale that the horse was 'sound and free from vice'.	A statement made after an agreement has been formed cannot amount to a representation.
Royscot Trust Ltd v Rogerson [1991] 2 QB 297	Concerned a misrepresentation by a car dealer to a finance company on the amount of a deposit paid by a customer.	Authority that damages for negligent misrepresentation are assessed on the same basis as fraudulent misrepresentation.
With v O'Flanagan [1936] Ch 575	Concerned the non-disclosure of a change in the value of a business since the initial discussions and the transfer.	Non-disclosure of a change in circumstances can amount to a misrepresentation.

@ Visit the book's companion website to test your knowledge

❖ Resources include a subject map, revision tip podcasts, downloadable diagrams, MCQ quizzes for each chapter, and a flashcard glossary

❖ www.routledge.com/cw/optimizelawrevision

5

Mistake

Revision objectives

Understand the law
- Can you outline the key areas where a mistake will be recognised at common law?
- What are the relevant characteristics of the three types of common law mistake discussed in this chapter?
- What is the effect of a finding of mistake on a contract?

Remember the details
- Can you remember the names of the principal supporting cases that highlight the different components of the definition of mistake?
- Can you explain the current position in equity regarding mistake?
- Can you relay the remedies available for mistake?
- Do you understand the principle of *nemo dat quod non habet* and its effect on a contract?

Reflect critically on areas of debate
- Are you able to discuss the rationale behind each of the different heads of mistake and pinpoint whether a claim would be a realistic option in a given scenario?
- Are you able to pinpoint any alternative courses of action in a given scenario?

Contextualise
- Can you explain when the alternative remedy of fraudulent misrepresentation may assist a claimant where a claim for mistake in identity would fail?

Apply your skills and knowledge
- Can you complete the problem question at the end of the chapter?

Chapter Map

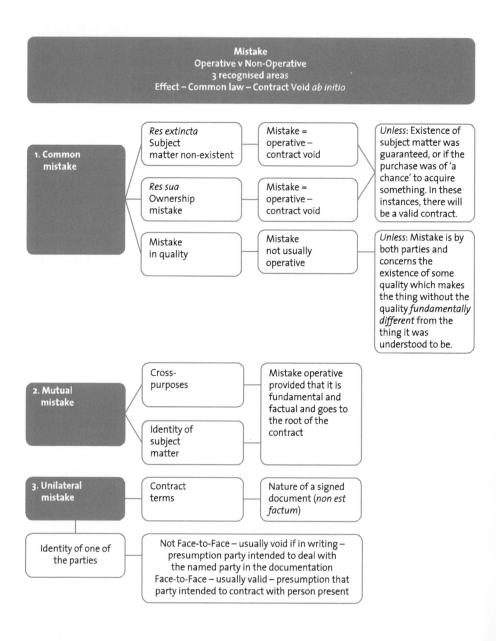

Mistake
Operative v Non-Operative
3 recognised areas
Effect – Common law – Contract Void *ab initio*

1. Common mistake

Res extincta
Subject matter non-existent

Mistake = operative – contract void

Unless: Existence of subject matter was guaranteed, or if the purchase was of 'a chance' to acquire something. In these instances, there will be a valid contract.

Res sua
Ownership mistake

Mistake = operative – contract void

Mistake in quality

Mistake not usually operative

Unless: Mistake is by both parties and concerns the existence of some quality which makes the thing without the quality *fundamentally different* from the thing it was understood to be.

2. Mutual mistake

Cross-purposes

Identity of subject matter

Mistake operative provided that it is fundamental and factual and goes to the root of the contract

3. Unilateral mistake

Contract terms

Nature of a signed document (*non est factum*)

Identity of one of the parties

Not Face-to-Face – usually void if in writing – presumption party intended to deal with the named party in the documentation
Face-to-Face – usually valid – presumption that party intended to contract with person present

Introduction

As a general rule, a mistake will not affect a contract. There is no doctrine of mistake as such, but the common law will recognise certain mistakes that are fundamental in nature. These types of mistake are known as *operative mistakes*, and will render a contract void.

Traditionally the courts have been reluctant recognise a mistake as being operative, mainly due to the extreme effect on a third party. A third party may have purchased goods innocently, only to find that they do not have good title (*nemo dat quod non habet*) and the goods have to be returned to the original owner.

Aim Higher

As you progress through this chapter, think about how the law in mistake could be simplified. If, for example, the rule that a person intends to contract only with the person he deals with were to be universally adopted (rather than solely for face-to-face-contracts), the law would be more transparent and a claim in fraudulent misrepresentation would sufficiently provide a remedy to assist the claimant who has been tricked by a fraudster. See the dissenting opinion of Lord Nicholls in *Shogun Finance Ltd v Hudson* [2003] and think about this idea as you work through the chapter. Be prepared to argue the position for or against this point.

Definition of mistake

Where an operative mistake is recognised, the contract will be void, *ab initio*. This means that the contract is treated as though it never existed and the parties are returned to their pre-contractual position. Where a mistake is not operative, the common law rules do not apply. Sometimes a solution can be found in equity. In equity a mistake will render a contract *voidable*, but it should be noted that an equitable remedy is subject to the maxims of equity and the discretion of the court. Operative mistakes fall into three categories:

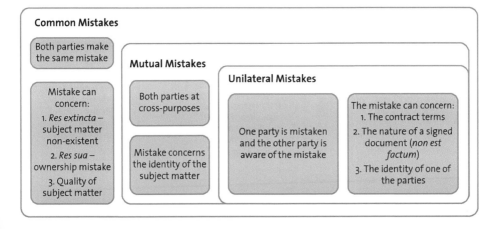

Common Mistakes

Both parties make the same mistake

Mistake can concern:
1. *Res extincta* – subject matter non-existent
2. *Res sua* – ownership mistake
3. Quality of subject matter

Mutual Mistakes

Both parties at cross-purposes

Mistake concerns the identity of the subject matter

Unilateral Mistakes

One party is mistaken and the other party is aware of the mistake

The mistake can concern:
1. The contract terms
2. The nature of a signed document (*non est factum*)
3. The identity of one of the parties

Common mistakes

Res extincta

This means that the subject matter of the contract did not exist at the time that the contract was formed. The parties will have contracted under the mistaken belief that the subject matter was in existence. In such instances the mistake will be operative and the contract will be void. An exception will occur if the offeror has guaranteed the existence of the subject matter.

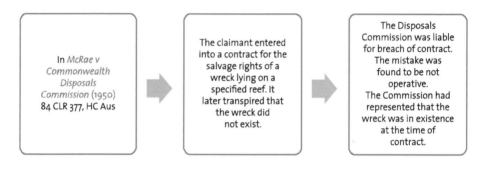

In *McRae v Commonwealth Disposals Commission* (1950) 84 CLR 377, HC Aus

The claimant entered into a contract for the salvage rights of a wreck lying on a specified reef. It later transpired that the wreck did not exist.

The Disposals Commission was liable for breach of contract. The mistake was found to be not operative. The Commission had represented that the wreck was in existence at the time of contract.

In *Couturier v Hastie* (1852) 5 HLC 673, the parties had agreed a sale on a cargo of grain which was in transit. Unbeknown to the parties, the captain had sold the grain during the voyage, as its condition had deteriorated. Whilst not decided on the principles of mistake, it is clear from the judgment that the contract was deemed void on the basis that the subject matter did not exist.

Where the subject matter of a contract does not exist, it is important to ascertain whether or not existence was guaranteed, or whether the purchase was of 'a chance' to acquire something. In these instances, there will be a valid contract.

Res sua

If a party mistakenly contracts to purchase something, which unbeknown to himself, he already owns, the mistake will be operative and the contract void. See below:

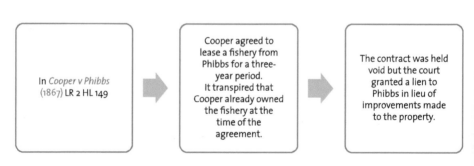

In *Cooper v Phibbs* (1867) LR 2 HL 149

Cooper agreed to lease a fishery from Phibbs for a three-year period. It transpired that Cooper already owned the fishery at the time of the agreement.

The contract was held void but the court granted a lien to Phibbs in lieu of improvements made to the property.

Mistake as to the quality of the subject matter

This means that where the subject matter of the contract is different in quality to that which has been agreed, the contract will *not* be void. The courts will not protect a party from a bad bargain. The mistake will be operative only if it is made by both parties and concerns the existence of some quality which makes the thing without the quality *fundamentally different* from the thing it was understood to be.

Case precedent – *Bell v Lever Brothers Ltd* [1932] AC 161

Facts: As a result of a reorganisation, Lever Bros negotiated an early termination severance package with two of its directors. It later transpired that Lever Bros could have legitimately terminated the contracts, without severance pay, due to irregular conduct by the directors. Lever Bros argued in the House of Lords that the contract was void on the basis of a fundamentally mistaken belief on all sides that the contracts were still valid and the individuals were entitled to compensation.

Principle: The mistake must be of material significance to render a contract void. It must go to the **root** of the contract. It must relate to a *term* of the contract rather than an expectation of the quality. Lord Aitken '... mistake will not affect assent unless it is the mistake of both parties, and is as to the existence of some quality which makes the thing without the quality essentially different from the thing it was believed to be'. The House of Lords held that Lever Bros got what it bargained for – the agreement was simply not of the value that they had anticipated.

Application: In a problem question you need to consider whether the alleged mistake is one that merely affects the *value or quality* of the deal, or whether the mistake is so fundamental that it renders the subject matter something *fundamentally different* to what the parties have agreed

---

In *Bell v Lever Bros* [1932], the House of Lords explained their decision by reference to a hypothetical contract for a painting. If both parties thought the painting was an old master and it turned out to be a modern copy, then the buyer would have no remedy in mistake unless the seller had represented that it was an old master. The buyer would simply have made a mistake as to the value of the contract, a factor which is insufficient to render a contract void for mistake. This area illustrates the importance of *caveat emptor* – let the buyer beware.

In the later case of *Leaf v International Galleries* [1950], which involved similar facts to the example above, Lord Denning held that a mistake concerning the identity of the painter of a picture of Salisbury Cathedral was irrelevant. The mistake related only to the quality of the contract, not to the subject matter of the sale. In essence, the parties got what they bargained for – a painting of Salisbury Cathedral.

Common Pitfall

Consideration of the ratio in *Leaf* may lead us to the belief that people could pass off non-original works as those of a master under this rule. That is not the case. If you look closely at the facts of *Leaf*, you will see that at no point was a representation made guaranteeing the identity of the painter. If there had been it is likely that the outcome of the case would have been different. It would be unjust to apply this rule universally in cases where there is a specific express term stating that a piece of work is an original. The case of *Peco Arts Inc v Hazlitt Gallery Ltd* [1983] highlights this point.

Further in *Associated Japanese Bank Ltd v Credit du Nord SA* [1988] a contract of guarantee for some machines, made on the basis that the specified machines were in existence, was held to be void when it transpired that the machines did not exist. It was found that the mistake had a suitably serious effect on matters that went to the root of the contract. Steyn J stated: '... the guarantee of obligations under a lease with non-existent machines was essentially different from a guarantee of a lease with four machines which both parties at the time of the contract believed to exist.'

Mutual mistakes

A mutual mistake can occur when both contracting parties have made different mistakes and are at cross-purposes. It can be said that there is no meeting of the minds (*consensus ad idem*). The mistake can relate to either the terms or the subject matter of the contract. The mistake must be a fundamental factual mistake and go to the root of the contract. For example, A is selling a Kindle and B thinks he is getting a mobile phone. Where the courts are unable to find an agreement and performance of the contract would be impossible, the contract will be held void for mistake.

On terms of the contract:

| In *Raffles v Wichelhaus* (1864) 159 ER 375 | → | Two separate ships carrying cotton, both known as 'Peerless' were due to depart from Bombay in October and December respectively. The defendant thought that the contract was for the October cargo and the claimant thought it was for the December cargo. | → | It was not possible to establish a consensus *ad idem*. Mistake was operative and the contract was held void for mistake. |

On subject matter of the contract:

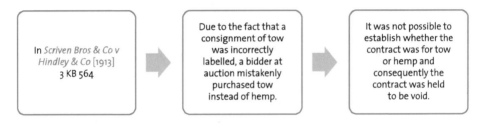

| In *Scriven Bros & Co v Hindley & Co* [1913] 3 KB 564 | → | Due to the fact that a consignment of tow was incorrectly labelled, a bidder at auction mistakenly purchased tow instead of hemp. | → | It was not possible to establish whether the contract was for tow or hemp and consequently the contract was held to be void. |

Aim Higher

In the case of **Smith v Hughes** (1871) LR 6 QB 597, a contract for new oats was upheld, notwithstanding the fact that the claimant was of the belief that he was purchasing old oats.

❖ Why could this not be classed as a mutual mistake?
❖ Were the parties at cross purposes?

TIP: What was the root of the contract?

Unilateral mistake

A unilateral mistake will usually fall into one of three areas:

| 1. Terms of the contract | ❖ *Hartog v Colin & Shields* [1939] 3 All ER 566 |

| 2. Nature of the signed document | ❖ *Saunders v Anglia Building Society* [1970] 3 All ER 961 |

| 3. Identity of one of the parties | ❖ *Cundy v Lindsay* (1878) 3 App Cas 459 – non face-to-face (*inter absentes*)
❖ *Lewis v Averay* [1971] 3 All ER 907 – face-to-face (*inter praesentes*) |

Terms of contract

A mistake will be operative where one party is mistaken on a material term of the contract and the other party is aware of the mistake. In *Hartog v Colin & Shields* [1939], a contract was held void due to a mistake on the pricing of some animal skins. In this particular trade the pricing policy for animal skins was common knowledge and the party trying to enforce the contract would have been aware of this. The mistake was found to be material.

Nature of the signed document (non est factum)

In order to find an operative mistake in *non est factum* the court must be convinced that there is a fundamental difference between the legal effect of a document signed and that to which the claimant thought he had signed. Carelessness will not suffice, as demonstrated in *Saunders v Anglia Building Society* [1970] where an old lady who signed a document without reading it properly, due to the fact that she had lost her spectacles, was bound by the content.

Note: If one party is mistaken and the other party is unaware of the mistake, the mistake cannot be operative; this was highlighted in the case of *Wood v Scarth* (1858), where the defendant was unaware that the claimant was mistaken in relation to the rental terms of a public house.

Mistaken identity

In order for a mistake concerning the identity of the other contracting party to be operative, the mistake must meet the following criteria:

| 1. The mistake must have been fundamental to the contract | 2. Proof must be provided that the mistaken party intended to contract with a different party than the one that they contracted with |

Non face-to-face contracts (*inter absentes*)

The two main cases in this area are *Kings Norton Metal Co Ltd v Edridge, Merrett & Co Ltd* (1897) and *Cundy v Lindsay* (1878). See below:

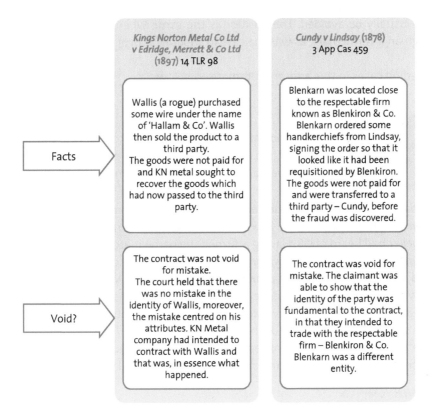

	Kings Norton Metal Co Ltd v Edridge, Merrett & Co Ltd (1897) 14 TLR 98	Cundy v Lindsay (1878) 3 App Cas 459
Facts	Wallis (a rogue) purchased some wire under the name of 'Hallam & Co'. Wallis then sold the product to a third party. The goods were not paid for and KN metal sought to recover the goods which had now passed to the third party.	Blenkarn was located close to the respectable firm known as Blenkiron & Co. Blenkarn ordered some handkerchiefs from Lindsay, signing the order so that it looked like it had been requisitioned by Blenkiron. The goods were not paid for and were transferred to a third party – Cundy, before the fraud was discovered.
Void?	The contract was not void for mistake. The court held that there was no mistake in the identity of Wallis, moreover, the mistake centred on his attributes. KN Metal company had intended to contract with Wallis and that was, in essence what happened.	The contract was void for mistake. The claimant was able to show that the identity of the party was fundamental to the contract, in that they intended to trade with the respectable firm – Blenkiron & Co. Blenkarn was a different entity.

The cases above illustrate that the courts will not allow a party to escape from a contract on the basis that a mistake has been made regarding the creditworthiness of the other party. The mistake will only be operative if it can be shown that the *identity* of the party is fundamental to the contract and that the other party is aware of the mistake.

The precedent in *Cundy v Lindsay* (1878) has been affirmed by the House of Lords in the more recent case of *Shogun Finance Ltd v Hudson* [2003]. The case also highlights the point that reasonable steps must have been taken to verify identity, if a case is to succeed in mistake.

Face-to-face contracts

Where parties conduct business face to face, there is a presumption that the seller intends to deal with the person in front of him. It is irrelevant that the person in front of him may be using a false name. In some instances, a person who has been tricked may be able to rescind the contract through a claim under fraudulent misrepresentation. However, this option is only available if the goods have not yet passed to a third party (remember: *nemo dat quod non habet*). In face-to-face transactions, the mistake will be deemed to relate to the *attributes* of the individual and not the individual himself. Such mistakes are non-operative and the contract cannot usually be avoided. The position is the same where the contract is made through an intermediary, as was the case in *Shogun* (above).

The leading cases in this area are summarised below:

Phillips v Brooks Ltd [1919] 2 KB 243	**Contract not void** – claimant intended to deal with the person in front of him – the mistake related to attributes. The jeweller would have transacted with any customer in his shop.

❖ A rogue (North) went into a jewellery shop, and chose some jewellery. Upon payment, the rogue told the jeweller that he was Sir George Bullogh (GB). The jeweller had heard of GB. Having affirmed the name matched the address listing in the phone directory, the jeweller accepted a cheque for some jewellery and allowed North to take part of his purchase (a ring) away. North then pawned the ring and the cheque to the jeweller was dishonoured. The jeweller sued the pawnbroker in conversion alleging that the contract was void for mistake. The contract was not void for mistake. Nor could the jeweller avoid the contract under fraudulent misrepresentation as he was too late to rescind – the goods had passed to the third party at the time the fraud was discovered.

Ingram v Little [1960] 3 All ER 332	**Contract void** – claimant intended to deal with the person whom the rogue purported to be, mistake was to **identity** rather than attributes (see below – a controversial decision)

❖ Two sisters advertised their car for sale. A rogue agreed a price with one of the sisters but his cheque was initally refused by one sister. The rogue informed the sister that he was PGM Hutchinson and that he had extensive business assets. Having confirmed that a person of this name and address was listed in the telephone directory, the sisters were satisfied that the information provided by the rogue was accurate. The rogue took the car and sold it on to a third party. Subsequently the cheque to the sisters was dishonoured. The sisters sued the third party in conversion on the grounds that the contract was void due to mistaken identity. Although the sisters were successful, this decision is generally regarded as wrong. The facts are not dissimilar to those pertaining in other cases in this area, where the decision has gone the opposite way (see *Lewis v Averay* below).

Lewis v Averay [1971] 3 All ER 907	**Contract not void** – claimant intended to deal with the person in front of him – the mistake related to attributes

❖ The claimant adversited his car for sale. The rogue agreed to pay the asking price and wrote out a cheque signed 'R A Green'. He produced a pass to Pinewood studios to support his statement that he was R A Green a well-known actor. The rogue was allowed to take the car which he quickly sold on to a third party. The cheque was dishonoured and the claimant sought recovery of the vehicle through conversion on the grounds that the contract was void for mistake. He was unsuccessful. Additionally, he could not claim under fraudulent misrepresentation as the goods had already passed to the third party when the fraud was discovered.

Up for Debate

Ingram v Little was not a unanimous decision – Lord Devlin dissented. In *Shogun Finance Ltd v Hudson*, Lord Millett considered the law in this area to be 'neither fair nor principled'. An innocent party will usually suffer whether or not the mistake is deemed operative. Is there a more equitable way to deal with mistakes made on identity in face-to-face contracts?

Mistake in equity

Where a mistake is not operative, equity can sometimes provide a remedy.

Equitable remedies can be broken down into three areas:

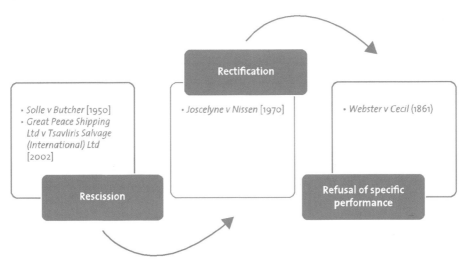

Rectification
• *Joscelyne v Nissen* [1970]

Refusal of specific performance
• *Webster v Cecil* (1861)

Rescission
• *Solle v Butcher* [1950]
• *Great Peace Shipping Ltd v Tsavliris Salvage (International) Ltd* [2002]

Rescission

Rescission was previously available where it would have been inequitable to allow a party to take advantage of a mistake (*Solle v Butcher* [1950]). Following the decision in *Great Peace Shipping Ltd v Tsavliris Salvage (International) Ltd*, the decision in *Solle v Butcher* is generally regarded as wrong. In the *Great Peace* case, the COA rejected the distinction between mistakes at common law and in equity. This is a rather complex area and appears to have a significantly diminished role since *Great Peace*.

Rectification

A document that does not accurately reflect the agreement reached between the parties can be revised by the courts to bring it in line with the anticipated agreement. This remedy was advanced in *Joscelyne v Nissen* [1970], where a father agreed with his daughter that she would buy his business and in return pay his residential energy bills. The contract did not express this 'continuing common intention' but, in agreeing to rectify the document, the court was satisfied that there was convincing proof of intention.

Refusal of specific performance

Specific performance is a discretionary (equitable) remedy. The court can refuse the remedy where it would be unconscionable to compel a party to fulfil their contractual responsibilities, or in circumstances where the other party was aware of the mistake and took advantage (*Webster v Cecil* (1861)). Specific performance will also be refused where the mistake arose as a result of a misrepresentation.

Up for Debate

The decision in *Great Peace Shipping Ltd v Tsavliris Salvage (International)* rejected the distinction between mistakes in law and mistakes in equity and took away a broad discretion previously afforded to the courts.
Lord Phillips:

> '... it is impossible to reconcile *Solle v Butcher* with *Bell v Lever Bros*. The jurisdiction asserted in the former case has not developed. It has been a fertile source of academic debate, but in practice it has given rise to a handful of cases that have merely emphasized the confusion of this area of our jurisprudence.'

The removal of discretion in this area has made the law in this area inflexible – is this a rational outcome?

Putting it into practice

Example problem question

Look at the scenario below, and then answer the following question:

Samuel went into Ellianna's art gallery, 'Animal Art' and expressed an interest in a marble sculpture of an eagle for sale at £6,000. Samuel informed Ellianna that he wished to purchase the sculpture as a birthday present for his wife and told Ellianna that he was Sir Benjamin Jones, the managing director of B Jones Fabrication Ltd, a large successful business located on the outskirts of town. Samuel produced a cheque book with B Jones Fabrication Ltd printed on it. Unbeknown to Ellianna, he had stolen the cheque book earlier that week from the director's car. Ellianna allowed Samuel to take the sculpture in return for the cheque signed by Samuel on behalf of B Jones Fabrication Ltd.

Two days later Ellianna was informed by her bank that the cheque had been dishonoured and Samuel has disappeared after selling the sculpture on to Cassandra for £4,000.

Advise Ellianna.

Example feedback

Introduction – State that all of the ingredients appear to be present to constitute a valid contract.

Identify the relevant area of law before progressing to advise Ellianna on whether she can recover the sculpture that she has been duped into selling to 'Sir Benjamin Jones'.

Area of Law is that of mistake and whether or not it will assist Ellianna in avoiding the contract and reclaiming her goods.

Explain the law

❖   Very few mistakes are recognised at common law and the reasons for this.
❖   There is a presumption of a valid contract.
❖   In some instances the courts will deem a mistake to be 'operative' and when this happens a contract will be void *ab initio*.

Narrow the area of law

❖   The mistake that needs to be addressed here falls under the head of unilateral mistake.
❖   It is termed unilateral because only one of the parties is mistaken.

Explanation

❖ Cover the factors necessary for a unilateral mistake to be operative.

❖ In essence, a unilateral mistake is where only one party to the contract has made a mistake and the other party *must be aware of the mistake*.

❖ The mistake must be fundamental as regards the *nature* of the promise made by the other party, a mistake about the quality is not sufficient.

❖ The presumption is to find for the existence of a valid and binding contract and it is for the person seeking to avoid the contract to rebut the presumption.

❖ The subjective test will apply in such circumstances.

❖ Where a mistake concerns identity and the seller is dealing with a person physically present before him (*inter praesentes*), there is a presumption that the seller intends to contract with the person present.

❖ In order for the mistake to be operative and the contract void, the question of the other party's identity must have been of fundamental importance to the innocent party.

❖ Discuss the key precedent that exists in this area; there are several cases that may be relevant.

Apply the law

To prove unilateral mistake, Ellianna must prove:

❖ an intention to deal with some other person;

❖ that the other party knew of her intention;

❖ that the identity was of fundamental importance; and

❖ that reasonable steps had been taken to verify the identity.

The facts here are similar to *Lewis v Averay* [1971] – Lewis advertised a car in a local newspaper. The rogue purporting to be RA Greene of Pinewood studios produced an identity pass and the seller allowed him to take the car. The cheque bounced and the rogue sold the car on to a third party. The court said that the contract was not void for mistake. Lewis had intended to deal with person in front of him irrespective of his identity. Similar actions occurred in *Phillips v Brookes* (1919). It is unlikely that *Ingram v Little* [1960] would assist here as no further steps were taken to identify Samuel's identity.

Whilst a claim in fraudulent misrepresentation could have been a possibility, it will not assist Ellianna because, at the time that she became aware of the fraud, the goods had been sold on to Cassandra, hence Cassandra will have acquired a good title.

The answer can be shown diagrammatically, and is a useful way to plan your answers when answering a scenario or problem question within an exam:

Explain which vitiating factor may be relevant here.

State the areas in which a mistake may be operative and the effect upon a contract.

Identify and define the area of mistake that is up for discussion in this scenario.
UNILATERAL MISTAKE.

Mistake made by one party.

Other party is aware of mistake.

Mistake must be fundamental in relation to the subject matter of the contract.

Mistake on quality will not suffice.

Person seeking to avoid the contract must rebut the presumption of a valid contract.

Identity must be of fundamental importance to the innocent party to render a contract void.

Subjective test face-to-face contracts – presumption of intention of the claimant to deal with the person in front of him.

Apply the law
Can Ellianna prove

(a) an intention to deal with some other person.

(b) that the other party knew of this intention.

(c) that the identity was of fundamental importance.

(d) that reasonable steps were taken to verify the identity.

It is unlikely that Ellianna will prove an intention to deal with some other person. She clearly intended to deal with the person in front of her.

Similar to the cases of *Phillips v Brooks* and *Lewis v Averay*.

The contract will NOT be void for mistake.

Ellianna will be unable to recover the sculpture from Cassandra.

Ellianna could attempt a claim in fraudulent misrepresentation but she would have to show that the contract was rescinded before the sculpture passed to Cassandra – this is highly unlikely.

Ellianna failed to take any steps to verify the identity of Sir Benjamin (Samuel).

The importance of checks on identity was highlighted in *Shogun Finance*.

It is clear that it was not the identity of Samuel that was important to Ellianna – she would have sold the sculpture to anyone – there is no suggestion whatsoever that she sold to Samuel because he was Sir Benjamin.

Table of key cases referred to in this chapter

Key case	Area of law	Principle
Bell v Lever Brothers Ltd [1932] AC 161	Concerned a contract for a severance package for two former directors. The company would have been entitled to terminate the contract for conduct reasons, but had not known this at the time.	Mistake as to the 'quality' of the subject matter of a contract will not render a contract void unless it is a mistake by both parties which renders the 'quality' as something totally different to what they had both anticipated.
Cundy v Lindsay (1878) 3 App Cas 459	Concerned a contract where a rogue imitated a well-established company in order to acquire goods. The goods were obtained and sold on to a third party. The plaintiff sued in conversion for the return of the goods.	The contract was void. The plaintiffs intended to deal with the reputable company that had been imitated. Identity was crucial here.
Hartog v Colin & Shields [1939] 3 All ER 566	Concerned the sale of some animal skins that were incorrectly offered by weight rather than by piece. This had a significant effect on the contract price.	Where a mistake occurs in relation to the terms of a contract and the other party is aware of the mistake, the mistake will be operative and the contract is void.
Ingram v Little [1960] 3 All ER 332	Concerned the sale of a car to a rogue who purported to be a man of wealth and significant business esteem. The plaintiff made checks on his identity and accepted a cheque which subsequently bounced. The plaintiff sued in conversion for the return of the car which had been sold on to a third party.	The contract was held void for mistaken identity. It is argued that the case was wrongly decided on the basis that the plaintiff contracted with the person in front of her.

Kings Norton Metal Co Ltd v Edridge, Merrett & Co Ltd (1897)	Concerned a contract where a rogue set up a bogus company in order to defraud the plaintiff. He then ordered goods and sold them on to a third party. The plaintiff argued that the contract was void for mistake.	The contract was not void. The plaintiff had intended to contract with the named company. The mistake concerned the attributes, not the identity of the company.
Lewis v Averay [1971] 3 All ER 907	Concerned the sale of a car. The plaintiff wrote a cheque in the name of RA Green whom he claimed was a famous actor. He produced a studio pass as identity. The cheque was dishonoured and the plaintiff sought to recover the car from a third party.	The contract was not void. The court held that the plaintiff intended to contract with the person in front of him. The mistake concerned attributes not identity.
McRae v Commonwealth Disposals Commission (1950) 84 CLR 377, HC Aus	Concerned a contract for salvage rights of a specific ship on a named reef. It transpired that the wreck did not exist.	A contract can be void where the subject matter is non-existent. However if its existence has been guaranteed, the contract will be valid.
Raffles v Wichelhaus (1864) 159 ER 375	Concerned a contract for the transportation of cotton. Two ships with the same name were due to complete a voyage, but at different times of the year. It was unclear which voyage the contract related to.	Where a mutual mistake occurs in relation to the subject matter of the contract and the mistake renders performance impossible, the mistake will be operative and the contract void.

@ **Visit the book's companion website to test your knowledge**

❖ Resources include a subject map, revision tip podcasts, downloadable diagrams, MCQ quizzes for each chapter, and a flashcard glossary

❖ www.routledge.com/cw/optimizelawrevision

6

Duress and Undue Influence

Revision objectives

Understand the law	• Can you outline the key instances where a contract may be void or voidable? • Can you recount the criteria for each of these areas? • Can you explain the effect of a finding of duress or undue influence on a contract?
Remember the details	• Can you remember the names of the principal supporting cases that highlight the different features of an operative mistake? • Do you understand the difference between legitimate and illegitimate pressure in duress and between duress and undue influence? • Can you relay the core requirements for a successful claim in undue influence? • Do you understand the different requirements of the separate classes of undue influence? • Can you recount the necessary criteria for a third party to be fixed with constructive notice and the action required to avoid such a finding?
Reflect critically on areas of debate	• Can you offer a view on whether the law currently draws a fair balance between legitimate and illegitimate pressure in the area of economic duress? • Are you able to discuss the rationale behind the different categories of undue influence and pinpoint which category would be appropriate when presented with a problem scenario in this area of law? • Are you able to discuss the rationale for the approach taken by the courts in fixing a lending institution with constructive notice in given circumstances?
Contextualise	• Do you feel relatively confident in ascertaining whether or not a claim for economic duress in a given problem scenario would succeed? • Can you draw a distinction between when a claim against a third party (i.e. constructive notice) is likely to be appropriate and when it is not?
Apply your skills and knowledge	• Can you complete the problem question on undue influence at the end of the chapter?

Chapter Map

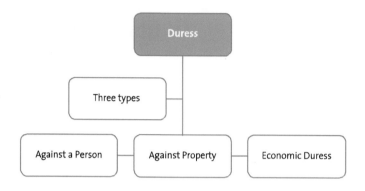

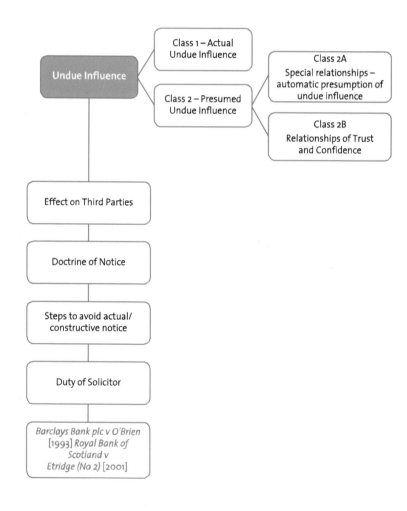

Duress and undue influence

Where a party has not entered into a contract voluntarily, the contract may be *voidable* due to duress or undue influence. The common law doctrine of duress will operate when a party has entered into a contract as a result of *illegitimate* pressure. The equitable doctrine of undue influence will be found when a party has entered into a contract as a result of excessive pressure or coercion. To understand this area of law fully, an analysis of the factors recognised by the courts as constituting vitiating factors under the two doctrines needs to be undertaken.

Recognised categories of duress

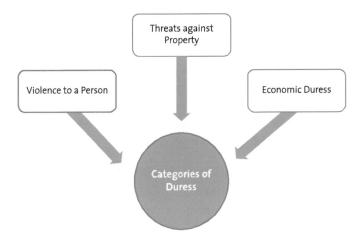

Violence to a person

This type of duress incorporates actual violence and threats of violence. Where a contract has been secured as a result of violence or a threat thereof, the party to whom the threats have been addressed can avoid the contract. Duress need not comprise the sole reason for contractual consent, but it must be *one* of the reasons.

Case precedent – *Barton v Armstrong* [1975] 2 All ER 265

Facts: The claimant was threatened with death if he did not purchase an allocation of shares from the defendant. The claimant purchased the shares but later tried to avoid the contract on the grounds of duress. It transpired that the threats were only part of the reason that the claimant purchased the shares; he was also persuaded by the fact that the acquisition of the shares was a good business transaction. The contract was declared voidable.

Principle: Even though the claimant may have still entered into the contract in the absence of the threats, the fact that the threats constituted *one of the* *reasons* for the claimant's contractual consent was sufficient to enable him to avoid the contract. The onus is on the defendant to prove that the threats had no influence on the claimant's choice to enter into the contract.

Application: In problem questions remember that duress does not have to be the sole reason for contractual consent. So do not be thrown off track if you are given a range of reasons; provided that duress is one of the factors, the contract can be avoided.

Threats against property/economic duress

Traditionally, precedent suggested that a threat against property could not amount to duress (see *Skeate v Beale* (1840)). However, there has been a shift in attitude, with the courts accepting in *Occidental Worldwide Investment Corporation v Skibbs A/S Avanti (The Siboen and the Sibotre)* (1976), that threats against property *can* amount to duress. Kerr J suggested that the real issue to be addressed is whether or not the contract has been agreed *'voluntarily'*.

Following *Occidental Worldwide Investment Corporation v Skibbs A/S Avanti (The Siboen and the Sibotre)* (1976) a further category of 'economic' duress has emerged. Economic duress will be recognised where evidence of improper economic pressure can be demonstrated. For example, if a large frozen food distributor threatened a small fish business with withdrawal of all future orders unless they cut the price of the current order by 60%, such action could constitute economic duress. The small company may rely so heavily on the business that to lose the contract would force them out of business altogether. The small fish company may accept the reduced price on the basis that they have no realistic alternative other than to do so if they want to preserve future business with the distributor.

In *The Siboen and the Sibotre* [1976], the threat that one party would go out of business if the other party did not re-negotiate the charter of two vessels was deemed as an action that could amount to duress. However it was found on the facts that the other party had agreed to the re-negotiation under commercial pressure rather than duress. Nevertheless, the case was the first to recognise that economic duress can render a contract voidable and this doctrine is now firmly embedded into contract law. To succeed under this head, a two-level approach was set out by Kerr J:

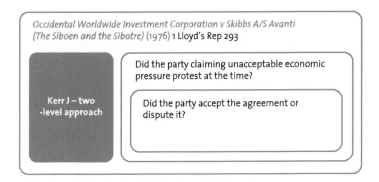

The criteria were later expanded in *Pao On v Lau Yiu Long* [1980] and *Universe Tankships v International Transport Workers Federation (The Universal Sentinel)* [1983]. In *Pao On*, Lord Scarman listed several factors that can be drawn upon to indicate whether pressure exerted in a given situation will be sufficient to constitute duress:

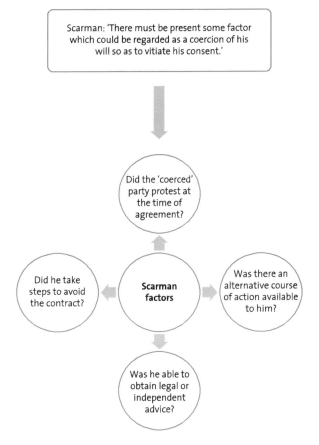

Lord Scarman – Pao On v Lau Yiu Long [1980] *3 All ER 65*

Common Pitfall

It is sometimes, incorrectly, assumed that the courts will allow a claimant to set aside a renegotiation of a contract concluded under pressure, which has later become onerous for him to perform. Remember commercial pressures are part of normal economic activity and, as such, these types of agreements will not always cross the line into illegitimate pressure.

An important factor in duress cases is whether there was a practical alternative *course of action* available to the claimant:

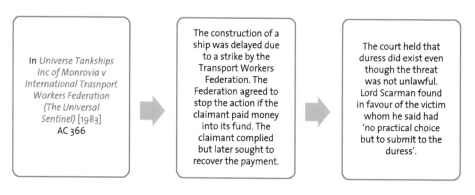

In *Universe Tankships Inc of Monrovia v International Trasnport Workers Federation (The Universal Sentinel)* [1983] AC 366

→

The construction of a ship was delayed due to a strike by the Transport Workers Federation. The Federation agreed to stop the action if the claimant paid money into its fund. The claimant complied but later sought to recover the payment.

→

The court held that duress did exist even though the threat was not unlawful. Lord Scarman found in favour of the victim whom he said had 'no practical choice but to submit to the duress'.

Threats of *unlawful action* will normally amount to duress (*Atlas Express Ltd v Kafco* [1989]) but closer analysis is required when assessing threats of *lawful action. CTN Cash & Carry v Gallagher* [1994] provides useful guidance. The case concerned a threat by the defendant company to withdraw the claimant's credit facilities if the claimant did not pay for some goods that had been stolen prior to delivery. The courts affirmed that a threat of lawful action *could* amount to economic duress where a party has *no other alternative*, or where the other party has *acted in bad faith* but, in this instance, the lawful threat of withdrawing credit facilities did not amount to economic duress.

Aim Higher:

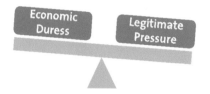

- Where do we draw the line between legitimate and illegitimate pressure?
- What factors will tip the balance?
- What do the courts say?

Summary

Where pressure has been exerted by one party on another and that pressure is deemed sufficient to amount to duress, a contract can be avoided. The difficulty is determining what will and what will not amount to illegitimate pressure. Sometimes a threat to break a contract will amount to illegitimate pressure and at other times it will not. In tackling a problem question it is necessary to look carefully at all of the stated factors to ascertain whether the pressure applied can be said to amount to a *coercion of will which has vitiated consent*. The answer is not always clear cut but the guidance provided by case law should help in outlining the factors to be considered in judging whether a claim for duress will succeed. The figure below summarises the three types of duress:

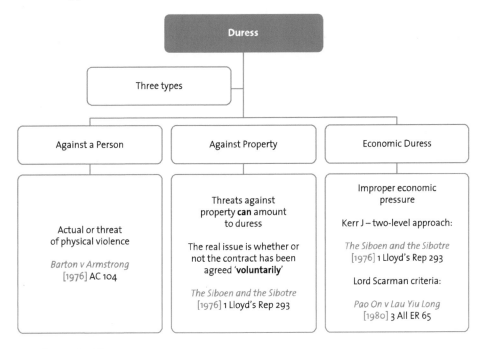

Undue influence

In the first part of this chapter, we attempted to gauge where the line could be drawn between legitimate and excessive pressure. Similarly, with undue influence, it is necessary to ascertain when influence goes beyond what is acceptable in an everyday context.

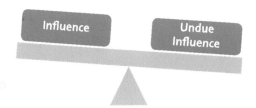

Undue influence is recognised in equity and a successful claim will render a contract voidable. Undue influence arises where a party can demonstrate that he has been disadvantaged in an agreement as a result of *improper pressure* applied by another party.

Undue influence can be broken down into two categories:

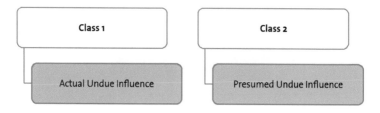

Actual undue influence

As the name suggests, Class 1 actual undue influence requires evidence that 'actual' undue influence has occurred, it is *never presumed*.

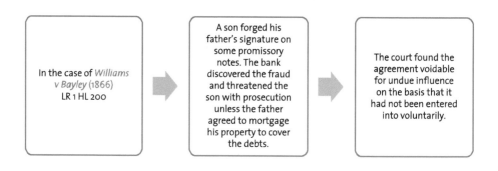

BCCI v Aboody (1990) provides a good example of actual undue influence. In this case, Mrs Aboody was bullied by her husband into signing a mortgage over the family home in favour of the bank as security for her husband's business debts. Whilst the Court of Appeal upheld actual undue influence, the transaction was not set aside as there had been no manifest disadvantage to Mrs Aboody. However, since the judgment in *CIBC Mortgages plc v Pitt* (1993), where actual undue influence has been established, it is no longer necessary to prove that the transaction was to the manifest disadvantage of the influenced party.

Presumed undue influence can be further sub-divided into classes: Class 2A Automatic Presumption of Undue Influence (special relationships) and Class 2B Presumed Undue Influence (relationships of trust and confidence).

Presumed undue influence

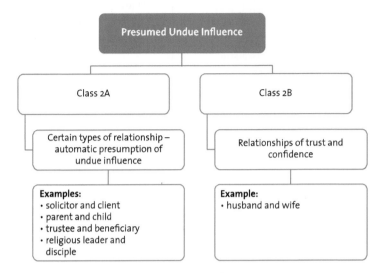

As illustrated above, where a certain type of 'confidential' relationship exists (Class 2A), an automatic presumption of undue influence will arise. Examples of confidential relationships include those of solicitor and client, parent and child etc. In such cases the influenced party must first show the existence of such a relationship and then show that the transaction is one that *calls for an explanation*. Provided the criteria are met, a rebuttable presumption of undue influence will have arisen. At this point, the burden will shift to the person alleged to have asserted the influence to refute the presumption. This can be done by proving that the other party entered into the agreement on his own volition (see *Allcard v Skinner* (1887)).

Under Class 2B Presumed Undue Influence, there is no 'automatic' presumption of undue influence. Instead, the claimant must prove that he has placed *trust and confidence* in the defendant. If he can prove this a presumption of undue influence will exist. The usual persons to fall within this category are husband and wife, but the category can extend to other relationships where the defendant can prove that a relationship of trust and confidence existed between the parties when the agreement was made:

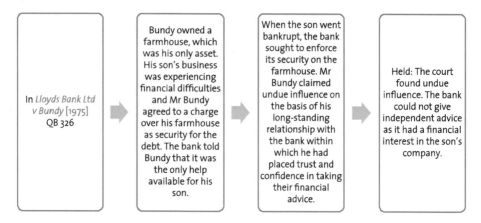

In *Lloyds Bank Ltd v Bundy* [1975] QB 326 ➤ Bundy owned a farmhouse, which was his only asset. His son's business was experiencing financial difficulties and Mr Bundy agreed to a charge over his farmhouse as security for the debt. The bank told Bundy that it was the only help available for his son. ➤ When the son went bankrupt, the bank sought to enforce its security on the farmhouse. Mr Bundy claimed undue influence on the basis of his long-standing relationship with the bank within which he had placed trust and confidence in taking their financial advice. ➤ Held: The court found undue influence. The bank could not give independent advice as it had a financial interest in the son's company.

Bundy is a rather unusual case. Undue influence will not normally arise simply due to a relationship existing between a banker and client (affirmed in *National Westminster Bank plc v Morgan* [1985]). It will only arise in instances where the bank has exerted significant influence (as in *Bundy*) but this is not commonplace.

To summarise Class 2 relationships, it can be said that an automatic presumption of undue influence will exist in class 2A relationships, but under class 2B, it is necessary to establish a relationship of trust and confidence between the parties. Proof can be brought forward to rebut such a relationship. The latter point was confirmed in *Royal Bank of Scotland v Etridge (No 2)* [2001] (see below).

Establishing a relationship of trust and confidence

Where a relationship does not fall into one of the automatic categories under class 2A, the reasons *why* one party could be argued to have placed trust and confidence in another need to be considered. Maybe the influenced person is in a position of vulnerability, for example an elderly person may place all of his trust in a carer, or a younger family member. Undue influence can also be presumed where the disadvantage conferred by a transaction is sufficiently serious to warrant the production of evidence to rebut the presumption that the agreement was secured by undue influence. In other words, where there is a transaction that calls for an explanation.

The presumption of undue influence can be rebutted by the alleged wrongdoer showing that the other party either *exercised their own judgment* or had *access to independent advice*. Independent advice from a solicitor or a financial adviser would normally be sufficient to show that the person was aware of the extent of the transaction. However, the alleged wrongdoer must still show that the person was not acting under their influence.

Undue influence – effect on third parties

Where a person is persuaded to enter into contract with a bank or creditor as a result of the undue influence or misrepresentation of another party (often husband and wife transactions), the undue influence can affect the transaction between the victim of the undue influence and the creditor. This commonly happens where the husband is acting as an intermediary between himself and the bank. Since *Royal Bank of Scotland v Etridge (No 2)* [2001], in all cases where the relationship between a surety and debtor is non-commercial, the creditor will be *put on notice* and must take reasonable steps to ensure that the surety is aware of the implications of the transaction upon him/herself. Where the bank has not taken appropriate steps to discharge this burden, the victim will be allowed to have the transaction set aside under the *doctrine of notice*. The main group falling within this category is that of husband and wife, but the category is not restricted to this group, as demonstrated in *Credit Lyonnais Bank Nederland NV v Burch* (1997) (a case which concerned an employer/employee relationship).

The doctrine is well illustrated in *Barclays Bank plc v O'Brien* [1993]:

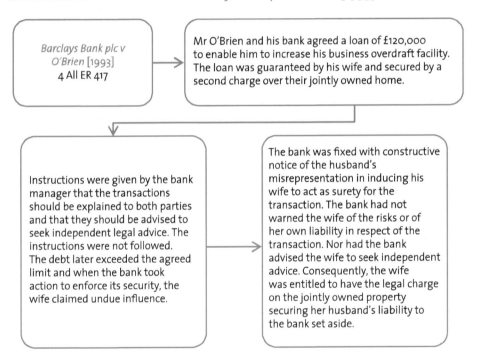

Barclays Bank plc v O'Brien [1993] 4 All ER 417

Mr O'Brien and his bank agreed a loan of £120,000 to enable him to increase his business overdraft facility. The loan was guaranteed by his wife and secured by a second charge over their jointly owned home.

Instructions were given by the bank manager that the transactions should be explained to both parties and that they should be advised to seek independent legal advice. The instructions were not followed. The debt later exceeded the agreed limit and when the bank took action to enforce its security, the wife claimed undue influence.

The bank was fixed with constructive notice of the husband's misrepresentation in inducing his wife to act as surety for the transaction. The bank had not warned the wife of the risks or of her own liability in respect of the transaction. Nor had the bank advised the wife to seek independent advice. Consequently, the wife was entitled to have the legal charge on the jointly owned property securing her husband's liability to the bank set aside.

In *Barclays Bank plc v O'Brien* (1994), Lord Brown-Wilkinson said:

Up for Debate

'A creditor is put on inquiry when a wife offers to stand surety for her husband's debts ... unless the creditor who is put on inquiry takes reasonable steps to satisfy himself that the wife's agreement to stand surety has been properly obtained, the creditor will have constructive notice of the wife's rights.'

Is it rational that knowledge of certain facts can be imputed upon a party (i.e. a bank), where actual knowledge of those facts does not exist? After all, if things go well and the husband's business is successful, the wife will share the financial rewards and benefits. Can such a protective approach therefore be justified in relation to the risks associated with such a transaction?

Thus, it can be seen that a creditor will be unable to enforce its security against a surety where the creditor is deemed to have *actual or constructive notice* of undue influence and it has not taken appropriate steps to ensure that the surety has been properly advised on the extent of the transaction.

Case precedent – *Royal Bank of Scotland v Etridge (No 2)* [2001] 4 All ER 449 (HL)

Facts: The case concerned a number of conjoined appeals concerning banks seeking possession of homes in circumstances where the wife had signed a charge or mortgage agreeing to act as surety for the debts of the husband on the family home.

Principle: The case is the leading authority on the fact that a bank will be put on enquiry whenever a wife stands as surety for her husband's debts. The bank does not have to show that it was aware of a relationship capable of giving rise to a presumption of influence; nor is there an absolute obligation on a bank to have a private meeting with the wife. However it is mandatory that the bank takes steps to satisfy itself that the wife has been appropriately advised. The bank can discharge this burden by insisting upon written confirmation from the surety's solicitor that the requisite advice has been given.

Application: In applying the rules, it is necessary to check that the surety has obtained advice from an independent solicitor. The person for whom they are acting as surety must not have been present at the meeting. In addition, the solicitor must have been provided with all information needed from the bank to ensure that the advice is accurate. If that information has not been forthcoming, the solicitor must decline to provide confirmation that the surety has been properly advised.

Duty of the solicitor

The minimum steps a solicitor should take when advising a surety are summarised below (using the example of the most common category of parties in transactions of this nature: husband and wife):

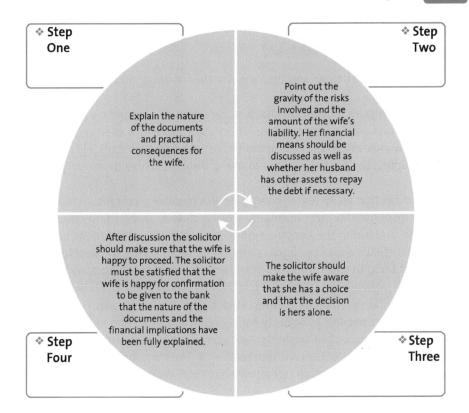

Step One

Explain the nature of the documents and practical consequences for the wife.

Step Two

Point out the gravity of the risks involved and the amount of the wife's liability. Her financial means should be discussed as well as whether her husband has other assets to repay the debt if necessary.

Step Four

After discussion the solicitor should make sure that the wife is happy to proceed. The solicitor must be satisfied that the wife is happy for confirmation to be given to the bank that the nature of the documents and the financial implications have been fully explained.

Step Three

The solicitor should make the wife aware that she has a choice and that the decision is hers alone.

Summary

Undue influence can make a contract voidable. Depending on the circumstances, undue influence can be *actual* or *presumed*. A finding of presumed undue influence requires proof of a relationship of trust and confidence. Some relationships will fall automatically within this category (Class 2A) whilst, for others, it is necessary to prove that a relationship exists (Class 2B). In the latter category, the presumption can be rebutted where it can be shown that the claimant received independent advice.

A third party, such as a bank, can be affected by undue influence or misrepresentation if it has notice of the factors constituting the undue influence. The bank can also be fixed with constructive notice where an agreement is disadvantageous to the surety/guarantor unless the bank can show that it took *reasonable steps* to ensure that the surety fully understood the extent of the transaction. The bank can discharge this burden by making sure that the surety has been provided with independent legal advice and that confirmation of such advice has been provided by the solicitor.

Putting it into practice

Example problem question:

Look at the scenario below, and then answer the following question:

Zak owns a furniture renovation business. He decided to extend his home to create a workshop and save on rental costs. He chose to raise the cash required for the extension by increasing his existing mortgage with Cashflow Bank. He met with the bank manager, Jagdip, who was an old friend from his school days.

Jagdip told Zak that an increased mortgage was possible on condition that the bank retained responsibility for arranging the architect, submitting the planning application and hiring the construction workers with direct payment being made from the mortgage advance. Jagdip said that he could secure the deal for a one-off payment of £600 to cover the costs of the architect and planning application.

The next day, Zak persuaded his wife, Laura, to sign the bank form. He told her that her consent was needed as security for his company's existing overdraft, without which he would go out of business. Not wanting her husband's business to fail, Laura hastily signed the form without reading it. The form included a declaration in bold print stating that that all signatories had received independent advice.

The bank instructed a firm of architects and secured the requisite planning consent. It engaged a company called Fastbuck & Co. to do the construction work. Zak was unaware that Jagdip owned shares in Fastbuck & Co.

The building work commenced while Laura was visiting her elderly mother in Scotland. However, on her return, she was dismayed to discover the true reason for the additional borrowing against their home and now seeks to avoid the contract.

In addition, Zak has just found out about the connection between Jagdip and Fastbuck & Co and is angry as he could have engaged a local well-established building company who could have completed the construction work for almost half of the cost.

(a) Advise Zak on whether or not he can avoid the transaction with the bank; and
(b) Advise Laura on whether or not she can avoid the transaction.

Example feedback

There are two potential instances of undue influence in the question: (i) *Zak v Jagdip (Cashflow Bank)*; and (ii) *Laura v Zak*.

(i) *Zak v Jagdip (Cashflow Bank)*

In order to avoid the transaction, Zak must prove that undue influence has arisen. The first task is to define undue influence:

❖ *Undue influence* is taking advantage of a relationship with someone to persuade or coerce that person into entering into a contract.

❖ There are two types of undue influence: Class 1 (actual undue influence) and Class 2 (presumed undue influence).

❖ Class 2 is further subdivided into Class 2A (certain categories of relationship where there is a presumption that they are relationships of trust and confidence, (e.g. doctor and patient) and Class 2B (other types of relationship – this is generally the category under which the relationship of husband and wife falls).

❖ The fact that Jagdip tells Zak that an increased mortgage is only possible if the bank arranges the plans, planning permission and the builders and that he does not tell Zak that he has shares in Fastbuck & Co may constitute *actual* evidence of influence meaning that Zak may have a claim in undue influence under Class 1.

❖ If this is not accepted as evidence of influence, Zak may still be able to make a claim under Class 2 undue influence. His relationship with Jagdip will not be a Class 2A relationship, as Bank/customer is not among the relationships where a presumption of trust and confidence will arise (as established in *Lloyd's Bank v Bundy*). We therefore need to look at a Class 2B claim.

❖ To succeed under Class 2B, Zak would have to prove that he placed significant trust and confidence in Jagdip. This may be possible as they are old friends (although if a long period has passed since their last acquaintance, this would weaken Zak's claim). It is not *usual* to find this relationship between banker and client. However, in *Lloyd's Bank v Bundy*, Mr Bundy had a relationship with his bank manager that spanned many years and, being elderly, he depended entirely on the bank manager for his financial advice. On this basis, the court accepted Mr Bundy's claim that there was a relationship of trust and confidence.

❖ Next, Zak would have to establish that the influence was 'undue'. The fact that Jagdip concealed his financial connection with Fastbuck & Co may constitute sufficient evidence.

❖ If so, the remedy available to Zak would potentially be rescission, rendering the contract voidable, at Zak's discretion. However, rescission is an equitable remedy, and, as such, even if Zak's claim is accepted by the court, the award of the remedy is at the court's discretion. The equitable maxim 'He who comes to equity must come with clean hands' could be argued here, and it could be strongly contended that Zak did not have 'clean hands' (i.e. the untruths told to his wife). Hence, there is a high probability that the remedy may not be granted.

(ii) *Laura v Zak (and the bank)*

Similar to Zak's claim against Jagdip and the Bank, it is possible that Laura may succeed with a claim against Zak under Class 1 undue influence. The fact that Zak lied to Laura about the purpose of the mortgage advance may be sufficient to constitute *actual evidence* of influence. If satisfied, the court may grant Laura the remedy of rescission.

❖ If Laura is unable to prove *actual* undue influence, she may succeed in a claim in undue influence under Class 2B.

❖ It was confirmed in *Barclay's Bank v O'Brien* that the husband/wife relationship is not a Class 2A relationship, thus there is no automatic presumption that this is a relationship of trust and confidence. Whilst some wives rely entirely on their husbands in all family financial affairs, in other marriages this is not the case. To have a successful claim under Class 2B Laura would initially have to prove that she placed a great deal of trust and confidence in Zak in relation to their financial affairs. If she can show this, she must also prove that this influence was *undue*. The fact that Zak misled her about the purpose of the loan may be enough to show this. She will probably also be able to show that the transaction was not to her advantage. We should note here that in *RBS v Etridge (No. 2)* the House of Lords established that 'manifest disadvantage', whilst not essential in establishing a claim under Class 2, is nevertheless an influential evidential factor. So, looking at this on the basis of evidence, it can be seen that Laura was told that the purpose of the loan was security for Zak's existing business overdraft, while the real reason was to allow Zak to extend their home to build a workshop. Laura could put up a strong argument that neither the true purpose, nor the untruthfully stated purpose of the loan benefited her; these factors together should provide persuasive argument to show that Zak's influence was undue.

❖ Notwithstanding a finding of undue influence against Zak, the courts will only allow Laura to avoid the contract and grant rescission if the Bank is deemed to have been 'fixed with constructive notice' of Zak's undue influence on Laura.

❖ Guidance in this area was initially provided by Lord Brown-Wilkinson in *Barclay's Bank v O'Brien* but, since this case, more detailed guidelines have been laid down by Lord Nicholls in *RBS v Etridge (No. 2)*. Banks must follow these guidelines to avoid being fixed with constructive notice.

❖ The guidelines state that where there is a suspicion of undue influence or manifest disadvantage to a surety/guarantor, the bank or building society should advise them to seek legal advice; they should not proceed with the transaction until they have received written confirmation from the solicitor that the surety/guarantor has been advised and, after being given the relevant advice, has indicated a wish to continue with the transaction.

❖ In the current scenario, there is a printed statement on the form that Laura has signed, indicating that the signatories have received independent advice. This falls short of the *Etridge* requirements that the bank must have received written confirmation from the solicitor before it proceeds with the transaction.

❖ In conclusion, therefore, it is likely that Zak's influence upon Laura will be found to be undue and it is also likely that the bank will have been fixed with constructive notice of the undue influence, having failed to absolve itself of its duty to take the necessary steps to ensure that Laura received independent legal advice. This being the case, the court can set aside the transaction with regard to Laura's liability to the Bank.

The answer can be shown diagrammatically. This is a useful way to plan answers when answering a scenario or problem question in an exam.

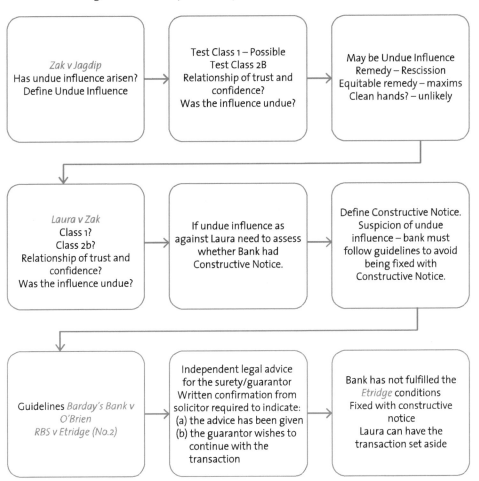

Table of key cases referred to in this chapter

Key case	Area of law	Principle
Barclays Bank plc v O'Brien [1993] 4 All ER 417	Concerned a guarantee made by a wife against her husband's overdraft. The husband had misrepresented the amount borrowed. The bank failed to properly inform the wife about the extent of the security and did not suggest that she took independent legal advice. The charge was set aside.	Where a bank has not fully explained a transaction to a surety and/or has not recommended that the surety take legal advice, it will be fixed with constructive notice of any undue influence used by the dominant party. A bank is put on enquiry where a transaction is not to the financial advantage of the surety, and where there are risks in the nature of a transaction.
Barton v Armstrong [1975] 2 All ER 265	Concerned a threat by one person to kill another if he did not execute a deed in his favour. This was not the sole reason that the threatened party agreed to contract.	An action for duress will be successful where duress has induced a person to enter into a contract. It need not be the only factor that has induced the contract.
Occidental Worldwide Investment Corporation v Skibs A/S Avanti (The Siboen and the Sibotre) [1976] 1 Lloyd's Rep 293	Concerned a threat of bankruptcy and inability to complete a contract if the other party did not lower their charges. The contract was avoided on the grounds of fraud, but the claimant would not have succeeded on the grounds of duress, as consent had not been vitiated as a result of the threat.	A contract can be avoided for economic duress, but the facts of this particular case did not support a finding of duress. It is necessary to show that the consent of the threatened party has been overborne to the extent that it has destroyed his intention to contract.

Pao On v Lau Yiu Long [1980] 3 All ER 65	Concerned a refusal to sell shares unless the other party undertook to subsidise all loss suffered by the claimants in carrying out their contractual obligations. This was found to be legitimate commercial pressure.	Lays down the key principles required to establish a claim for economic duress. Did the party protest? Any independent advice? Any alternative choices available? What steps were taken to avoid the contract?
Royal Bank of Scotland v Etridge (No 2) [2001] 4 All ER 449 (HL)	Concerned several conjoined appeals concerning banks seeking possession of homes where a wife had signed a charge or mortgage to secure debts of the husband on the family home.	The current authority in this area was reviewed and the rules were restated and clarified. Following on from *O'Brien*, a bank must ensure that the wife has received independent advice and certification that she has formed an independent judgment.
North Ocean Shipping Co Ltd v Hyundai Construction Co Ltd, The Atlantic Baron [1979] QB 705	Concerned a threat by ship builders to terminate the construction of a ship unless the buyers paid an additional 10% above the agreed price. The price was paid, but the buyers later sought to avoid the contract. The claim was unsuccessful as the buyers had affirmed the contract by paying the additional sum and had also delayed their action too long to successfully avoid the contract.	A claim may not succeed where a contract that is 'voidable' has been affirmed. Also delay is a bar to rescission; hence prompt action is needed where an injured party wishes to avoid a contract for duress.

@ Visit the book's companion website to test your knowledge

❖ Resources include a subject map, revision tip podcasts, downloadable diagrams, MCQ quizzes for each chapter, and a flashcard glossary

❖ www.routledge.com/cw/optimizelawrevision

7

Illegal Contracts and Contracts in Restraint of Trade

Revision objectives

Understand the law
- Can you outline the main areas of illegality? What is the criteria for each category?
- Can you explain the criteria needed for a restraint of trade clause to be upheld?
- Can you list the instances where the courts will not enforce a contract due to lack of capacity?

Remember the details
- Can you remember the names of the principal supporting cases for each category of illegality and the areas where lack of capacity is an issue?
- Can you relay the details and ratio of the main cases on restraint of trade?
- Can you explain the reasoning behind the decision in *Nordenfelt v Maxim Nordenfelt Guns and Ammunition Co* [1894].

Reflect critically on areas of debate
- In light of the case law in this area, does the attitude of the judiciary reflect current sociological trends and moral attitudes when making decisions on contracts contrary to public policy? Can you provide some examples?
- Does the law in relation to contractual liability of minors need revisiting?
- Does the current state of the law on contracts in restraint of trade strike a fair balance between the parties?

Contextualise
- Are you confident in judging whether a claim for illegality will succeed on the grounds of public policy in a given problem scenario?
- Are you confident in analysing a set of facts and drawing a reasoned conclusion upon whether a specific clause is likely to be found in restraint of trade?

Apply your skills and knowledge
- Can you complete the problem question at the end of the chapter?

Chapter Map

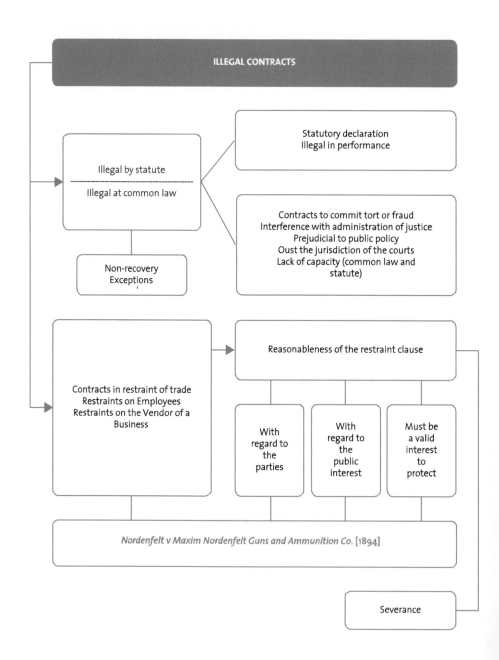

ILLEGAL CONTRACTS

Illegal by statute

Illegal at common law

Statutory declaration
Illegal in performance

Contracts to commit tort or fraud
Interference with administration of justice
Prejudicial to public policy
Oust the jurisdiction of the courts
Lack of capacity (common law and statute)

Non-recovery
Exceptions

Contracts in restraint of trade
Restraints on Employees
Restraints on the Vendor of a Business

Reasonableness of the restraint clause

With regard to the parties

With regard to the public interest

Must be a valid interest to protect

Nordenfelt v Maxim Nordenfelt Guns and Ammunition Co. [1894]

Severance

Introduction

The law will prevent an individual from profiting from illegal behaviour. In certain instances an otherwise valid contract will be unenforceable where it has been declared illegal. In such cases, any money or property transferred under the contract is irretrievable. A distinction is drawn between contracts that involve the commission of a statutory offence and those that are void under the common law as contrary to public policy. See below for the main areas of illegality:

Contracts illegal by statute	Contracts illegal at Common Law
Statute may declare a contract illegal, for example, the **Competition Act 1998**	An agreement to commit a crime, a tort or a fraud
Statute may prohibit an act, but declare that it shall not affect validity of contract, for example, the **Consumer Protection Act 1987**	An agreement to defraud the Inland Revenue (*Napier v National Business Agency* [1951]).
Statute may prohibit an act but not stipulate its effect on the contract. The status of the contract will be a matter of interpretation for the court *Re Mahmoud and Ispahani* [1921]	Contracts damaging to the country's safety or foreign relations
The courts are reluctant to imply a prohibition when this is not clearly indicated in the statute (*Hughes v Asset Managers* [1995])	Contracts interfering with the course of justice, for example, contracts to give false evidence
	Contracts tending to promote sexual immorality (*Pearce v Brooks* [1866])
	Contracts leading to corruption in public life (*Parkinson v Royal College of Ambulance* [1925])

Contracts illegal as formed

An illegal contract is void *ab initio*, meaning that the contract will be treated as though it has never existed. Because the contract never existed, no action can be taken for breach of contract. Thus in *Pearce v Brooks* [1866], the owner of a coach of unusual design was unable to recover the cost of hire from a prostitute who had hired it to attract clients.

A further example of non-recovery can be observed in *Parkinson v College of Ambulance Ltd* [1925], where Colonel Parkinson was unable to recover the money he had donated to the defendants on the understanding that they would secure a knighthood for him because such a contract was illegal.

Exceptions to the rule of non-recovery

❖ Parties not equally at fault, i.e. one party is unaware of the illegal nature of the contract.
❖ Where transferor can make his claim without relying on the contract (*Bowmakers v Barnet Instruments* [1945]).
❖ Where part of the contract is lawful, the court will not sever the good from the bad.
❖ Where the transferor repents and repudiates the contract before performance (*Tribe v Tribe* [1996]).

Exceptions

Contracts illegal in their performance

A contract may not be illegal at the outset but may become illegal during performance, for example, a carrier may break the law by driving whilst under the influence of alcohol whilst delivering goods. He will be punished, but the contract will not necessarily be void. A claim by the innocent party to enforce the contract in these circumstances is likely to succeed. Thus in *Archbolds v Spanglett* [1961], Spanglett contracted to carry Archbold's whisky in a van which was not licensed to carry any goods other than his own. Archbold was unaware of this and could therefore recover damages for breach of contract. Contrast this with *Ashmore, Benson, Pease & Co v Dawson Ltd* [1973], where a lorry had been overloaded but the other party was aware of this breach. Here, the claimant could not recover damages as he had participated in the illegality.

In some instances, the party at fault may enforce the contract, if the illegality is incidental. For example, in *Shaw v Groom* [1970], a landlord who failed to provide his tenant with a rent book, as required by law, was allowed to sue for unpaid rent. The purpose of the statute was to punish the landlord's failure to supply a rent book, not to render the contract void. Again, in *St John Shipping v Rank* [1957], a ship owner was allowed to recover some freight, even though he had overloaded his ship in contravention of statute.

Contracts contrary to public policy

There are several types of contract that can fall under this head. With the exception of contracts in restraint of trade (covered under a separate head), the main areas are shown below:

Contracts prejudicial to the administration of justice	❖ Where a party attempts to use a contract to prevent the law being upheld against him, it will be void (*Harmony Shipping Co v Davis* [1979]).
Contracts to oust the jurisdiction of the courts	❖ These contracts are void (*Baker v Jones* [1954]). Note the exception under the Arbitration Act 1996.
Contracts promoting sexual immorality	❖ Traditionally such contracts are void (*Pearce v Brooks* [1866]). However the courts are now unlikely to find a sexually immoral contract void unless it involves a criminal offence (*Armhouse Lee Ltd v Chappell* (1996)).

Capacity

A court will refuse to enforce a contract if one of the parties lacks the capacity to make the agreement. The following table summarises contracts that may fall within this category:

Limitations on Capacity		
Minors Exceptions: – Necessaries – Beneficial contracts of service – Minors' Contracts Act 1987	Mental Disability – Affairs under control of Mental Capacity Act 2005 – Unable to appreciate nature of transaction	Intoxication Incompetent to contract – liable to pay a reasonable price for goods sold and delivered

A minor is a person under the age of 18. Contracts with a minor can be voidable but it will depend upon the circumstances. Contracts for necessaries are enforceable. Section 3(3) of the Sale of Goods Act 1979 provides that a minor must pay a reasonable price for necessaries. Necessaries are goods deemed suitable to the condition in life of the minor and to his actual requirements (*Nash v Inman* [1908]). A beneficial contract of service, such as one of education or employment will bind a minor if it is substantially for the minor's benefit, so in *Chaplin v Leslie Frewin*

(Publishers) Ltd [1966], a book contract with a minor was regarded as a contract of service and thus binding on the minor. Again in *Proform Sports Management Ltd v Proactive Sports Management Ltd* [2006], a contract for representation services between a 15-year old footballer and an agent was not deemed to be a contract for necessary services. *Mercantile Union Guarantee v Ball* [1937], is authority for the fact that trading contracts with a minor will not be enforced.

Under the Minors' Contracts Act 1987, an otherwise void contract can be ratified when the minor reaches the age of 18. The contract is then enforceable by either of the parties. Certain contracts are binding unless the minor repudiates within a reasonable time; such contracts are for commodities of a permanent nature, such as shares, a lease, or a partnership agreement.

Up for Debate

Is the age of recognition of a minor now out-of-date in modern times with regard to contracts for the purchase of goods and services? Most 16-year-olds now have access to a bank account and many have part-time jobs. They are legally old enough to engage in activities such as employment, sex and smoking. Should they not therefore be liable for *all* their own voluntary transactions?

Contracts in restraint of trade

Contracts in restraint of trade are the most significant category of illegal contract.

A contract in restraint of trade is *prima facie* void, but the courts will uphold a restriction if it can be established that the restraint protects a legitimate interest that is reasonable between the parties and with regard to the interest of the public.

The modern doctrine of restraint of trade is set out in *Nordenfelt v Maxim Nordenfelt Guns and Ammunition Co* [1894]:

> ### Case Precedent – *Nordenfelt v Maxim Nordenfelt Guns and Ammunition Co* [1894] AC 535
>
> **Facts:** A manufacturer of guns and ammunition sold his business. As part of the sale agreement he contracted not to engage in this type of business anywhere in the world for 25 years.
>
> **Principle:** The worldwide ban was upheld for the full duration. Lord MacNaghten stated that, in normal circumstances, restraints of trade are void, but acknowledged an exception to the rule where the restraint can be proven to be reasonable. In defining the term 'reasonable' he declared that a restriction needs to be reasonable with reference to the interests of the parties concerned, and reasonable in the interests of the public.
>
> **Application:** In problem questions ensure that you test whether the clause holds up against *all* of these factors.

Categories of restraint

Restraints on employees

There is a presumption that a provision within a contract restricting the type of employment an employee can engage in once leaving the company seeking to rely on the restraint is void. The presumption can be rebutted by evidence showing that the clause is *reasonable*. For example, the clause may have been included in the contract to protect a trade secret or to prevent solicitation of clients.

Restraints on the vendor of a business

Again a clause preventing competition *per se*, will be void, but a clause preventing the seller of a business from setting up directly in competition with the buyer, or from soliciting their clients could be valid if the interest is deemed to be one that warrants protection. The payment for the business may well have included an element for the goodwill of the operation. Also, the interest must not extend further than is reasonable to protect the contended interest and must not be contrary to public interest. If a hairdressing business was sold in a particular town, a clause preventing the opening of a salon anywhere else within the UK is unlikely to succeed.

To recap, the criteria for a valid restraint of trade clause are summarised below:

There must be a valid interest

- *Herbert Morris Ltd v Saxelby* [1916] 1 AC 688 –
- Lord Shaw – two types of interest that can legitimately be protected:
  1. Sale of business – clause to prevent seller from acting in direct competition,
  2. Contract of employment – clause to protect trade secrets and to prevent solicitation of clients.

The restraint must be reasonable

- *Mason v Provident Clothing Co* [1913] AC 724 – clause concerning geographical extent of a restriction in a densely populated area held to be excessive
- *Fitch v Dewes* [1921] 2 AC 158 – clause on geographical extent held to be reasonable and required to protect the interests of the business of a former employer.

The restraint must be within the public interest

- *Wyatt v Kreglinger and Fernau* [1933] 1 KB 793 – a covenant that a former employee would not compete in the wool trade was held to be in breach of the public interest.

An analysis of what is reasonable

In determining whether or not a restraint is reasonable, the court will consider the *nature, duration* and the *geographical extent* of the clause. Covenants that expand beyond what the court deems reasonable will be unenforceable. Rulings will vary depending upon the nature of a business. For example, in *Nordenfelt* (discussed above), a worldwide ban preventing the vendor of a business from dealing in guns and ammunition was deemed reasonable owing to the very narrow market for this product type. Whereas in *Goldsoll v Goldman* [1915], the geographical extent of a restriction in the imitation jewellery market was held to be too wide. There are many case illustrations:

Restrictive dealing/*solus* agreements

Sometimes an individual may agree to work for only one employer or to sell only a particular manufacturer's product. Such *solus* agreements are valid if reasonable. See below:

There must be an interest meriting protection > The agreement must be reasonable in relation to the interest > **The agreement must not be contrary to the public interest**

In considering a *solus* clause, the courts must consider several factors:

Case precedent – *Esso Petroleum Co Ltd v Harper's Garage (Stourport) Ltd* [1967] 2 WLR 871

Facts: A garage owner entered into separate *solus* agreements for two garages he owned, to purchase all of his petrol from Esso. One agreement was for four years six months (in return for a discount on the petrol) and the other ran for 21 years (in return for a mortgage). The agreement included an undertaking not to sell to a purchaser unless they entered into similar covenants.

Held: The House of Lords indicated that both interests merited protection, but could only be enforced if they were reasonable. It concluded that the 21 year agreement was unreasonable as it attempted to look too far into the future, but the shorter agreement was reasonable.

Application: Analyse the facts carefully. Ensure that you apply the reasonableness test taking into account all factors that have been drawn out in case law. Look at the **nature, duration and geographical extent** of the clause.

The Competition Act 1998 made significant changes to competition law enforcement in the United Kingdom. The Act equips the Office of Fair Trading with powers to investigate potential anti-competitive practices.

Severance

Severance of the objectionable part of the contract must not alter the nature (as distinct from the extent) of the original contract. The illegal restraint will not be severed if it forms the main purpose of the restraint, or if severance would significantly alter the scope and intention of the agreement. In *Attwood v Lamont* [1920], the court refused to sever restrictions on a tailor that prevented him from competing with any department of the store that employed him. The court stated that this was a covenant 'which must stand or fall in its unaltered form'.

For the blue pencil test to operate, it must be possible to sever the illegal part of the clause simply by deleting words in the contract. The court will not add or rearrange words or in any way redraft the contract. In *Mason v Provident Clothing Co Ltd* [1913], the House of Lords refused to redraft a promise not to work within 25 miles of London. However, in *Goldsoll v Goldman* [1915], a dealer in imitation jewellery promised not to deal in real or imitation jewellery either in the UK or abroad. Dealing in real jewellery and dealing abroad were severed, leaving a valid contract in restraint of trade.

Aim Higher

In drafting a restraint of trade clause what factors must be considered in relation to:

❖ The nature of the business – How wide should the restriction be with regard to the range of activities and areas of expertise
❖ Duration
❖ Unusual covenants
❖ Consideration provided for the agreement
❖ Geographical extent
❖ Non-solicitation clauses

Summary

An illegal contract cannot be enforced. There are several categories of illegality, many of which include public policy. Contracts in restraint of trade often give rise to litigation. These contracts are *prima facie* void. The presumption can, however, be rebutted if certain special factors exist that are accepted to render the restraint valid. For rebuttal to be successful, the restraint clause must be reasonable both with regard to the parties to the contract as well as the interests of the public. Factors such as the duration of the restraint and the area of the restraint are relevant in reaching conclusions here. Restraint of trade clauses can be found in contracts of employment; contracts for the sale of a business and in *solus* agreements. The following flowchart may assist in analysing the effect of a restraint of trade clause:

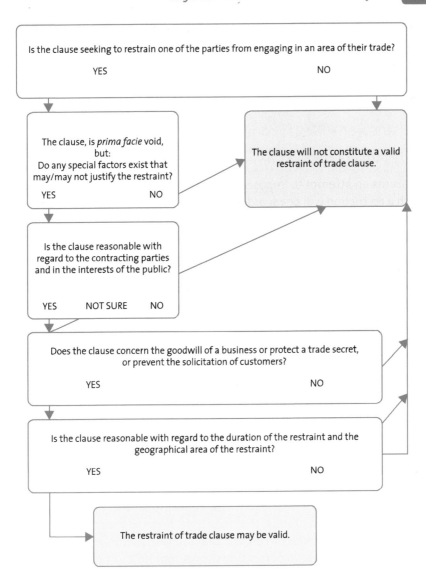

Putting it into practice

Look at the scenario below, and then answer the following question: Billy owns a shop in Taliswell, a large town. His business mainly consists of selling and repairing Ecospin washing machines, a brand new revolutionary energy-saving design. Billy's is the only shop in Taliswell which sells this type of washing machine. Billy is now considering opening another shop in a small town called Waddington, some five miles from Taliswell. Billy plans to sell his shop in Taliswell. The prospective purchaser is Whiteflakes plc, a national firm which owns a chain of electrical shops, and specialises in Ecospin washing machines. This firm wants Billy to agree not to open another shop selling Ecospin washing machines, any other make of washing machine, or any other laundry equipment anywhere in the UK for the next eight years.

Advise Billy.

Model answer – illegal contracts

Identify subject area

* Concerns an attempt to impose a restriction on the vendor of a business.
* Such a restriction will be regarded as being in restraint of trade and therefore *prima facie* illegal.
* Billy will only be bound by the restriction if Whiteflakes can rebut the presumption of illegality by showing that the restraint is reasonable to protect a legitimate interest.
* Even if it is unreasonable as worded, the court may be prepared to enforce it if the scope can be narrowed by taking out some part of the restriction.

Define the legal principles

* Starting point for this kind of restraint is the House of Lords case – *Nordenfelt v Maxim Nordenfelt* [1894].
* Held that all covenants in restraint of trade are *prima facie* contrary to public policy and void.
* Recognised that the presumption could be rebutted if the restraint could be shown to be reasonable with reference to both the interests of the parties and the public interest.
* For the restraint to be reasonable, Whiteflakes must show that they have a *legitimate interest* to protect; that the scope of the restraint does not extend further than is *reasonable* to protect that interest; and that there is no *general public interest* at stake in permitting the restriction.

Apply the law

Legitimate interest

* This is satisfied. Where a person sells a shop as an ongoing business, goodwill is an important aspect of the sale. A good reputation and established customers are both valuable business assets.
* It is evident that Billy will increase the price of the business to include these elements in its value. It is accepted that the protection of the goodwill in a business being bought is a legitimate interest which can be protected by a reasonable restriction. This is what happened in *Nordenfelt*.

❖ Such a clause will benefit the vendor as well as the purchaser, because if the vendor were not prepared to accept an obligation not to compete, it is likely that he would have difficulty selling his business, or he would almost certainly have to accept a lower price for the business.

Is the restraint reasonable to protect that interest?

❖ Whiteflakes obviously has an interest to protect. The restraint covers the sale of any make of washing machine and other laundry equipment, anywhere in the UK for eight years.
❖ In order for the restraint to stand, it will have to be considered reasonable in respect of scope, area and time.
❖ The clause is likely to fail these tests.
❖ Billy's business mainly concerned Ecospin washing machines, whereas the restraint extends to washing machines and other laundry equipment. It seems that the bulk of Billy's business is in Ecospin washing machines. A restraint which extends far beyond this area is likely to be regarded as unreasonable.
❖ Whiteflakes must tailor the restraint to the scope of the business which they are purchasing, not the scope of their own business (*British Reinforced Concrete Engineering Co Ltd v Schelff* [1921]).
❖ In *Nordenfelt*, a worldwide restriction was found to be reasonable. In this case the restriction is to the UK market only. From this case, it seems that the area must relate to the interest being protected. It is unlikely that Billy would have any serious impact on the trade of Whiteflakes by opening up a shop in an area in which he was unknown.
❖ There are likely to be areas in the UK where Whiteflakes have no existing shops that would be affected by Billy's competition.

On the facts, it appears that the area and the scope of the restraint are too wide.

Length of restriction

❖ Eight years – need to consider, if Billy opened a shop within the next eight years would he be likely to retain any of his existing customers? This would have an effect on the goodwill of the business sold to Whiteflakes. This aspect of the restraint may be reasonable.
❖ Courts could sever the unreasonable parts of the restraint and give effect to what is reasonable. See *Goldsoll v Goldman* [1915] – strike out offending words, and if what is left makes sense, the agreement can continue.

Applying the facts to the problem

It is fairly simple to narrow the scope of this clause by cutting out the phrases 'any other make of washing machine, or any other type of laundry equipment'. May also make the area less wide, i.e. substitute anywhere in the UK for a more localised area.

General public interest
Not contrary to public interest.

The answer can also be displayed in diagrammatic form:

Identify the law	❖ Restriction on the sale of a business. ❖ *Prima facie* void unless presumption can be rebutted.
Define the law	❖ Leading case *Nordenfelt v Maxim Nordenfelt* [1894]. ❖ Presumption can be rebutted if the restraint can be shown to be reasonable in the interests of the parties and the public interest. ❖ Whiteflakes must show that they have a **legitimate interest** to protect; that the scope of the restraint does not extend further than is **reasonable** to protect that interest, and that there is no **general public interest** at stake.
Apply the law	❖ Need to consider. (a) Is there a legitimate interest capable of being protected? (b) Is the restraint reasonable to protect that interest in respect of scope, area and time?
Apply the law	❖ Whiteflakes do have an interest to protect – laundry equipment and Ecospin washing machines – a restraint extending beyond Ecospin machines is likely to fail. ❖ The geographical area is likely to be too wide. It is unlikely that Billy's business will affect Whiteflakes if it is located in a different region. ❖ The time may be reasonable, but is open to argument as to whether he would retain any of his previous customers after this length of time. ❖ Severance may be possible – *Goldsoll v Goldman* [1915].

Table of key cases referred to in this chapter

Key case	Area of law	Principle
Attwood v Lamont [1920] 3 KB 571	On leaving the tailoring department of a store, the defendant covenanted not to work as a tailor, dressmaker or draper within 10 miles of Kidderminster.	*Held*: The restraint was too wide in relation to the activity restrained.
British Reinforced Concrete Engineering Co. Ltd v Schelff [1921] 2 Ch 563	A national company making road reinforcement products took over the business of a small company specialising in the selling of loop road reinforcements. The contract contained a clause restricting the smaller company from establishing a new business within a 10-mile radius.	*Held*: The restriction was void. It did not protect a proprietary interest. The small company specialising in loop road reinforcements was no threat to the much larger business who sold road reinforcements in general.
Esso Petroleum Co Ltd v Harper's Garage (Stourport) Ltd [1968] AC 269	Concerned a *solus* agreement relating to two petrol stations that the owner would purchase petrol from Esso only. A short agreement was valid, but a longer one was invalid.	A restraint of trade clause must be reasonable between the parties and must not be of excessive duration or be in breach of the public interest.
Forster & Sons Ltd v Suggett (1918) 35 TLR 87	A works manager entered into a covenant not to engage in glass-making anywhere within the UK.	*Held*: The covenant was enforceable to protect a trade secret. The manager had acquired knowledge of a secret glass-making process.
Home Counties Dairies v Skiltontd Ltd [1970] 1 ALL ER 1227	A restraint on a milkman not to serve or sell milk or dairy produce to, or solicit orders for milk or dairy produce from any person or company he had dealt with in the last six months as an employee in the course of his employment was challenged.	*Held*: The restraint was void as it extended far wider than necessary to protect the interest that it intended to protect.

Key case	Area of law	Principle
M & S Drapers (A Firm) v Reynolds [1957] 1 WLR 9	Concerned a clause that a sales representative could not solicit former customers for five years.	*Held*: The clause was unenforceable due to its excessive duration.
Mason v Provident Clothing Co [1913] AC 724	Concerned a clause relating to the geographical extent of a restriction in a densely populated area.	The geographical extent of a restraint of trade must not be excessive, taking into account all *Nordenfelt* factors.
JA Mont (UK) Ltd v Mills [1993] IRLR 173	The manager of a paper tissue company was made redundant after 20 years of service. His severance package included a clause that he would not work for another paper tissue company for 12 months.	*Held*: The covenant was too wide.
Nordenfelt v Maxim Nordenfelt Guns and Ammunition Co [1894] AC 535	Concerned the sale of a guns and ammunition business. As part of the sale agreement the buyer contracted not to engage in this type of business anywhere in the world for 25 years.	A restraint of trade clause must be reasonable with reference to the interests of the parties concerned, and reasonable in the interests of the public. It must not be unreasonable in its scope, duration or geographical extent.
Wyatt v Kreglinger and Fernau [1933] 1 KB 793	Concerned a covenant that a former employee would not compete in the wool trade.	A restraint of trade clause must not be in breach of the public interest, i.e. restrict a service.

@ **Visit the book's companion website to test your knowledge**

- Resources include a subject map, revision tip podcasts, downloadable diagrams, MCQ quizzes for each chapter, and a flashcard glossary
- www.routledge.com/cw/optimizelawrevision

8 Discharge of Contract

Revision objectives

Understand the law
- Can you outline what 'discharge of contract' means?
- Can you explain the different ways in which a contract may be discharged?

Remember the details
- Can you explain the exceptions to the rule of strict performance?
- Can you explain what is meant by anticipatory and repudiatory breach?
- Can you outline the legal requirements needed for the doctrine of frustration to apply?
- Can you outline the legal effects of frustration?

Reflect critically on areas of debate
- Can you explain what happens to the parties' obligations in case of discharge by breach of contract?
- Do you understand the different explanations for the theoretical basis of the doctrine of frustration?
- Do you agree with the outcome and the reasoning in *Krell v Henry*?

Contextualise
- Do you understand the different contexts of the different forms of discharge of contract and how they will operate in the typical commercial setting?
- Do you understand the different legal consequences of discharge for the parties?

Apply your skills and knowledge
- Can you answer the question at the end of this chapter?

Chapter Map

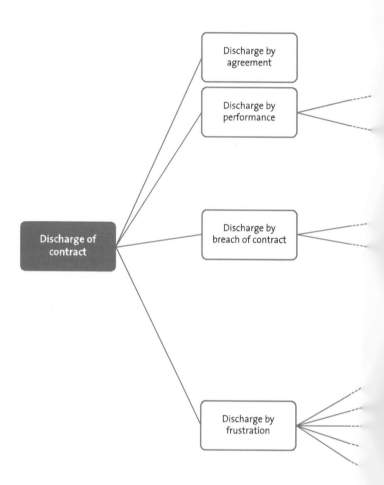

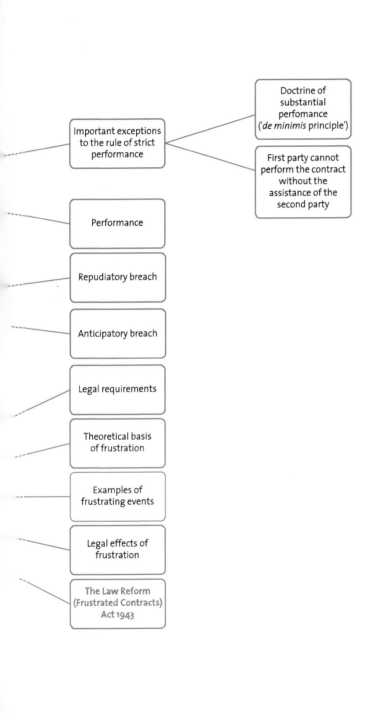

Important exceptions to the rule of strict performance

Doctrine of substantial perfomance ('*de minimis* principle')

First party cannot perform the contract without the assistance of the second party

Performance

Repudiatory breach

Anticipatory breach

Legal requirements

Theoretical basis of frustration

Examples of frustrating events

Legal effects of frustration

The Law Reform (Frustrated Contracts) Act 1943

Introduction

Once formed by offer, acceptance and consideration an agreement becomes an enforceable contract: for the duration of this contract, each party must perform his contractual obligations as specified by its terms with the consequence that, if either party fails to so perform, the disappointed party may go to court to seek contractual remedies against the non-performing party. This chapter considers the duration of the performance obligations in the contract. In this context, it is important to note that, just as the primary contractual performance obligations have a starting point – at formation – so they have an end point which arrives when the contract can be said to be discharged.

Discharge of contract (sometimes called 'termination of contract') may happen in several ways:

❖ by (express or implied) agreement that the parties are discharged from their respective obligations to perform under the contract;
❖ by full and proper performance of the contract obligations;
❖ by a sufficiently serious breach of contract by one party to allow the innocent party to thereafter treat the contract (and any of his outstanding performance duties under it) as discharged from that point in time; and
❖ if it becomes impossible to perform the contract for unforeseen reasons independent of the actions of either party such that the contract and the performance due under it are automatically discharged by the doctrine of frustration.

Why is the issue of discharge of contract important?

As discharge of contract sets the point in time when primary performance obligations end, it is essential to understand the law concerning the three types of discharge of contract in order to know:

(a) whether your own performance obligation remains to be completed or is at an end;
(b) what your options are concerning any given breach of contract either threatened or committed by the other party;
(c) whether and, if so, how, the doctrine of frustration applies to automatically discharge the contract and its performance obligations, as a matter of law, from the time of the frustrating act.

Common Pitfall

Don't be fooled into thinking that because discharge of contract sets an end point to the duty to perform primary contractual obligations it means that **ALL** legal liabilities under the contract therefore end: discharge of contract does **NOT** destroy those legal liabilities which have arisen prior to the point of discharge. In other words, *do not confuse a **discharged** contract with a contract that is **void**.*

The difference between a discharged contract and a void contract

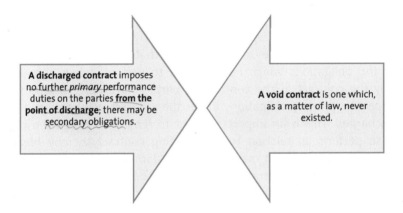

A **discharged contract** imposes no further *primary* performance duties on the parties **from the point of discharge**; there may be secondary obligations.

A **void contract** is one which, as a matter of law, never existed.

Discharge by agreement

As a contract is created by agreement, it may be discharged ('terminated' or 'extinguished') by agreement between the contractual parties. Consideration will generally be required for such an agreement to be enforceable. Consequently, one has to differentiate between contracts which have been wholly executed on one side (meaning: one party has performed all its obligations under the agreement) and those which are executory on both sides (meaning: both parties still have obligations to perform – see Chapter 2 for more details on consideration). With regard to the former, the party seeking to be discharged must show either a release by deed or some consideration (this is known as 'accord and satisfaction', see *British Russian Gazette and Trade Outlook Ltd v Associated Newspapers Ltd* [1933]) in place of, or in addition to, its existing obligation. With regard to the former, the mutual release from their respective duties under the contract expressed by each party will usually be enough to be regarded as 'good' consideration to make the discharge by agreement enforceable.

Discharge by agreement may occur in the following situations:

❖ A contract may, by a *termination clause*, expressly confer a right of discharge, especially in commercial contracts.

❖ A contract may be discharged by an *express agreement* to terminate it.
❖ A contract may be discharged by *implied agreement* between the parties, e.g. where the parties create a second contract inconsistent with the intention that the original contract should remain in force or where it may be inferred from the parties' conduct that the original contract should be terminated.

(See Hugh Beale (ed.), *Chitty on Contracts*, 31st edn, chapter 22 for further reading on this.)

Discharge by performance

Probably the most obvious way in which a contract can be discharged is by performance of the parties' respective primary contractual obligations. The general rule regarding performance of contract is that each party must *precisely* perform the obligations which he promised to perform when agreeing to be bound by the contract: if the contractual parties have done exactly this, then their respective primary obligations under the contract will be deemed to have been discharged. This is an important point to remember because a party who fails to so perform in relation to a subsisting contract thereby breaches his performance obligations and may be sued for damages arising from his breach. Consequently, unless the contrary has been agreed between the parties subsequent to the formation of the contract, each contracting party is entitled to insist upon receiving *exactly* what he was *specifically* promised he would receive under the contract.

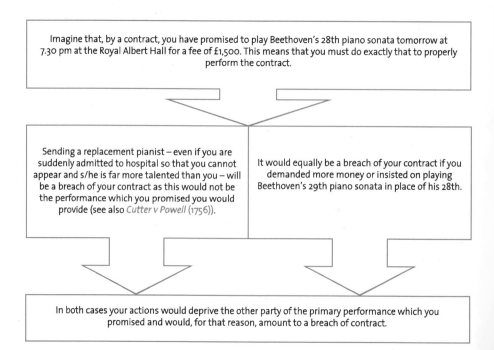

Imagine that, by a contract, you have promised to play Beethoven's 28th piano sonata tomorrow at 7.30 pm at the Royal Albert Hall for a fee of £1,500. This means that you must do exactly that to properly perform the contract.

Sending a replacement pianist – even if you are suddenly admitted to hospital so that you cannot appear and s/he is far more talented than you – will be a breach of your contract as this would not be the performance which you promised you would provide (see also *Cutter v Powell* (1756)).

It would equally be a breach of your contract if you demanded more money or insisted on playing Beethoven's 29th piano sonata in place of his 28th.

In both cases your actions would deprive the other party of the primary performance which you promised and would, for that reason, amount to a breach of contract.

As even a brief consideration of the facts provided by this example makes clear, it is possible to envisage many situations in which the promised performance would be difficult or impractical: it is in such situations that it is necessary to know whether the contract, and its future performance obligations, survive or have been discharged as your client will need to know:

❖ what his options are, and, importantly,
❖ whether he must still perform or is now free from the contract and may now sell goods to Jerry which were originally contracted to go to Tom.

There are certain exceptions to the general rule of strict performance of the contract but it must be remembered that these exceptions are narrowly construed by the courts and frequently fail to displace the general rule of strict performance. Do NOT assume these exceptions are 'the norm': these exceptions are truly exceptional.

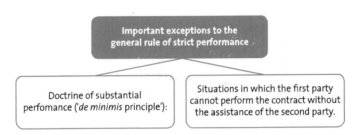

Important exceptions to the general rule of strict performance

Doctrine of substantial perfomance ('*de minimis* principle'):

Situations in which the first party cannot perform the contract without the assistance of the second party.

Doctrine of substantial performance (the '*de minimis* principle')

The **first exception** may be known either positively as the doctrine of substantial performance or negatively as the *de minimis* principle (from the Latin maxim: '*de minimis non curat lex*' which translates as 'the law does not concern itself with trivial matters'). In either case, the party alleged to be in breach argues that he has so nearly done everything which was required that his performance is sufficient to refute the breach of contract claim: *if the court can be persuaded*, the exception will excuse utterly trivial instances of non-performance.

The difficulty in practice is that litigation tends to demonstrate that the contracting parties do not share the view that the defect in performance is trivial. This practical problem is neatly illustrated by the following cases:

❖ *Margaronis Navigation Agency Ltd v Henry W Peabody & Co of London Ltd* [1965] which demonstrates the usual difficulties of convincing a court of the triviality of a failure in performance in a commercial case;
❖ *Hoenig v Isaacs* [1952] which is a somewhat unusual case where the court took a more charitable view of a claim by an interior decorator that he had rendered substantial performance to his client; and
❖ *Bolton v Mahadeva* [1972] which demonstrates the more typical view regarding the issue of substantial performance.

Up for Debate

A question which you may encounter in coursework or exam is why it might be a bad idea to routinely allow a contractor to start a job, leave it unfinished and allow him to claim a proportion of the agreed fee. In this context, you might want to consider the position of the householder who has employed a builder who leaves the job unfinished (see B McFarlane & R Stevens, 'In defence of *Sumpter v Hedges*' (2002) LQR 569).

The first party cannot perform the contract without the assistance of the second party

The **second exception** concerns situations in which the first party cannot perform the contract without the assistance of the second party, e.g. by the second party accepting its attempted payment or accepting its attempted delivery. If the defendant refuses to accept proper payment (or, as in *Startup v Macdonald* (1843), he refuses to admit the claimant onto his premises to deliver in accordance with the contractual agreement), he cannot then object that the claimant has not properly performed: in such a situation it is enough for the claimant to genuinely and unreservedly offer to perform or to 'tender' performance in accordance with the contract. This has the effect that, if one party can show that he has so indicated a willingness to tender his performance, and that the other party has wrongly rejected it, he will be deemed to have performed if the other party then attempts to allege that he has not so performed.

What form of performance does the law require?

Allegations of breach of contract are frequently countered by the assertion that proper performance has actually been tendered: a claim alleging a breach of contract will be refuted if the party allegedly in breach can show that he has performed all of his contractual obligations. This poses the question of what the courts will regard as satisfactory/sufficient performance, i.e. what form/level/ standard of performance the law requires. To resolve the matter, the court must first establish what form of contractual performance the contract required and then consider whether the evidence indicates that sufficient performance has been provided to refute the claimed breach of contract.

First, the court has to interpret the contract so as to ascertain the nature of the obligation which is owed under the contract. This is a question of law.

Then, the court examines if the actual performance satisfies the requirements as set out in the contract. This is a question of mixed fact and law because the court has to determine whether the facts (i.e. what has actually been performed) live up to the performance standard as prescribed by the relevant contractual provisions which define the obligation in question.

Taken together, these two points allow the court to draw its conclusion as to whether a contractual obligation has been fulfilled satisfactorily, i.e. whether or not the facts of a particular case amount to sufficient performance.

How the courts approach the question whether a party's performance is sufficient/satisfactory in the eyes of the law

As the diagram shows, the most important indicator of the form of performance required will be the provisions of the contract itself: the court will consider these provisions to try to establish the intentions of the parties concerning performance. The court will additionally consider any evidence of subsequent agreement by the parties to vary the original contract provisions concerning performance. Though each case will turn on its own particular contract terms, the common law has built up a range of interpretative provisions which, in the absence of evidence that the parties intended otherwise, will indicate the assumed meaning of various standard provisions concerning contract performance. Some examples of such interpretative conditions relating to the determination of performance obligations are listed below.

Time

The time allowed for by a contract for its performance may throw up a number of interpretative issues:

If the contract is silent on when a party must perform, or uses words which do not indicate a definite period of time (e.g. 'Jack will perform promptly ...'), the court will assume that *a reasonable time* must have been intended.

What will be a reasonable time will depend upon the nature of the contract at issue and what the parties are deemed to have intended, *Bunge Corporation v Tradax Export SA* [1981].

If the contract is drafted to contain a provision which either explicitly fixes a time period for its performance or states that '... *time is to be of the essence* ...' in the performance *of the term which is breached*, the court will presume that the time provision is a condition (see Chapter 3 on Terms).

Thus once it expires without due performance, the innocent party may treat the failure to perform as a breach of condition, *Lombard North Central Plc v Butterworth* [1987]. Once it is plain that time IS of the essence in the eyes of the court, almost any delay will allow discharge of the contract: in *Union Eagle Ltd v Golden Achievement Ltd* [1997], a delay as short as 10 minutes would have sufficed. For the effect of waiving breaches of a time of the essence term and how to then successfully bring the contract to an end for repeated such breaches, *Charles Rickards Ltd v Oppenheim* [1950].

If the contract as originally drafted did not originally make the time for performance be of the essence, it is not possible for one contracting party to unilaterally convert the time provision into a condition the breach of which will then immediately entitle the termination of the contract: it is however possible for this party to serve notice upon the party in default to make time be of the essence after the expiry of a specified reasonable new notice period.

If the new period elapses without performance and the innocent party is thereby deprived by the delay of a substantial part of the benefit which he hoped to receive under the contract, he may plausibly argue that the disregard of the period for performance specified in the notice represents evidence of a repudiatory breach of contract by the party in default.

If the contract as originally drafted did not originally make the time for performance be of the essence, it is not possible for one contracting party to unilaterally convert the time provision into a condition the breach of which will then immediately entitle the termination of the contract.

It is however possible for this party to serve notice upon the party in default to make time be of the essence after the expiry of a specified and reasonable notice period. If the new period elapses without performance and the innocent party is thereby deprived by the delay of a substantial part of the benefit which he hoped to receive under the contract, he may plausibly argue that the disregard of the period specified in the notice represents evidence of a repudiatory breach by the other party.

If the performance of the contract is expressed in relation to a duration measured in days, the 'days' in question will usually be assumed to include weekends and public holidays unless the contrary is indicated (e.g. 'working days' would not include those days on which work was unusual such as the weekend, bank holidays and other public holidays, *Lafarge Aggregates Ltd v London Borough of Newham* [2005] EWHC 1377).

A day is assumed, unless there is contrary evidence in the contract, to run from one midnight to the next midnight. Normally if the contract requires that a party does something (e.g. make a payment) by a certain day he is allowed the entirety of that day to so perform and cannot be held in breach of his performance obligation until the commencement of the next day. The position is different if a party is required by a particular day to give a notice or other formal document to a person or to an office: then the assumption is that the notice must be given within the office hours of that day.

If the performance of the contract is expressed in relation to a duration measured in months, the 'months' in question will be assumed to be calendar months (despite the fact that months are of different durations).

If a period of time measured in 'months' is to be computed *from* or *after* a given date, that day is excluded from the computation, and the period elapses at midnight on the corresponding day of the month of expiry, *Dodds v Walker* [1981].

Payment

The performance required concerning the 'payment' obligation is equally prone to issues of interpretation. Once again, the contract will be consulted by the court to try to establish what the parties intended should happen concerning the payment obligation. The court will additionally consider any evidence of a subsequent agreement by the parties to vary these contract provisions.

Common Pitfall

In this context, it is important to remember that a claim for the payment of a debt due under a contract is *radically* different to a claim for damages for breach of an obligation under that contract (see below). It is a bad blunder to try to reduce the amount due in debt on the basis of non-mitigation, remoteness or causation.

Claim for payment of a debt due	Claim for damages for breach of contract
The *debt claim* requests that the court orders payment of a definite sum specified in the contract which has fallen due but not been paid, *White and Carter (Councils) v McGregor* [1962].	A *damages claim* requests that the court calculates a compensatory sum subject to proof of causation, remoteness and the duty of the claimant to mitigate his losses – none of these concepts are relevant to a claim for the payment of a debt (see Chapter 9 on remedies for more details).

Subject to the above, and in the absence of contrary intentions appearing from the contract or from later binding agreements between the parties, the court will assume the following in relation to the obligation of payment in connection with the performance of a contract:

Payment of a debt will be assumed to be required to be made in full in legal currency, i.e. in cash. There is no requirement that any other method of payment (e.g. by a negotiable instrument such as a cheque) will be accepted as amounting to performance.

Though the parties to most contracts can later agree to different methods or forms of payment, it is important to be sure that such agreements are themselves *de facto* 'enforceable' in the eyes of the law: a subsequent agreement varying a contract which originally stipulated – whether expressly or by default of expression – payment in cash to allow payment by cheque will probably NOT be binding unless there is fresh consideration for the subsequent agreement.

If the contract requires payment into a bank account specified by the creditor, the payment is deemed 'received' once the creditor's bank (as agent of the creditor) has received the payment from the debtor so as to allow the creditor the full use of the payment *as if received as cash*.

Thus money paid by cheque to a bank for the benefit of its client was not technically deemed received when the bank made a book entry indicating its receipt but only when the payment was cleared through the banking system so as to be fully at the disposal of the client, *The Chikuma* [1981]. Note, however, the strong criticism in (1981) 97 LQR 379.

If either the *place or* the *time of payment* are **not** specified by the contract, they must be deduced by the Court from the contract and its surrounding circumstances, i.e. the matter is one of construction of the contractual terms.

If no place of payment is stipulated, the general rule is that the debtor must pay the creditor at his place of business, *The Eider* [1893]. If there is a provision concerning the time of payment, it would be advisable to use clear words if it is intended to elevate this provision to the status of a 'condition', e.g. s. 10(1) of the Sale of Goods Act 1979.

Discharge by breach of contract

The significance of a breach of contract, in relation to the issue of discharge, is that if the innocent party is confronted with the right type of breach, he may also elect to treat the breach as discharging the contract, and his unperformed primary performance obligations, thereby 'ending' the contract and thus transforming the other party's breached primary performance obligations into secondary obligations to pay the innocent party damages to remedy the breach. The main question to be considered here is *when* will the innocent party be able to respond to an actual or threatened breach of contract by so treating the contract as discharged?

The importance of understanding this issue is best revealed by considering the facts of a case where the innocent party, wishing to escape from future payment obligations under a contract, wrongly treated the other party's undoubted breach of a term (which promised that a particular ship would be seaworthy) by allowing it to discharge the contract: the result was that the innocent party was itself sued for breach of contract for wrongfully repudiating its contract to hire the ship *Hongkong Fir*.

Case precedent – *Hongkong Fir Shipping Co Ltd v Kawasaki Kisen Kaisha Ltd* [1962] EWCA Civ 7

Facts: The Ship Owner hired its ship by a special contract called a time charterparty to the Charterer for 24 months. Under this contract, though the Charterer had the ship, the Ship Owner provided the crew and had certain continuing contractual obligations including that the ship was seaworthy. The Charterer hired the ship to use it for the carriage of goods by sea. Unfortunately, as well as the ship's engines being old and temperamental, there were initially problems with understaffing and alcoholism in the engine room crew: consequently substantial repairs were required. Though the Charterer was not liable for hire charges during these periods, the Charterer could not use the ship for 20 weeks because of the breakdowns – this was a clear breach of the seaworthiness term by the Ship Owner. The Charterer notified the Ship Owner that its repeated breaches of the seaworthiness term had discharged the contract and also any further performance obligations due to the Ship Owner from the Charterer. The Ship Owner admitted the breach of the seaworthiness clause (and a liability in damages) but did not agree that the breaches of this unclassified term were serious enough to entitle the Charterer to treat the contract as terminated (or 'repudiated'). The Ship Owner successfully sued the Charterer for wrongfully attempting to repudiate the contract.

The Queen's Bench Division and then the Court of Appeal each found for the Ship Owner and awarded damages against the Charterer (less a sum to represent breaches of the seaworthiness clause by the Ship Owner) because, although the Ship Owners were admittedly in breach of a clause of the time charterparty as the vessel was unseaworthy on delivery by reason of an insufficient and incompetent engine room staff, seaworthiness was not a condition of the time charterparty a breach of which entitled the Charterer at once to repudiate the contract. Consequently, as the Charterer lost both cases he also had to pay all the legal costs for both sides of this litigation.

Principle: Innocent party's ability to treat the contract as discharged as a consequence of an actual or threatened breach of contract.

Application: The case makes the important point that though a breach of a contractual term always allows the innocent party to claim contractual damages, it DOES NOT also always allow the innocent party to treat the contract as discharged by (and from) this breach. This is an important point to remember when confronted with a scenario involving the issue of discharge by breach of contract.

The importance of the nature of the breach of contract for the question of discharge

Q.: How do we decide whether the innocent party can or cannot opt to treat the breach as discharging it from further contract performance?

A.: It depends upon the nature of the *actual* or *threatened* breach of contract:

A total refusal to perform by one party amounts to a **renunciation / repudiation** of the contract and, without more, allows the other innocent party to treat the contract as discharged, *The Mihalis Angelos* [1971].	If a less than total refusal to perform is at issue, e.g. a party cannot, or refuses to, comply with one of the contract terms, the options before the innocent party will depend upon the classification of the breached contract term: only where contractual terms classified as 'conditions' have been breached (including equivalent breach of innominate terms) will the innocent party be able to accept the opportunity to repudiate and thereby end the contract on the basis of its discharge by breach.

Repudiatory breach

Thus, for the contract and the subsequent obligations to be treated as discharged by breach, the innocent party must be confronted by what is known as a *repudiatory breach*, i.e. either by a total renunciation of performance – in which case there can be no argument that the innocent party may decide to treat the contract as discharged – or by a breach of a primary contract term which *the court* will classify as amounting to a breach of condition or a serious breach of an innominate term.

Remember that a contract is not discharged ('terminated') automatically upon the occurrence of a repudiatory breach. Rather, a repudiatory breach gives the innocent party a right to elect between treating the contract as 'at an end' (sometimes referred to as 'accepting the breach') or affirming the contract (sometimes referred to as 'rejecting the breach').

Anticipatory breach of contract

Anticipatory breach of contract deals with another aspect of the question of *when* an innocent party can act in response to a threatened breach of contract. The term 'anticipatory breach' denotes the situation in which one party is confronted with words or actions by the other party which make it – prior to performance – (expressly or impliedly) plain that the other party will either not perform the contract at all or will commit a repudiatory breach of it. The case of *Hochster v De La Tour* (1853) established that an innocent party so confronted may immediately decide to treat the contract as at an end, thereby terminating its own future performance obligations, and also allowing an immediate damages claim based on the other party's anticipatory renunciation of performance. This is known as the innocent party's 'right to elect'.

However, it should be remembered that the concession this offers to the innocent party is however subject to the often problematic requirement that the anticipatory breach must *unambiguously* threaten the renunciation either of the entire contractual performance or of at least a condition (or equivalent innominate term) allowing repudiation by the innocent party.

Some important points to note regarding discharge by breach

| Who makes the decision of how to react to the repudiatory or anticipatory breach? | It is solely for the innocent party to decide upon its preferred course of action. Though the party in breach can make suggestions, and may even attempt to incentivise one response over the other by offering to replace the old contract with a new one – which if accepted is sometimes called 'discharge by agreement' – the decision (i.e. 'the election') whether or not to treat the contract as discharged belongs to the innocent party. The innocent party must elect either to |

	end the contract (and also its own outstanding performance obligations) by accepting that the other's renunciation (or repudiatory breach) shall have this consequence, or must decide to 'affirm' the contract that is – despite the breach – to treat the contract as continuing to allow later performance or legal action in relation to the other's breach, *White and Carter (Councils) v McGregor* [1962].
What happens when the innocent party elects to treat the contract as discharged?	At the moment, when the innocent party makes an election favouring discharge he brings the possibility of performing the primary obligations of the contract – including any performance obligations that he owes to the party in breach – to an end. Though this action is sometimes called 'terminating the contract' it is more accurate to speak of 'transforming the contract' as the election changes the breached primary performance obligation of the other party into a secondary performance obligation to pay damages to the innocent party for the breach of contract (*Photo Production Ltd v Securicor Transport Ltd* [1980]). The contract is NOT destroyed by such 'termination' but can no longer be performed in the same way once the innocent party elects to treat it as discharged: thus the party in breach cannot thereafter compel the innocent party to accept his overdue primary performance after the innocent party has elected to accept the repudiation (*Xenos v Danube and Black Sea Railway* (1863)).
What if the innocent party elects to affirm the contract?	If the innocent party elects to affirm the contract, despite the breach by the other party, the contract and the primary obligations continue for the benefit of both contracting parties. Thus, in this situation, the party in breach can compel the innocent party to accept an overdue primary performance – subject to paying damages for any losses arising from his original breach of contract: the innocent party will itself breach the contract if it refuses to accept this performance.
	As the effect of affirmation is that the contract is still notionally operative as far as *both* parties are concerned, either may take advantage of subsequent events which allow discharge of the contract.
How long may the innocent party spend in considering its options?	If the innocent party takes too long to reach a decision, it risks the loss of its right of election by either the operation of legislation (e.g. s 11(4) of the Sale of Goods Act 1979) or by reason of its own unreasonable delay, *Stocznia Gdanska SA v Latvian Shipping Co (No.2)* [1999] some delay is allowed and it is sometimes said that delay alone will not amount to

affirmation. The question of how long an innocent party has to consider its options will thus turn on the facts: a period of time that may be unreasonably long for a contractual relationship where time is clearly in short supply may be reasonable in the context of a more sedate contractual relationship (*Force India Formula One Team Ltd v Etihad Airways PJSC* [2010]).

Another matter for the innocent party to consider is that events may overtake him; the contract could be discharged independently of his election by a repudiatory breach he commits or by an unforeseen frustrating event, see *FercoMetal v Mediterranean Shipping Co* [1989] and *Avery v Bowden* (1855).

Common Pitfall

With regard to exams or coursework questions, don't merely assume/state that the innocent party has affirmed the contract; you *need* to show that he, in the scenario at hand, has actually done so. This means that you *need to* consider the following points in your answer:

(a) Does the innocent party know of the facts from which the breach has arisen? AND ALSO
(b) Does the innocent party know that he has the option to elect between the two courses of action of affirmation or accepting the repudiation, *Peyman v Lanjani* [1985]?

Assuming that the innocent party has this knowledge, he may affirm expressly (by informing the other party) or impliedly (by acting in such a manner as to indicate to a reasonable person an intention to continue with the contract despite the other's breach).

Discharge of contract by frustration

A contract will be discharged by frustration if a qualifying unforeseen event arises independently of the actions or decisions of the contracting parties which makes further performance of the contract impossible: this form of discharge is automatic, it occurs immediately by operation of law (without action by the parties) at the time of the frustrating event. Once a contract is discharged by frustration, all unperformed performance obligations under that contract end, as does any possibility of either party compelling further performance under that contract.

Common Pitfall

Discharge of contract by frustration is a regular essay and exam topic but is often poorly answered. To successfully address this topic in an assessment it is necessary to:

(a) set out the results of discharge of contract by frustration; and
(b) to consider matters **objectively** from BOTH sides; and
(c) to demonstrate an awareness of the larger issues of legal certainty which are raised by the doctrine of frustration.

A student who, when answering a question set, ignores legal certainty and, because he is *outraged* by what he *subjectively* considers an 'unfair' result, advises that party 'A' should sue party 'B' for not performing a contractual obligation which no longer exists, is unlikely to score many marks. The same fate will befall a student who wishes to use the doctrine of frustration where it plainly cannot be used (usually to escape a bad bargain) because he thinks that his solution would be 'fair'.

Before proceeding any further with frustration, three basic points need to be made:

Frustration concerns unforeseen events which arise after a contract is formed and make its performance impossible: frustrating events must arise independently of the actions of the contracting parties. The situations in which frustration will arise are thus always unexpected for BOTH parties: to regard this as 'unfair' for one party is to miss the point of the frustrating event and – more importantly – to miss the point of frustration as a legal doctrine.

When it can be used at all, *which will be rarely*, frustration acts to automatically discharge the contract for both contracting parties – *frustration is not concerned with subjective 'fairness'* (the Law Reform (Frustrated Contracts) Act 1943 offers some relief from the unexpected hardships that frustrating events can impose but only applies to certain contracts).

Because *frustration does not concern itself with subjective 'fairness'*, the parties to commercial contracts expressly will include terms in their written contracts to minimise the circumstances in which the contract could unexpectedly and unpredictably be discharged by frustration. To the extent that the parties have covered an eventuality by a term in their contract – such as a *force majeure* clause – the doctrine of frustration cannot apply.

This fact greatly reduces the practical scope of the doctrine of frustration, even when its requirements are seemingly made out.

The courts are genuinely reluctant to allow contracts to be discharged by frustration and take a restrictive (if not downright sceptical) view of allegations of any but the clearest examples of frustrating events. The courts have no desire to help one party who now wishes to escape what has, for him, become a less attractive contract. If the contract is commercial in nature there will be even less judicial willingness to apply the doctrine in any but the most clear cut cases.

This judicial reluctance is attributable to the violence that such loose use of the doctrine would do to the principle that enforceable contractual agreements should be upheld – *the whole law of contract is based on this principle: if unchecked, the doctrine of frustration could put all legal certainty in contract law at risk.*

Aim Higher

A student who correctly sets out the law concerning the requirements of the doctrine of frustration and also demonstrates an informed awareness of the three points above will score a higher mark than one who fails to accurately demonstrate the law, or blunders with regard to the abovementioned points.

The legal requirements for the doctrine of frustration to apply

1   An enforceable contract must have been concluded between the parties *before* the alleged frustrating event occurs: *if there is no contract in existence at this time, frustration – which operates to automatically discharge a contract – obviously cannot apply.*

2   The contract must NOT provide for the event which is argued to be frustrating: *a frustrating event is one which is unexpected and unforeseen.*
    In *Bunge SA v Kyla Shipping Co Ltd* [2012] there could be no frustration arising from the severe damage to the ship because the contract expressly provided for the event of such damage arising and even for the damage not being covered by an insurance policy.

3   The potential frustrating event must **NOT** arise from the act or decision of either contract party: *if the reason the contract cannot be performed is because of an act or decision made by one party there is no frustration.*
    This important principle was re-confirmed by the Court of Appeal in *J. Lauritzen AS v Wijsmuller BV (The Super Servant Two)* [1990]. The contract allowed Wijsmuller the liberty of moving Lauritzen's heavy drilling rig by using *either* of its two barges (the Super Servant One or the Super Servant Two). The contract could not therefore be frustrated when *one* of the two barges was unintentionally lost at sea. That the other barge had been booked on other contracts was irrelevant: Wijsmuller could still perform the original contract even though to do so would require it to cancel (and therefore breach) the other bookings concerning the surviving barge. There was no frustration because of the existence of the provision in the contract for performance by an alternative vessel. Had performance by only one vessel been specified, and had that vessel then been so lost, Bingham LJ was willing to assume that there *would* have been frustration on the assumed facts.

4   The potential frustrating event must make it impossible to perform the contract – *not* merely more difficult or more expensive.
    Many cases fail on this point, e.g.

    ❖   The closure of the Suez Canal did *not* amount to frustration of a contract of carriage of goods by sea – though it doubled the transport costs – because the contract did NOT specify that the Suez Canal was the *only* delivery route which could be taken, *Tsakiroglou & Co Ltd v Noblee Thorl GmbH* [1962].

❖ A shortage of labour and bad weather meant that a building contract intended to take 8 months took 22. The contract was *not*, therefore, frustrated. The possibility of such delays was not so unexpected as to radically change the nature of the contract to which the parties had originally agreed (*Davis Contractors v Fareham Urban DC* [1955]).

❖ A decision by a local council which closed the only access road to a warehouse that the claimant rented from the defendant did *not* therefore frustrate the lease for any part of the 5 years it still had to run, even though the warehouse was effectively unusable for 20 months (*National Carriers Ltd v Panalpina (Northern) Ltd* [1981] where the House of Lords held that the landlord **could** continue to demand rent from his tenant during the 20-month period).

❖ An unexpected decision by the Secretary of State to 'list' a Victorian warehouse (thereby drastically reducing its immediate commercial value) did *not* frustrate a contract of sale of the Warehouse despite being announced by the Government 2 days after the contract was signed, *Amalgamated Investment & Property Company v John Walker and Sons* [1977]. Though the listing decision prevented the buyer's immediate plan to re-develop the building, the court held that this event did NOT prevent performance of the *contract* of sale.

What is the theoretical basis of frustration?

This simple question does not, yet, have a simple answer. The doctrine of frustration has grown from case law and thus has developed by unplanned fits and starts from one case to another at different periods of time and in response to different events: even the Law Reform (Frustrated Contracts) Act 1943 arose as a result of the *Fibrosa* case (see below). Matters are complicated because the judges who have expressed a view on the legal basis of frustration have been cautious not to undermine the certainty of contract law. A further complicating factor in discerning the legal basis for frustration is that aspects of the doctrine overlap with the law of Unjust Enrichment (which is itself in the process of development).

There have been *two major explanations* of the basis of frustration. The original explanation – which is now judicially discredited – tried to base the doctrine (and its legal effects) on the judicial implication of a term into the contract (necessarily 'a condition') that the parties contracted on the basis that performance remained possible: thus, the explanation argued, if unforeseen events made performance impossible, the implied condition operated to terminate further performance obligations and by so doing discharged the contract. There are a number of logical problems with this explanation:

1)	2)	3)
It is artificial for the court to pretend that the parties intended to contract on the basis of an implied term concerning events which were necessarily unexpected and are not present in the contract.	It is also most unlikely that the parties will BOTH agree – after all, they will be litigating *a dispute* – that the unexpected and unforeseen event in question should act to discharge them both from all further contract performance.	When neither contracting party is at fault, it is arguably unjust for the court to help one and thereby disadvantage the other when he demands performance (or compensatory damages for non-performance).

Despite these objections, frustration was, for many years, said to be based upon an implied term. This explanation was offered in the first case establishing the doctrine of frustration (*Taylor v Caldwell* (1863) and thereafter was regularly cited with approval, e.g. by Lord Loreburn in *FA Tamplin Steamship Co Ltd v Anglo Mexican Petroleum Products Co Ltd* [1916]).

Case precedent – *Taylor v Caldwell* (1863) 3 B&S 826

Facts: A music hall was hired to the claimant for a series of concerts he planned to stage there. The claimant made extensive preparations for these concerts at considerable expense to himself. Before the day of the first performance, the music hall accidentally burned down. The claimant could not give any concerts and, facing great financial losses, sued the defendant hall-owner for breach of contract based on the failure to supply the venue in a suitable condition as per the contract. As the law then stood – *don't forget that this was the case which introduced the Doctrine of Frustration* – if a party promised by an enforceable contract that he would do a lawful thing he would be held liable in damages for failing to do it (*Paradine v Jane* (1647)).

Principle: A term that performance should remain possible might be implied into the contract with the potential effect of discharging future performance when an unforeseen event, which was the fault of neither party, occurs to make performance impossible.

Application: This finding allowed the defendant to escape liability for breach of contract as the 'missing' performance (providing the venue) was due *after* the date of discharge. (N.B. Because frustration discharges the contract it prevents either party from claiming subsequent performance (or any remedies for non-performance) due *after* the frustrating event (i.e. the fire).)

Aim Higher

Showing awareness and, indeed, knowledge of how a particular doctrine (see below in relation to the issue of frustration) has developed is, especially in relation to essay questions, an indispensable asset which will help you to gain a higher mark.

The doctrine of frustration as laid down in *Taylor v Caldwell* was developed in *Jackson v Union Marine Insurance Co Ltd* [1874] to apply in circumstances where performance was so delayed as to make the contract contemplated by the parties a different contract altogether. The case concerned a ship hired *for a specific voyage* (from Liverpool to Newport and thence, with a cargo, to San Francisco). The ship ran aground outside Liverpool where it was so badly damaged that it could not be used for some seven and a half months. The court found that the contract had been frustrated and this was confirmed on appeal.

The significance of this case is that **the commercial purpose of the contract** was clearly accepted as itself being capable of being frustrated – this was a development from the older cases which tended to feature frustration arising from the unforeseen destruction of something vital for the performance of the contract. The case can also be read as a pre-cursor of what is now regarded as the modern explanation of the basis of the doctrine of frustration, i.e. **a radical change in the contractual obligation**.

In 1956 the House of Lords re-examined the doctrine of frustration in the case of *Davis Contractors Ltd v Fareham UDC* and firmly rejected the implied term explanation. Instead Lord Radcliffe, after considering the earlier cases, said:

> '... perhaps it would be simpler to say at the outset that frustration occurs whenever the law recognizes that without default of either party a contractual obligation has become incapable of being performed because the circumstances in which performance is called for would render it a thing radically different from that which was undertaken by the contract. Non haec in foederaveni. It was not this that I promised to do.'

Since this case the orthodox explanation for the basis in law and in theory of the doctrine of frustration has been that it operates because there has been a radical change in the contractual obligation. The 'modern' approach makes it plain that the court must:

a) start by construing the meaning of the ACTUAL terms of the contract; and	b) consider these terms (and the performance they require) in the context of the facts known to the parties *at the time of the formation of the contract*; and	c) consider these matters OBJECTIVELY in the light of what is normal commercial practice for the given type of contract.

Davis Contractors has been repeatedly followed and approved (*National Carriers Ltd v Panalpina (Northern) Ltd* [1981] and *The Super Servant Two* [1990]). The test was re-examined in *Edwinton Commercial Corp v Tsavliris Russ (Worldwide Salvage & Towage) Ltd (The Sea Angel)* [2007] where the enquiry was said to involve the court in a 'multi-factoral approach' to consider:

❖ the terms of the contract;
❖ its context;
❖ what the parties may objectively and jointly be regarded as having thought and known – particularly as to issues of who was to bear the risk – at the time the contract was formed; and
❖ the nature of the alleged frustrating event.

The Sea Angel saw the court reject a claim that a contract to hire an oil tanker for 20 days (to assist a salvage specialist in transporting a cargo of oil from a stricken ship to safety) was frustrated by the wrongful impounding of the tanker *after the oil had all been transported* but before the tanker was formally delivered back to its owner: the commercial purpose of the 20-day contract had been performed and it could not be regarded as having been frustrated by delay resulting from the impounding as such risks were known to the salvage industry and arguably reflected in the terms. *The Sea Angel* was followed in *Bunge SA v Kyla Shipping Co Ltd* [2012].

What may amount to a frustrating event?

Thus far most of the cases considered have failed to demonstrate frustration: this is normal. For the reasons outlined above, frustration is difficult to establish. Difficult is not, however, the same as impossible: below are some – but not all – of the situations in which frustration has been regularly found and might be found again.

Common Pitfall

DO NOT forget that each contract must be examined individually *even if a matter does fall into one of the categories* below:

(a) Destruction of the subject matter: see *Taylor v Caldwell* (1863) (outlined above).
(b) Outbreak of war: The outbreak of war – or a conflict of equivalent effect – will often frustrate a contract, either because the other contracting party thereby becomes an 'enemy alien' or because the conflict simply prevents performance (see *Fibrosa* below). Also, in a time of war, the State may impose internal laws which restrict commercial behaviour so as to frustrate existing contractual arrangements between its own subjects (*Denny, Mott and Dickinson Ltd v James B Fraser & Co Ltd* [1944]).
(c) Cancellation of the event which induced the contract *may* sometimes frustrate its commercial purpose: The first attempt at a coronation for King Edward VII was cancelled. Of the many cases which followed this unforeseen event, the doctrine of frustration was held to discharge the contract in *Krell v Henry* [1903] but not in *Herne Bay Steam Boat Co v Hutton* [1903].

Up for Debate

In *Krell v Henry*, the contract was to rent rooms for two days (but only during the hours of daytime) which overlooked the planned route of the Coronation processions: a hefty price of £75 was demanded by Krell (the owner of the flat) and Henry agreed, paying £25 in advance. When Krell sued for the balance, Henry successfully defended by arguing that the cancellation of the coronation had discharged the contract by frustration. In *Herne Bay Steam Boat Co v Hutton*, Hutton hired a steamboat for two days to allow paying passengers to see a Naval Review and to cruise around the fleet at anchor (which had congregated for the expected coronation). The cost of the hire was £250, of which £50 was paid in advance: the illness of the monarch led to the cancellation of the Naval Review on the 25 June, three days before it was due. At this point the owners asked Hutton for instructions but received no reply. The owners used their boat to take other passengers around the fleet at anchor and then demanded the balance of the £250 from Hutton, who argued that the hire contract had been frustrated and discharged on the 25 June. The Court of Appeal found no frustration on these facts.

When considering the different outcomes of these cases, reflect upon the following questions:

(a) Why did Henry abandon that part of his counterclaim which – at first – requested the return of the £25 he had paid in advance?
(b) £75 in 1903 is roughly equivalent to £7,000 today. Did this influence the courts?

(c) Did either contract have a commercial aspect?
(d) Was it still possible to perform either contract despite the cancellation?

In this context, be aware that *Krell v Henry* has been judicially criticised and confined to its facts by senior judges, see pp. 528–9 of *Maritime National Fish Ltd v Ocean Trawlers Ltd* [1935] AC 524 which records not only the collective disquiet of the members of the Privy Council who heard this case (Lords Atkin, Tomlin, Macmillan and Wright) but also that of Lord Finlay LC in *Larrinaga v Société Franco-Americaine des Phosphates* [1922].

What is the legal effect of frustration?

Frustration discharges the contract automatically at the time at which the frustrating event occurs: neither party can be compelled to perform any contractual obligation after that time. The inconvenience this may create for the parties is illustrated by the *Fibrosa* case which led to the passage of the Law Reform (Frustrated Contracts) Act 1943.

Case precedent – *Fibrosa Spolka Akcyjna v Fairburn Lawson Combe Barbour Ltd* [1943]

Facts: By a contract dated July 1939 a Polish company agreed to buy a machine which was to be made and then shipped to Poland by an English company. When the contract was signed, the Poles paid £1,000 towards the cost of the machine 'on account'. Before the machine was built, the Polish port to which it was to be shipped was occupied by the advancing German army: the contract was thus discharged by frustration as of that date. The main question before the court was: could the Poles recover the £1,000 paid on account for a contract that would now not be performed?
The difficulties by which the Poles were faced were:

(a) the common law regards discharge of contract by frustration as ending any further future performance obligations (i.e., in this case, the obligation of the sellers to continue to make the machine, or to deliver it); and
(b) the fault-free nature of discharge by frustration prevents any claim for breach of contract for non-performance (if so sued the makers would simply have pointed to the discharge of the contract that had previously contained their performance obligations).

The House of Lords allowed the claim for £1,000 to proceed on the basis that in this case there had been a 'total failure of consideration' because the Poles had received *nothing* of what they had contracted for.

Principle: Where there is a total failure of consideration, money paid or payable in advance is recoverable under the doctrine of frustration.

Application: This decision allows recovery of money (paid or payable in advance) on a basis which had previously been understood only to be available for contracts that were invalid from the beginning (*ab initio*) and by so doing, overruled *Chandler v Webster* [1904] (which had taken the opposite, literal view that, as the frustrating event only discharged *future* performance obligations, it could not allow a party who had contracted to pay a deposit AND the balance *before the frustrating event* to avoid paying BOTH to the other party for NOTHING in return).

Up for Debate

Though it is difficult to fault the objective justice of the result in the *Fibrosa* case, the problem of how to best deal in an objectively fair way with the unexpected and unforeseen event which renders performance impossible was not fully solved by extending the possibility of a claim for a *total* failure of consideration. Consider the position if the Poles had received a small part of the thing for which they had contracted: in this case there could be no claim for a *total failure of consideration* and the problem would remain unsolved. Equally, if the facts were adjusted to make the money payable only on receipt of the machine in Poland, there could be no claim by the maker for payment for any work it had done before the frustrating event.

The Law Reform (Frustrated Contracts) Act 1943

The *Fibrosa* case illustrated the need for a means of allowing **objective** fairness and **objective** justice to prevail by allowing the court to equalise the distribution of money or benefits left in the wrong hands by the unpredictable automatic discharge of contract brought about by frustration. The Law Reform (Frustrated Contracts) Act 1943 attempts to do just this.

For the Act to apply the following are required:

a) The contract must have become frustrated under common law principles.	b) The contract must be governed by English law.	c) The contract must NOT be one of the four types listed in s 2(5) of the Act.	d) The parties must not have contracted out of the Act via s 2(3).

If the Act applies there are two sub-sections which allow the court to adjust objective unfairness between the parties:

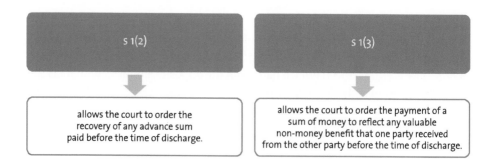

s 1(2)

allows the court to order the recovery of any advance sum paid before the time of discharge.

s 1(3)

allows the court to order the payment of a sum of money to reflect any valuable non-money benefit that one party received from the other party before the time of discharge.

There are not many cases concerning these provisions – many potential cases are resolved by arbitration rather than by litigation – however, two cases illustrate the basic operation of the Act:

❖ *BP Exploration Co (Libya) v Hunt (No 2)* [1982] saw the court faced with a claim by BP under s 1(3) of the Act concerning benefits that its work had conferred on its business partner (Hunt) in a joint venture to find and extract oil from the Libyan desert. The joint venture was successful in finding the oil but shortly after the oil started to flow, control of the Libyan State was seized by Colonel Gaddafi: BP were swiftly expelled and their Libyan oil revenues terminated. Approximately a year later, Hunt was similarly expelled. BP asked for a sum to reflect its contribution to the profits enjoyed by Hunt in the period prior to his expulsion: the court awarded such a sum to BP.

❖ In *Gamerco SA v ICM Fair Warning (Agency) Ltd* [1995] a contract to promote a concert by the rock band 'Guns N' Roses' was held to have been frustrated when the promoter's licence to use the Spanish stadium was revoked shortly before the concert because the Spanish authorities had safety concerns regarding the structural integrity of the stadium. Could the promoter recover the advance payment it had made to the management of the band? The claim was allowed under s 1(2) and, though a deduction to reflect the other party's expenses was possible, the court decided against allowing this deduction in the interests of justice.

Aim Higher

Read the judgment in *BP Exploration Co (Libya) v Hunt (No 2)* [1979] 1 WLR 783 given by Robert Goff J (later Lord Goff) at first instance – there has rarely been a clearer account of how the **Law Reform (Frustrated Contracts) Act 1943** should operate.

Putting it into practice

'The Doctrine of Frustration does not routinely allow a party to escape from contracts which have become bad bargains'. Explain and discuss this statement.

Example feedback

To properly answer this question it should first be noted that you are asked *to explain* AND *to discuss* the statement: *you must do both*. Also, when so doing, you must demonstrate your knowledge to the marker: the best to do this is to provide a legal authority to back up the point you have made. Think of such authorities (whether cases or legislation) as the punctuation to any sentence: you would not miss off a necessary full-stop, so do not miss off the necessary authority! You will notice that only a few authorities are needed: so learn the facts and law of those which can serve for more than one purpose, e.g. *The Super Servant Two* [1990]. Don't worry about memorising foreign words/names: a shortened name which makes it clear to which authority you are referring will suffice *in an exam*.

1 Explain the statement

This requires the consideration of the following points:

(a) What is the doctrine of frustration?

The doctrine of frustration is a creation of case law and automatically discharges a contract which, because of unforeseen reasons independent of the contracting parties, has become 'impossible' to perform, *The Super Servant Two* [1990]. Such a discharge of contract automatically brings any outstanding obligations under the contract to an end (*Taylor v Caldwell* (1863)). Frustration rarely applies in practice because though events often make a contract less economically desirable for one party they do not often make it impossible (as a matter of law) to perform that contract (*Davis Contractors v Fareham UDC* [1952]).

(b) What is required for the doctrine of frustration to operate?

In principle, frustration can only apply if there is already a contract in place before the alleged frustrating event (*Amalgamated Investment & Property Company v John Walker and Sons* [1977]). The frustrating event must be unforeseen; this means that the contract must not make explicit provision for the event: if the contract sets out what is to happen if the venue burns down, a fire will not frustrate that contract, *The Super Servant Two* [1990]. and the frustrating event must arise independently of the contracting parties (*The Super Servant Two* [1990]). The frustrating event must make it impossible – in the legal sense – to perform the original contract: unforeseen cost will not suffice (*Tsakiroglou & Co Ltd v Noblee Thorl GmbH* [1962]); unforeseen delay is rarely enough, *Davis Contractors v Fareham UDC* [1955] (but see *Jackson v Union Marine Insurance Co Ltd* [1874] where delay did suffice).

(c) What is the legal effect of discharge of contract by frustration?

The discharge is automatic, occurring by operation of the law, forwards from the time of the frustrating event. The awkwardness of this result is to some extent mitigated by a) the concession made by the House of Lords in *Fibrosa Spolka Akcyjna v Fairburn Lawson Combe Barbour Ltd* [1943] allowing a claim for total failure of consideration and b) by the creation of the Law Reform (Frustrated Contracts) Act (1943) which may apply to certain frustrated contracts to allow the court to make orders to equalises transfers of money and benefits prior to the frustrating event (*BP Exploration Co (Libya) v Hunt (No 2)* [1979]).

2 Discuss the statement

This requires making explicit reference to the statement in order to assess its accuracy as well as the question if (and to what extent) it could be more precisely or accurately expressed:

(a) Is the statement accurate?

The statement is broadly accurate in its claim that frustration does not ROUTINELY allow a contracting party to escape a bad bargain. Frustration applies to unforeseen events and automatically discharges performance obligations from the date of the frustrating event; it may well be the case that sometimes a contracting party may appear to escape a bad bargain because of frustration. This, however, is pure coincidence and may well be subject to a claim brought under the Law Reform (Frustrated Contracts) Act 1943. The crucial point is that the badness of the bargain is irrelevant to the operation of the doctrine of frustration. As explained by Lord Radcliffe in *Davis Contractors v Fareham UDC* [1955], the legal basis of the doctrine is that the '...circumstances in which performance is called for would render it a thing radically different from that which was *undertaken by the contract*.... "It was not this that I promised to do".' So e.g. if a party promised by a contract to take goods by the Suez canal and the canal was unexpectedly closed because of armed conflict, this would be a frustrating event. If however that party had promised to take goods from A to B (assuming but not stating IN THE CONTRACT that the Suez canal was the only economically viable route) the same closure would not amount to a sufficiently radical change from the bargain recorded in the contract to activate the doctrine of frustration (*Tsakiroglou & Co Ltd v Noblee Thorl GmbH* [1962]).

(b) Discuss the reasons why the doctrine of frustration is so narrow.

Here you should demonstrate your knowledge of:

❖ the objective nature of the doctrine – that it is not concerned with subjective complaints of unfairness; and
❖ the likelihood that a standard form contract will already provide for the eventuality, e.g. *Bunge SA v Kyla Shipping Co Ltd* [2012]; and
❖ the danger to contractual certainty which a loose application of the doctrine of frustration would pose for the whole law of contract.

The facts of *The Super Servant Two* [1990] are useful here as even the fact that performance of the original contract would now – after the loss of one of the two tugs mentioned in that contract – require the breach of other later contracts was not a good enough reason to argue that there had been a sufficiently radical change in the original contractual obligation undertaken to discharge the contract by frustration.

3 Conclude

A good answer provides a brief conclusion of the issues discussed to present a coherent and complete picture to the examiner. This also helps to leave a favourable impression on the examiner's mind, e.g. 'For the reasons discussed above, it can be seen that the statement is accurate'.

Table of key cases referred to in this chapter

Key case	Area of law	Principle
BP Exploration Co (Libya) v Hunt (No 2) [1982] All ER 925	Discharge by frustration – Law Reform (Frustrated Contracts) Act 1943	The value of the valuable benefit under s 1(3) is to be calculated as the 'end product' which is valued before the frustrating event.
Fibrosa Spolka Akcyjna v Fairburn Lawson Combe Barbour Ltd [1943] AC 32	Discharge by frustration	Where there is a total failure of consideration, money paid or payable in advance is recoverable under the doctrine of frustration.
Hongkong Fir Shipping Co Ltd v Kawasaki Kisen Kaisha Ltd [1962] EWCA Civ 7	Discharge by breach	Although a breach of a contractual term always allows the innocent party to claim contractual damages, it DOES NOT also always allow the innocent party to treat the contract as discharged by (and from) this breach.
J. Lauritzen AS v Wijsmuller BV (The Super Servant Two) [1990] 1 Lloyds Rep 1	Discharge by frustration	The potential frustrating event must NOT arise from the act or decision of either contract party: there is no frustration if the contract cannot be performed because of an act or decision made by one party.

@ **Visit the book's companion website to test your knowledge**

❖ Resources include a subject map, revision tip podcasts, downloadable diagrams, MCQ quizzes for each chapter, and a flashcard glossary

❖ www.routledge.com/cw/optimizelawrevision

9

Remedies

Revision objectives

Understand the law

- Can you outline the different remedies which may be awarded for breach of contract?
- Can you explain how equitable and common law remedies differ?

Remember the details

- Can you outline and explain the requirements for an action in debt?
- Can you outline and explain the requirements for specific performance?
- Can you outline and explain the requirements for an injunction?
- Can you outline and explain the requirements for the award of contract damages?

Reflect critically on areas of debate

- Following the case of *Co-operative Insurance Ltd v Argyll Stores (Holdings) Ltd* [1998], what role – if any – remains for specific performance in contract law?
- Why might an award of damages recovering restitutionary loss potentially be considered problematic?

Contextualise

- Do you understand how the equitable remedies of specific performance and injunction operate?
- Do you understand the effects which causation, remoteness and mitigation have on the claimant's ability to claim damages?

Apply your skills and knowledge

- Can you answer the question at the end of this chapter?

Chapter Map

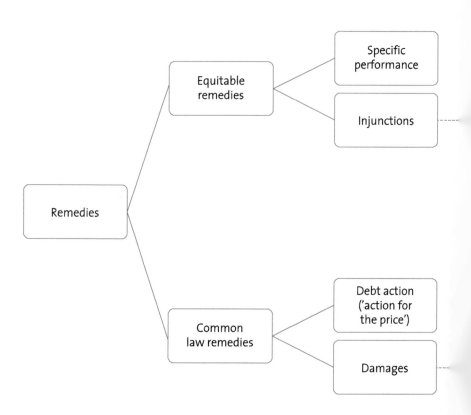

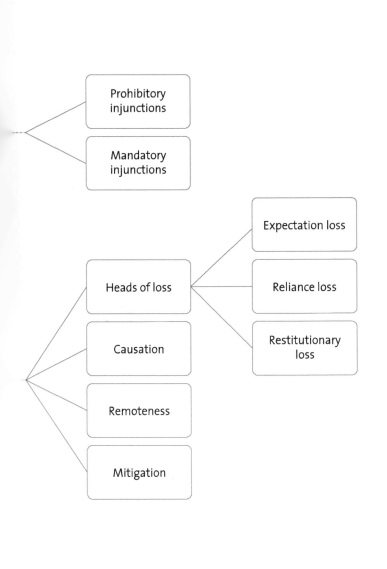

Remedies

If a contracting party does not properly perform his primary contractual obligations the other party may 'enforce' the contract by seeking one or more remedies from the court.

Common Pitfall

Don't be fooled into thinking that this 'enforcement' of the contract usually takes the form of a remedy compelling the party in default to perform the contract: in fact such an order (called 'specific performance') is *very* unusual in general contract law cases. In typical contract cases the remedy sought and awarded will be a money remedy rather than such a performance remedy. The money remedy can take the form of either an order that the party in default must pay the unpaid sum due (called a 'debt action') or of an order that the party in default pays compensation (called 'damages') to the innocent party for the contractual losses caused by his breach of contract.

Four contractual remedies are examined in this chapter: debt, damages, specific performance and injunction. Of these, debt and damages are each frequently encountered common law remedies whereas specific performance and injunction are less frequently encountered equitable remedies.

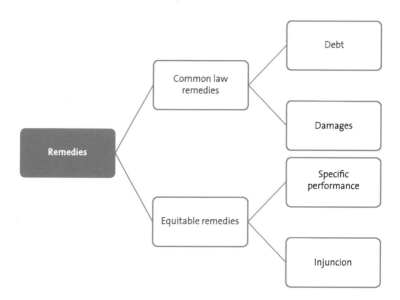

Why is it important to be able to differentiate between different remedies?

It is important to know what each remedy offers the claimant and what is required to use each remedy: the choice which remedy to pursue is with the claimant and it is necessary to make an informed choice when selecting the best remedy for the situation.

Common law remedies

Debt

A debt action (sometimes called '*an action for the price*') is used by a seller or supplier to recover a definite sum of money which, *according to the contract*, he is now owed by the other party but which he has not yet received (e.g. the price of the goods supplied).

To use this remedy it is necessary that:

(a) the contract expressly specifies that the defendant shall pay a definite price or sum to the seller / supplier for the goods / services supplied, *and*	(b) the claimant has performed *all* of his contract obligations, *and*	(c) the defendant has NOT paid the definite price or sum when it fell due in accordance with the terms of the contract.

Debt claims are very common in practice (see s 49 of the Sale of Goods Act 1979), more so even than claims for contractual damages. The advantage of a debt claim for the claimant is, as the claim is simply for the money owed under the contract, that *there is no need for the court to work out how much money should be awarded to the successful claimant*: the remedy will be the sum specified in the contract. Therefore issues such as *causation, remoteness* and *mitigation* – which are of crucial importance to a claim for the remedy of damages – are *irrelevant* to a claim in debt. As illustrated by *White and Carter (Councils) v McGregor* [1962], this can make a significant difference to the position of the defendant:

Case precedent – *White and Carter (Councils) v McGregor* [1962] AC 413

Facts: W & C placed adverts for local businesses on council refuse bins and charged for this service. McGregor, a local garage, advertised in this way for three years. McGregor was asked if it would renew the contract for another three years. McGregor's representative said: 'Yes', but later that day sent a letter to say: 'No'. W & C accepted the initial 'yes' as extending the contract for another three years and refused to accept the attempted repudiation and treated the renewed contract as subsisting. W & C placed new adverts on the refuse bins and demanded payment as specified in the contract. McGregor refused to pay and *was sued in debt*. McGregor argued that W & C should be required to *mitigate* the losses founding its claim (as would have been the case had W & C sued for the different remedy of damages). At the point when McGregor purported to cancel the renewal of the contract, W & C had no suffered claimable losses and so – had it sued for damages – could only have sued for nominal damages absent mitigation.

The House of Lords allowed W & C to sue in debt and refused to apply mitigation concepts belonging to the action for damages to the conceptually distinct action for debt.

Principle: As long as the claimant qualifies to bring a claim, the decision as to which claim he brings is his and his alone; he is under no duty to pick a remedy that suits the defendant!

Application: The case is unusual on the facts as it was possible for W & C to complete its performance without any further assistance from McGregor: had this not been the case, W & C could not have sustained a debt action as it could not have performed all of its own obligations. It is important to keep this in mind when considering a claim in debt.

Damages for breach of contract

This common law remedy provides a sum of money to reasonably, but not unduly, compensate one contract party for the admissible losses caused to him by the breach of contract by the other party. A damages claim is the default contract remedy and arises *as of right* (i.e. without any judicial discretion) – at least in its nominal form – whenever one contracting party has not properly performed those obligations which he owes to the other. If the claimant can prove such a failure in performance, he will *always* be awarded damages.

Common Pitfall

Although damages are available as of right, don't forget to consider the amount of recoverable damages: there is no point in bringing a claim for £50 of damages if the costs of so doing are £50,000. The amount (or *quantum*) of damages awarded depends on various factors concerning the claimant's losses. If more than nominal damages are to be awarded for a breach of contract (e.g. only £5 was awarded in *Obagi v Stanborough (Developments) Ltd* [1993] meaning that the claimant had to pay the defendant's costs too) the claimant must prove that he has suffered *claimable losses*.

Losses will only be claimable as damages if:

a) the claimant has suffered a type of loss the law recognises ⇨ what type of loss?

b) the breach of contract caused the losses which are claimed ⇨ causation?

c) the losses are not deemed too 'remote' as a matter of law ⇨ remoteness?

d) the claimant made a reasonable attempt to mitigate the losses arising from the defendant's breach ⇨ mitigation?

These requirements have led to many cases concerning the right way for the court to determine the correct amount of compensation it should award as damages for breach of contract. It is possible for the parties to try to avoid these complications if they set out in advance in the contract what the damages will be by means of a liquidated damages clause. If the sums specified in the contract represent **a genuine pre-estimate of loss** resulting from the breach (and are **not** unenforceable penalty clauses) the court will uphold such clauses, *Dunlop Pneumatic Tyre Co. Ltd v New Garage and Motor Co. Ltd* [1915].

Aim Higher

Questions on damages are often poorly answered for two reasons:

(a) students do not discuss the procedural and evidential aspects of a damages claim conducted before a court in terms of what will be argued and disputed by claimant and defendant;
AND/OR
(b) students do not demonstrate any appreciation of how the different rules concerning the operation of damages can interact with each other to affect the final award.

Therefore, to do well in questions concerning remedies you MUST **expressly consider the facts and evidence** *together with* **all relevant rules concerning the remedy at issue.**

The most common exam and essay questions dealing with contractual remedies ask about aspects of the damages remedy: it is therefore essential that you understand the different steps involved in analysing a damages claim and how each step may interact with the other steps. The four steps to consider are:

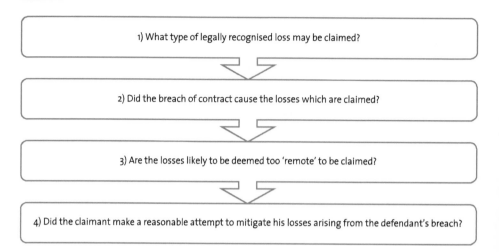

1) What type of legally recognised loss may be claimed?

2) Did the breach of contract cause the losses which are claimed?

3) Are the losses likely to be deemed too 'remote' to be claimed?

4) Did the claimant make a reasonable attempt to mitigate his losses arising from the defendant's breach?

Step 1: What type of legally recognised loss may be claimed?

It is important to remember that the overriding aim behind an award of contract damages is compensatory: this prevents a claimant from being unfairly enriched, e.g. by recovering damages multiple times for the same loss. The claimant chooses which of the three heads of loss (*expectation loss, reliance loss or restitutionary loss*) his damages claim falls under; he cannot receive compensation more than once for any given type of contractual loss.

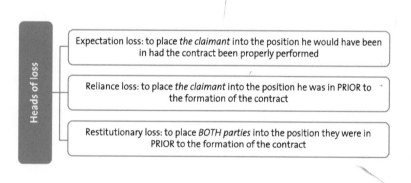

Heads of loss

Expectation loss: to place *the claimant* into the position he would have been in had the contract been properly performed

Reliance loss: to place *the claimant* into the position he was in PRIOR to the formation of the contract

Restitutionary loss: to place *BOTH parties* into the position they were in PRIOR to the formation of the contract

Although unusual, it is *not* impossible to claim and receive damages including BOTH an expectation loss (i.e. the lost *net profit*) AND a reliance loss (i.e. the incidental expenses) as long as it is proper to award both and the loss is not duplicated), see e.g. *Western Web Offset Printers Ltd v Independent Media Ltd* (1995) where a properly mitigated claim for *gross profits* – i.e. profits including the claimant's expenses *and* lost net profits – was allowed.

In practice, the choice of head of damages is sometimes effectively made by the (non)availability of the evidence required to plausibly quantify an expectation loss (see *Anglia Television v Reed* [1972]) but note that speculative damages *which are not too remote* can be awarded (see *Chaplin v Hicks* [1911]).

Expectation loss

This is the most frequently claimed type of contractual loss. Expectation loss is based upon the idea that the claimant is entitled to be placed – *in so far as money can achieve this* – in the position he would have expected to be in had the contract been properly performed (*Robinson v Harman* (1848)). The claimant may claim damages to reflect *either the profits he has lost* because of the other party's breach of contract, *or* to reflect *the bargain he has lost* because of the other party's breach of contract. Remember that the issue of *evidence* is crucial for both types of expectation loss: *if you cannot convince the court that your claim is plausible, it will NOT award you substantial damages!*

Loss of profits

A claim for loss of profits requires the claimant to prove what his profit would plausibly have been had the contract been performed. *Prima facie* this exercise is carried out by comparing the *market values* of what – if anything – was 'provided' to the claimant at the time specified by the contract and the market value of what he should have received at that time. The Sale of Goods Act 1979 specifically provides such a *prima facie* rule via ss 50, 51 and 53. However, the legislation and the courts recognise that such an approach may not always be apt:

❖ For example, if the goods are to be re-sold by the buyer *and this is known to the seller*, see e.g. *Bence Graphics International Ltd v Fasson UK* [1998] with regard to s 53(3) of the Sale of Goods Act 1979.
   OR

❖ More generally, if events subsequent to the date of breach are relevant in avoiding over-compensation, see e.g. *Golden Strait Corp v Nippon Yusen Kubishika Kaisha (The Golden Victory)* [2007].

Loss of bargain

A claim for loss of bargain requires the claimant to demonstrate that the sum he claims properly represents his actual losses arising from the lost bargain. It is possible to look at the loss of bargain claim from two different perspectives:

❖ The court could award damages to provide the claimant with the difference in the value between the bargain he received and the bargain he expected to receive;
OR

❖ The court could award damages to provide the claimant with the cost of curing/remedying/reinstating the losses arising from the lost bargain.

The choice between these two options is complicated when there is a large difference between the damages which would be awarded under each method of compensating the claimant for his lost bargain: the court has to decide *on the evidence* whether the appropriate figure to compensate – without overcompensating – the claimant for his loss of bargain is the difference in value or the cost of cure. Usually in cases concerning defective building work the cost of cure is appropriate, see e.g. *Harbutt's Plasticine Ltd v Wayne Tank and Pump Co. Ltd* [1970]. If, however, there appears to be a real risk of overcompensation, the usual rule will be displaced and only the difference in value will be awarded. This issue is best illustrated by the following important case:

Case precedent – *Ruxley Electronics and Construction Ltd v Forsyth* [1996] AC 344

Facts: The claimants were to build a swimming pool in the defendant's garden with a deep end for diving that was 7 feet and 6 inches deep. In breach of contract the deep end was only 6 feet deep in the diving zone: the pool was however perfectly safe for diving. The defendant refused to pay anything further for the pool and was sued by the claimant for the £39,000 which he owed. The defendant counter-claimed on the basis of the breach of contract alleging that he had suffered a loss of bargain because the pool was not as specified in the contract: he claimed circa £21,500 (the cost of curing the breach of contract by re-building the pool to the correct depth).

The trial judge refused to allow the cost of cure claim and awarded only £2,500 in damages to Forsyth's for loss of amenity: Forsyth was ordered to pay what he owed. On appeal the Court of Appeal awarded Forsyth the cost of cure (£21,500). The House of Lords reversed the Court of Appeal and re-instated the decision of the trial judge.

Principle: If the cost of cure is entirely disproportionate to the losses actually suffered *and risks overcompensating the claimant* the court will refuse to award the cost of cure and will only award the difference in value.

Application: This case illustrates the relevant criteria to be taken into account when considering the question of when the cost of repair can be awarded and also the importance of the evidence in assessing the appropriate remedy.

Suggested further reading: B. Coote, 'Contract Damages, Ruxley, and the Performance Interest' [1997] CLJ 537.

The 'exception' to the rule: non-pecuniary losses

As stated above, expectation loss is based upon the idea that the claimant is entitled to be placed – in so far as money can achieve this – in the position he would have expected to be in had the contract been properly performed. *Normally*, this means that damages will *only* be awarded for financial losses. However, damages for non-pecuniary losses may be awarded if it was within the parties' contemplation that such losses were not unlikely to result from the breach. Thus, *damages for non-pecuniary losses* are sometimes awarded in *consumer contracts*: as such contracts are not motivated *entirely* by profit, such 'losses' (e.g. for loss of amenity) are feasible, see *Farley v Skinner* [2001]. However, it should be noted that the quantum of damages awarded for non-pecuniary losses should be a 'modest' sum (*Watts v Morrow* [1991]).

Reliance loss

Reliance loss offers an alternative to the claimant who does not wish to claim for the loss of the bargain or profit he expected to make: reliance loss means that the claimant claims the *expenses* he incurred by *relying on the proper performance of the contract*. The most common reason to claim reliance losses rather than expectation losses is that it is too difficult – as a matter of evidence – to calculate and prove a plausible money value for the expectation loss. This is shown by the following case:

Case precedent – *Anglia Television v Reed* [1972] 1 QB 60

Facts: The claimants contracted with Reed, an American actor, that he would appear in a film they were producing. Shortly before filming began, Reed withdrew from the production in breach of contract; this caused the film project to collapse. As it was impossible to know how much profit (if any) the unmade film might have made, the claimants sued Reed for the expenses they had already incurred by acting in reliance on his coming to the UK and performing the contract.

The Court of Appeal refused Reed's appeal and required him to pay the claimant's expenses, even those which occurred before the date of his contract with the claimant.

Principle: It is the choice of the claimant whether he claims the reliance loss or the expectation loss.

Application: This case illustrates the major alternative to a claim for an expectation loss and is useful when the ascertainable reliance costs are high and the expectation losses are very uncertain in terms of quantification and might be nil.

It should be noted that, by opting to claim the reliance loss, the claimant cannot recover more than what he would have been entitled to if the breach had not occurred, i.e. if the contract had been properly performed (*CCC Films (London) Ltd v Impact Quadrant Films Ltd* [1984] and *C & P Haulage v Middleton* [1983]). In the same context, it should also be remembered that for the defendant to resist a claim for damages brought under the reliance head of loss *the defendant* must prove to the court that the claimant would not have recouped his claimed expenses even if the contract had been performed (see again *CCC Films (London) Ltd v Impact Quadrant Films Ltd* [1984] and *C & P Haulage v Middleton* [1983]).

Restitutionary loss

This head of loss seeks the recovery of a benefit which has accrued to the defendant because he has not performed the contract. The aim of this head of loss is to place BOTH parties (*not just the claimant as in the reliance head of loss*) in the position in which they were prior to the formation of the contract: thus, a claim under the restitutionary head of loss asks the court to order that the defendant account for the profits he has made by breaching the contract by paying them to the claimant.

Aim Higher

Restitutionary loss is the most controversial and unclear head of contract damages as it often seems that when the court has awarded such damages it has done so for reasons which come perilously close to attempting to punish a 'wrongdoer': this is possibly most clearly seen in the case of *Attorney General v Blake* [2001] where the House of Lords prevented the notorious traitor, soviet spy, and prison escapee George Blake from receiving payments from his book publisher for his memoirs. This indicates the tension implicit in the restitutionary head of damages as also demonstrated by *Wrotham Park Estate Co. Ltd v Parkside Homes Ltd* [1974] and *Surrey County Council v Bredero Homes Ltd* [1993]. Having read these two cases, you might want to consider the question of why the outcome differed in each case.

Suggesed further reading: C Rotherham, 'Wrotham Park damages' and account of profits: compensation or restitution? LMCLQ 2008, 1 (Feb, 25-55).

Step 2: Did the breach of contract cause the losses which are claimed?

This point acts as a limitation on the claimant's ability to recover damages for breach of contract. The claimant is only entitled to claim damages for those losses which were actually caused by the breach of contract: if the losses were NOT caused by the breach of contract (e.g. because they would have arisen anyway or because they were wholly attributable to another cause), they cannot be claimed from the defendant via the damages remedy.

Common Pitfall

As may be imagined, the claimant who seeks an award of damages will often face the argument that the defendant's breach of contract did NOT cause the claimant's losses. Unfortunately, student answers often deal with this point rather inadequately by taking either the claimant's or the defendant's word for granted instead of properly analysing the issue in view of the facts presented by a given scenario. In this context, it is worth remembering the following: as the court may be faced with conflicting accounts of the true causation of the loss, it will have to resolve the dispute by considering the evidence in light of the basic question: 'Did the defendant's breach of contract cause the claimant's losses'? The answer to this question will turn on the court's *assessment of the evidence* admitted by each contract party; each case will differ. A good illustration of the operation of such a causation dispute is provided by the case of *C & P Haulage v Middleton* [1983] which confirmed the general principle that the breach of contract must actually cause the losses to arise as a matter of fact.

Step 3: Are the losses likely to be deemed too 'remote' to be claimed?

This point acts as another limitation on the claimant's ability to recover damages for breach of contract. The concept of remoteness in relation to the calculation of damages is concerned with the determination of the point at which a claim for damages will be rejected because the connection between the causative event – in this context: the breach of contract – and the loss caused by that event is deemed to be too tenuous. The cases in this area of contract law often appear complex but in essence all they are trying to determine is the location of the point noted above: the complexity arguably arises when senior judges try to lay down general and abstract methods of determining the presence or absence of contractual remoteness.

The best approach for a law student is to focus on understanding the classic case of *Hadley v Baxendale* (1854). This case saw Alderson B set out a practical two-limbed test against which the claimable losses could be tested: if the loss cannot fit under *either* limb it is too remote and cannot be claimed. The test and its effects can be summarised as follows:

❖ First limb: The defendant is liable for losses which may fairly and reasonably be considered *as arising naturally* (i.e. according to the usual course of things) from such a breach of contract.

❖ Second limb: The defendant is also liable for losses which may reasonably be supposed to have been *in the contemplation of BOTH parties when the contract was made* as the probable result of its breach.

How the *Hadley v Baxendale* test works

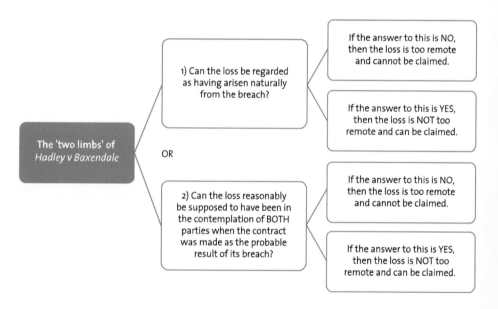

The most recent major case to consider the *Hadley v Baxendale* test (which has stood the test of time well) is *Transfield Shipping Inc v Mercator Shipping Inc (The Achilleas)* [2008]. (Remember: it is always beneficial if you can show to the examiner that your knowledge of a particular principle is up to date.)

Facts

In 2003 the claimant hired a ship from the defendant subject to a latest return date of 2nd May 2004. The cost of hiring such a ship then rose such that by April 2004 the hire rate had more than doubled. In April 2004, one day after the defendant had given formal notice that it would return the ship to the claimant by 2nd May 2004, the claimant contracted to hire the returned ship to another party at a very high daily rate of hire. Under this new contract the ship had to be delivered to the new hirer by the 8th May 2004. The defendants returned the ship nine days late on the 11th of May. In the meantime the market price for ship hire had fallen: to prevent the new hirer from cancelling the new hire contract on the 9 May the claimant had to reduce its daily hire rate by $8,000 per day. The claimants sought damages representing the resulting loss of profits at $8,000 per day for every day of the new hire contract. The defendants countered that the claimants were only entitled to such damages for the 9 late days and that those damages would be calculated as the difference between the contract rate of hire and the market rate of hire during the nine days in question.

Reasons

The claim for loss of profit of $8,000 per day for the entirety of the new hire contract after the re-delivery of the ship was too remote: the losses did not arise naturally and nor could they be regarded as having been in the reasonable contemplation of the parties in 2003 when the first contract of hire was entered into. Instead, the loss was said to be the result of the market conditions which were extremely volatile.

Decision

The House of Lords rejected the extensive claim by the claimants and only allowed the loss of profits claim for the nine late days: the damages claimed for subsequent losses of profits (after the return of the ship) were too remote under both limbs of the *Hadley v Baxendale* test.

Other cases which have considered the *Hadley v Baxendale* remoteness test have usually focused on the second limb of the test and thus *have turned on the evidence as to what was known by each contracting party* about the contract and the potential losses at the time the contract was made, e.g.:

❖ *Victoria Laundry (Windsor) Ltd v Newman Industries Ltd* [1949]: late delivery of an industrial boiler to a laundry would only allow a damages claim for losses under the first limb of *Hadley v Baxendale*. An attempt to claim losses connected with a lucrative dyeing government contract failed under the first limb because it was not 'normally arising' and failed under the second limb because the contract was *unknown* to the seller of the boiler at the time the contract was made.

❖ *Balfour-Beatty Construction (Scotland) Ltd v Scottish Power plc* [1994]: the claimants were not able to claim losses arising from a power cut caused by the defendants that interrupted and hence ruined what needed to be a continuous pour of concrete in a construction project. Such a loss did not fit under either the first or second limb of *Hadley v Baxendale* because the loss was unusual and because there was *no evidence* that the need for a continuous pour was known to the defendants.

Stap: 4 Did the claimant make a reasonable attempt to mitigate his losses arising from the defendant's breach?

Mitigation (sometimes also called the 'duty to mitigate') refers to a set of rules which act, again, as a limitation of the claimant's ability to recover damages for breach of contract: thus, after successfully proving that a loss has been caused by the defendant's breach of contract which is also not too remote it is then necessary to consider the issue of *mitigation* of loss.

Essentially, mitigation has the effect that the claimant, after accepting that the contract is at an end, can only recover those losses which he could not have avoided by taking reasonable steps. What amounts to reasonable steps is a question of fact and thus depends upon the circumstances of each case (*Payzu v Saunders* [1919]).

The rules usually referred to under the heading of the 'duty to mitigate' are:

| 1) The claimant can only recover damages for those losses caused by the defendant's breach which he could not have avoided by taking reasonable steps. | 2) The claimant cannot recover for mitigated/ avoided losses, even if he took more steps to avoid losses than could be reasonably be expected of him under point 1. | 3) The claimant can recover further losses or expenses incurred in taking reasonable steps to mitigate the loss caused by the defendant's breach of contract. |

The burden of proof is on the defendant to show that the losses claimed as damages by the claimant could have been reduced or avoided had the claimant taken reasonable steps to so mitigate them. If the claimant responds by demonstrating *either* that the steps suggested by the defendant were NOT reasonable, *or*, that he has made a reasonable effort (judged against the circumstances of the case) to mitigate his claimed losses, the claimant will still be able to claim those losses. If however the claimant either declines to mitigate, or, cannot show a reasonable attempt to do so, the court will then reduce his claim to take into account what it believes would have been a reasonable level of saving by mitigation. In this context, it should be noted that a claimant need not succeed in any attempt he makes to mitigate his losses: the requirement is merely that he must make a reasonable attempt to mitigate: the claimant who attempts to mitigate may even unintentionally *increase* his claimable losses to include the additional costs of what was a reasonable attempt to mitigate his losses which failed and increased his costs and losses (*Gebruder Metelmann GmbH & Co v NBR (London) Ltd* [1984]).

Common Pitfall

If the breach of contract is anticipatory (see Chapter 8) there is no need to consider mitigation if the contract is still capable of being treated (and is treated) as subsisting by the innocent party: mitigation *only* becomes relevant once the contract is *unambiguously* accepted as having been discharged by breach (see *White and Carter (Councils) Ltd v McGregor* [1962]).

How mitigation works

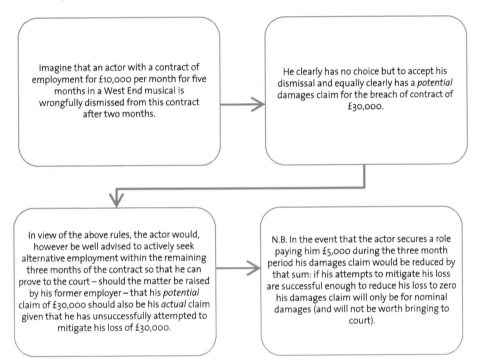

Imagine that an actor with a contract of employment for £10,000 per month for five months in a West End musical is wrongfully dismissed from this contract after two months.

He clearly has no choice but to accept his dismissal and equally clearly has a *potential* damages claim for the breach of contract of £30,000.

In view of the above rules, the actor would, however be well advised to actively seek alternative employment within the remaining three months of the contract so that he can prove to the court – should the matter be raised by his former employer – that his *potential* claim of £30,000 should also be his *actual* claim given that he has unsuccessfully attempted to mitigate his loss of £30,000.

N.B. In the event that the actor secures a role paying him £5,000 during the three month period his damages claim would be reduced by that sum: if his attempts to mitigate his loss are successful enough to reduce his loss to zero his damages claim will only be for nominal damages (and will not be worth bringing to court).

The above indicates that mitigation can significantly reduce – or even wipe out – a damages claim and thus may make litigating a damages claim pointless (see e.g. *British Westinghouse Electric and Manufacturing Co Ltd v Underground Electric Railways Co of London Ltd* [1912] where mitigation was so effective that it cancelled out all of the losses attributable to one part of the breach of contract claim).

Equitable remedies

Specific performance

A claim for specific performance asks the court to make an order that compels the party in breach (or about to be in breach) to perform his unperformed contractual obligation as per the terms of the contract. If this order is disobeyed, the party in breach commits a criminal contempt of court which may be punished by a fine and/ or by imprisonment. As specific performance is an equitable remedy, it can only act *in personam*, i.e. upon a named person whether a 'natural person' (e.g. a human being) or a 'legal person' (e.g. a company limited by shares).

Common Pitfall

Remember that this remedy will only be awarded if the party who is the target of the order of specific performance is within the territorial jurisdiction of the English court: this remedy is hence useless if the target is based outside England & Wales and has no assets within this jurisdiction.

The award of specific performance requires that the following requirements are satisfied:

(a) Damages would NOT be an adequate remedy: this also applies to injunctions (see below). This hurdle is often very difficult to overcome as damages would usually be an adequate remedy; orders of specific performance are therefore comparatively rare. However, if the subject matter of the contract is *unique*, *damages* would NOT be adequate and so an order of specific performance might be appropriate. Also, if the contract is for 'Land' (including various interests in 'Land'), specific performance is frequently – but not always – available as each piece of 'Land' is legally deemed to be unique. Furthermore, if the contract is for goods, an order of specific performance is also available if the goods are truly unique; e.g. a contract to buy a specific painting by Picasso could potentially be enforced by an order of specific performance as that painting would be unique. Unique is interpreted literally, see *Société des Industries Metallurgiques SA v The Bronx Engineering Co Ltd* [1975], where the Court of Appeal refused to grant specific performance concerning an industrial machine that, though large expensive and slow to make, was capable of being re-ordered from its manufacturers and hence was not unique.

(b) The remedy of specific performance is sometimes subject to a requirement that there must be sufficient *mutuality* concerning its award: the court will be reluctant to order one party to perform if there is no way of compelling the other party to then perform his own later contract obligations. Thus if only one party can make a successful claim for specific performance *at the time of application* and the performance of the other party has not yet been tendered the court may refuse to make an award (*Flight v Bolland* (1828)). The time at which mutuality must be present is, according to *Price v Strange* [1978], the date of the hearing.

(c) It must be 'equitable' – in the technical rather than the ethical sense of this word – between the parties in the circumstances of the instant case for the court to exercise its discretion to grant the remedy of specific performance (this also applies to injunctions (see below)): equitable remedies are *not* awarded 'as-of-right' but are said to be *discretionary*.

Common Pitfall

It should be remembered that an admissible claim for the common law remedy of damages will ALWAYS give rise to an award of damages (even if the damages awarded are actually only nominal) whereas an admissible claim for an equitable remedy *may not* result in the grant of the equitable remedy if the rules concerning the judicial exercise of the equitable discretion indicate otherwise. It is important to realise that the rules concerning the use of the equitable discretion are quite rigid: they neither permit a judge to 'make-it-up-as-he-goes-along' nor do they look only to the interests of one party, see e.g. *Webster v Cecil* (1861) where one party sought an order of specific performance to compel the other party (the seller) to convey land to him for the sum of £1,250, i.e. the sum offered by the seller by reason of a mathematical error which the buyer noticed and immediately sought to exploit by accepting the offer at a price which he knew was £1,000 too low. This case also shows one guiding principle of the operation of the equitable discretion: 'He who comes to Equity must do Equity'. In *Webster v Cecil* the court used its discretion to refuse the claimant an order of specific performance because of his own inequitable conduct in knowingly exploiting the defendant's obvious mistake. If however there is no evidence that the party seeking specific performance acted in an inequitable manner, then the order of specific performance may be granted as in this instance the claimant would be considered as having come to equity AND having done equity (see e.g. *Tamplin v James* [1879]).

Further factors affecting the operation of the court's equitable discretion in relation to the grant of specific performance as well as injunctions (see below) include:

(a) Unreasonable delay by the claimant may activate the Doctrine of Laches (pronounced *lay-cheese*) and defeat his claim for an equitable remedy. What is 'unreasonable' will depend on the circumstances of the case.

(b) 'He who comes to Equity must come with clean hands': in practice this means that a claimant may not plead a matter to the court which discloses his own inequitable conduct.

(c) There will be no order of specific performance or injunction concerning any contract which requires the defendant to *positively* carry out personal services or employment for another person.

(d) There will be no order of specific performance or injunction if undue future supervision of the order will be required of the court (*Co-operative Insurance Ltd v Argyll Stores (Holdings) Ltd* [1998]).

Aim Higher

When considered earlier by the Court of Appeal (*Co-operative Insurance Ltd v Argyll Stores (Holdings) Ltd* [1996]), the conduct of the defendants (which was deemed by the court to be motivated by 'gross commercial cynicism' per Leggatt LJ at p.295) was a factor in the willingness of that court to reverse the judge at first instance and to grant the requested order of specific performance. In the House of Lords in the following year Lord Hoffmann rejected this approach and observed: '*Both landlord and tenant in this case are large sophisticated commercial organisations and I have no doubt that both were perfectly aware that the remedy for breach of the covenant was likely to be limited to an award of damages. The interests of both were purely financial: there was no element of personal breach of faith*' (at p. 18). Consider, in light of Lord Hoffmann's comments, what role remains for specific performance in relation to contract law.

Injunctions

The equitable remedy of injunction is in many respects similar to the remedy of specific performance. Thus, many of the same rules and equitable principles apply and the same consequences will arise (via contempt of court) if a party disobeys an injunction. When requesting an injunction the claimant asks the court to make an order that either prohibits (via a *prohibitory injunction*) a party from breaching a contractual undertaking as expressed in a *negative* sense, or, compels (via a *mandatory injunction*) a party to do a *positive* thing.

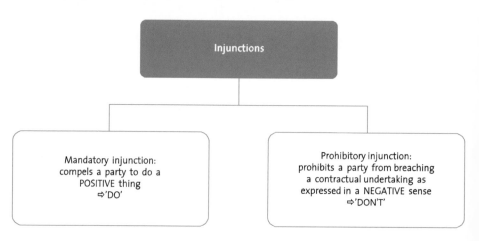

Of the two types of injunctions, mandatory (or positive) injunctions are rarer in contract cases as the remedy of specific performance usually suffices. By contrast, prohibitory injunctions are quite common in relation to certain types of non-compete contract terms, e.g. as found in employment contracts or in contracts for the sale of a business as a going concern:

❖ Thus if on the sale of his business a party promises that he will not compete with the buyer for a period of five years, that buyer can apply to the court for a prohibitory injunction to prevent such competition during the relevant five-year period.

❖ More controversial are those cases where an employee who has *explicitly* promised by his contract that he will not work for another employer for a certain period of time is then restrained by an injunction from breaching this express contract term. The court will not compel positive personal performance by an injunction as to do so would be to make the employee the slave of the other contracting party; however it will restrain an employee from breaching an express promise not to work for others during a period of time specified in the contract (assuming this period to be deemed reasonable – on the facts – by the court), see *Warner Bros Pictures Inc v Nelson* [1937] and *Page One Records v Britton* [1968].

Putting it into practice

Jeremy, a well-known television personality, saw a 1985 Audi Quattro for sale at his local garage for £16,000. After a test drive Jeremy agreed to buy the car for £16,500 if the garage would service its suspension. The garage fixed a number of small problems with the suspension to bring it up to the Audi service specification for road use. Yesterday, while Jeremy was driving the car at speed around a corner in a race against a Stratos rally car in a disused quarry, its suspension failed leading to a crash which wrote off the Audi. The race was being filmed for a popular television programme about cars. Already annoyed with the total loss of the Audi (which, as a result of his own clerical blunder, was not insured against racing damage), Jeremy was further annoyed to learn that the cost of filming being abandoned was £15,000 for his television production firm.

On a close inspection of the crashed Audi it became clear that one of the suspension components fitted by Jeremy's local garage was for a 1986 Audi; because of this Jeremy blames the garage for *all* of his losses and wishes to sue the garage for breach of contract to recover:

(a) £16,500 he paid for the car;
(b) £15,000 for the lost day of filming; and
(c) for his personal disappointment with the driving experience offered by the Audi Quattro as serviced by the garage.

Advise Jeremy of his prospects of recovering these losses via the law of contract.

Example feedback

This question deals with the remedy of damages for breach of contract. Anyone who suffers a breach of contract can sue for damages: this remedy, unlike specific performance, is available as of right. In practice, a claimant must be able to show that he has suffered losses which the law recognises as claimable and which the evidence shows to be claimable in his case. Jeremy must thus establish (a) that there has been a breach of contract; (b) that the losses he wishes to claim fall under one of the available 'heads' of contract damages; and (c) that in the circumstances of the case he can claim these losses.

This means that, if Jeremy cannot establish a breach of contract, his claim will fail. Also, if Jeremy cannot then place a claim under a recognised head of damages that claim will fail. Finally, if Jeremy cannot then show that the evidence supports his claim for substantial damages the claim will fail and he will only receive nominal damages.

Consequently, the following questions need to be addressed to assess Jeremy's prospects to recover:

Was there a breach of contract?

The contract Jeremy had with the garage was to buy and service the car in accordance with his instructions. If the garage has not properly performed this contract it will be in breach of contract and Jeremy may sue it for contract damages. The difficulty is that we do not know that the use of a 1986 suspension component represents a breach of contract: possibly the components are interchangeable? As we do not have enough information to decide we will *assume* that the components are NOT interchangeable and therefore amount to a breach of contract.

Are Jeremy's alleged losses theoretically recoverable in contract law?

Contract law allows for three 'heads' of damages: expectation damages (which attempt to put the 'victim' in the position in which he would have been had the contract been performed), reliance damages (which compensate the 'victim' for expenditure made in reliance on the performance of the contract) and restitutionary damages (which attempt to prevent undue enrichment and are not relevant on these facts).

Jeremy's claim (a) falls under the expectation head of loss: as he was not seeking to make a profit from the purchase of the car he can only ask for compensation for his 'loss of his bargain' (*Ruxley Electronics and Construction Ltd v Forsyth* [1996]). The court could either award damages to compensate for the diminution in value of the car or for the cost of curing the defects: as the car has been written off both figures would be substantial. As the case of *Ruxley* shows, the courts are reluctant to overcompensate a claimant: Jeremy would only be allowed to claim the lower of the two figures.

Claim (c) also belongs under the expectation head of damages as a claim for non-pecuniary loss: such claims are only allowed in cases which are non-commercial

(*Farley v Skinner* [2001]). Though Jeremy does not seem to want to sell the car, he does appear to be using it in a commercial context and this will prevent a claim for non-pecuniary loss.

Claim (b) is a reliance-based claim as in *Anglia Television v Reed* [1972]: Jeremy seeks the costs expended and lost in relying on the proper performance of the contract and the continued functioning of the car; subject to the comments below he can bring this claim.

Are Jeremy's alleged losses actually recoverable in contract law?

For each of his surviving claims Jeremy must show that the breach of contract caused his loss and that the losses were not too remote as a matter of law. Mitigation is not obviously relevant on these facts.

Causation: a claimant may only claim damages for losses that were directly caused by the breach of contract (*C & P Haulage v Middleton* [1983]). It may be difficult for Jeremy to show that the alleged breach of contract caused the crash from which the losses resulted. Though the matter will turn on the evidence of causation, it may be wondered whether the cause of the crash was the use of a 1986 suspension component or a combination of his driving and use of a road car as a racing car/rally car in a disused quarry. If Jeremy or the decision to use the car in this fashion, caused the loss, there will be no claimable substantial losses against the garage. It would be reasonable to expect the garage to vigorously contest this issue by attempting to prove that Jeremy's crash would still have occurred regardless of the alleged breach by the garage (*CCC Films (London) Ltd v Impact Quadrant Films Ltd* [1984]). As we do not know enough about the evidence we will *assume* that the alleged breach of contract can be proven to have caused the claimed losses: thus the next point to consider is the issue of remoteness.

Remoteness: if the link between the causative event and the loss is deemed too remote (as a matter of law) under *both* of the limbs of *Hadley v Baxendale*, then none of the claims will succeed.

The first limb of *Hadley v Baxendale* allows claims for losses which either arise 'naturally' according to the usual course of things or may fairly and reasonably be considered as arising from such a breach of contract. Is it likely that Jeremy's unusual claims will fall under this limb of the test? The matter will turn on the evidence but from the facts – and assuming causation – it may be that none of Jeremy's surviving claims will fairly and reasonably be considered as arising naturally from such a breach of contract.

The second limb of the test concerns more abnormal types of loss and will allow recovery of losses that may reasonably be supposed to have been in the contemplation of BOTH parties *when the contract was made* as the probable result of its breach. Again the evidence will be decisive on this point: was it known to the garage how Jeremy planned to use the Audi? It seems not as the suspension was only subject to road use specifications. Equally, would it be reasonable for the garage to know – unless Jeremy told them – that the car was one that was to be used off-road in a quarry to film a television programme?

Conclusion

Unless Jeremy can prove that he told the garage that he was to use the car as he did use it and that this use was to be filmed, his first and second claims will fail for being too remote: all will depend upon what Jeremy can prove he told the garage when he bought the car. Jeremy's third claim is not permissible under a contract law claim as non-pecuniary losses are not recoverable in a commercial context.

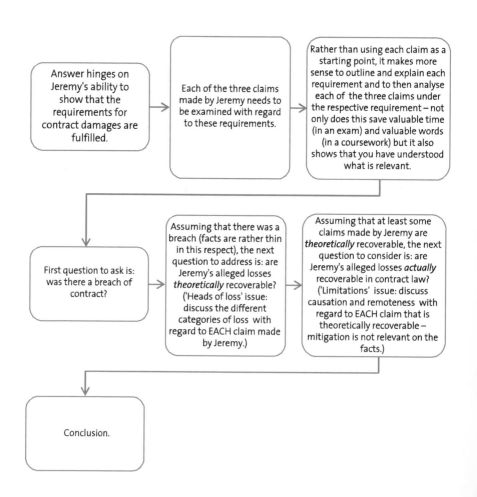

Table of key cases referred to in this chapter

Key case	Area of law	Principle
British Westinghouse Electric and Manufacturing Co Ltd v Underground Electric Railways Co of London Ltd [1912] AC 673	Mitigation	If the claimant successfully mitigates the entirety of his losses he cannot claim more than nominal damages concerning such 'losses'.
C & P Haulage v Middleton [1983] EWCA Civ 5	Causation and reliance loss	The defendant's breach of contract must actually have caused the claimant's losses. Further, damages for breach of contract are not intended to put the injured party in a better position than that he would have in had the contract been properly performed.
Co-operative Insurance Ltd v Argyll Stores (Holdings) Ltd [1998] AC 1	Specific performance/ injunctions	Specific performance is not usually an appropriate remedy for commercial disputes. Also, the court will neither grant specific performance nor an injunction if undue future supervision of the order will be required of the court.
Gebruder Metelmann GmbH & Co v NBR (London) Ltd [1984] 1 Lloyd's Rep 614	Mitigation	The claimant need only make a reasonable attempt to mitigate: he will not be penalised – with the benefit of hindsight – for so doing just because his losses increase.
Hadley v Baxendale (1854) 9 Ex 341	Remoteness	A loss will be too remote to be claimed as damages unless the evidence shows that the loss in question is one which either: (a) could fairly and reasonably be considered as arising naturally (i.e. according to the usual course of things) from such a breach of contract; *or* (b) which may reasonably be supposed to have been in the contemplation of BOTH parties when the contract was made as the probable result of its breach.

Key case	Area of law	Principle
Surrey County Council v Bredero Homes Ltd [1993] 1 WLR 1361	Damages	If the breach of contract causes no loss to the claimant, the appropriate award is nominal damages.
Warner Bros Pictures Inc v Nelson [1937] 1 KB 209 AND *Page One Records v Britton* [1968] 1 WLR 157	Injunctions	Though a court will not compel a person to positively undertake employment under a contract, it will prohibit a person from breaching a promise not to do work for a rival (without agreement) or not to compete (assuming both restrictions to be reasonable on the facts).
Wrotham Park Estate Co Ltd v Parkside Homes Ltd [1974] 1 WLR 798	Damages	The award of damages may include a share of the profits made by the party in breach.

@ **Visit the book's companion website to test your knowledge**

❖ Resources include a subject map, revision tip podcasts, downloadable diagrams, MCQ quizzes for each chapter, and a flashcard glossary

❖ www.routledge.com/cw/optimizelawrevision

Index